GREAT CITIES OF THE WORLD

WHITE STAR PUBLISHERS

CONTENTS

TEXTS
Marco Cattaneo
Jasmina Trifoni

PROJECT EDITOR
Valeria Manferto De Fabianis

COLLABORATING EDITORS
Enrico Lavagno
Elisabetta Gargagli

GRAPHIC DESIGN
Paola Piacco

© 2005 White Star S.p.a.
Via Candido Sassone, 22/24 -
13100 Vercelli, Italy
www.whitestar.it

Translation: Catherine Bolton

ISBN 88-544-0096-3

REPRINTS:
1 2 3 4 5 6   09 08 07 06 05

Printed in Cina
Color separation by
Chiaroscuro, Turin

INTRODUCTION

Until just a few thousand years ago, man lived as a hunter and gatherer, but the end of the last Ice Age ushered in a phase of rapid population growth due to improved climatic conditions. Several groups of *Homo sapiens*, probably extended families, abandoned their nomadic lifestyle to settle in areas where fertile soil and a wealth of resources guaranteed food for everyone for long periods of time.

Since then, the history of man has suddenly accelerated, but this is just one of the many effects that discoveries and technology have had on our civilization. Our forebears quickly learned to select the plant species that contained the right nutritional substances for their diet. And it was in these fledgling stable settlements that man began to domesticate plants species as well as animals such as sheep, goats and cattle. Villages and larger settlements were thus established, and with them the groundwork was laid for a structured society, in which our ancestors began to allocate different roles and functions. These primitive experiences at coexistence eventually spawned what the Greeks called the *polis*, the Romans the *urbs* or *civitas*, and modern man the city.

Big cities have prospered in both the ancient and recent past, making an extraordinary contribution to the evolution of humankind. The power of great empires arose from their development of these cities. There were many legendary cities in antiquity, but several stand out, such as the Egyptian capitals of Memphis and Thebes. More than 5000 years ago, a written language was already being used in these cities, a language that went beyond ideographic symbolism and ultimately laid the foundation for the earliest alphabets. And, of course, there was Babylonia, the magnificent capital of the kingdom of Hammurabi, the ruler who in about 1700 BC put together history's first code of law. These are unequivocal signs of the maturity of those early societies, and of their vitality and capacity to generate structured cultures.

Over the centuries, cities gradually became the heart of human activities. For example, we can cite Athens, Rome and Constantinople (later named Byzantium and now Istanbul), one of the liveliest and most fought-over urban centers of all time. Moving ahead in history, we can cite the great mercantile powers of the Middle Ages – Italy's maritime cities like Venice, which dominated the Mediterranean for centuries – as well as Renaissance marvels like Florence. There are the cities of the Hanseatic League in Northern Europe, from Lübeck to Bergen, Bruges and even London. Between the 16th and 17th century, London's strategic position would help it become the capital of one of the most powerful empires in history. Each of these extraordinary cities enjoyed periods of astonishing wealth and splendor, powerfully promoting knowledge, art, architecture and, later, industrial development. Several of them are still considered among the most important cities in the world, while others have gradually waned, losing their influence and ultimately facing periods of difficulty and, in some cases, decline. Nevertheless, each of them has left an indelible mark on at least one era in the history of humanity.

In the past fifty years, however, the urban scenario has burst onto the horizon of our everyday life as never before. Likewise, never before have there been metropolises of 20 or 30 million inhabitants, whose extent and level of crowding are changing the very models of human coexistence.

Today, 3 billion people are concentrated in urban areas, and 650 million of them (about population) population live in the world's 300 most populous cities. By 2007 urban residents will outnumber the population of rural areas for the very first time in history, and according to the United Nation's Population Division, by the year 2030 they will number 5 billion, versus a rural population of 3.2 billion.

At the turn of the 20th century, nearly all the great cities were located in Europe and North America, with

London, New York, Paris and Berlin dominating the modernization process in a world that heard the growl of the first cars and saw the earliest skyscrapers go up (the term was coined in the United States in 1880 to refer to the first buildings that exceeded 10 to 20 floors in height). According to the most recent forecasts, however, by 2030 all the biggest cities will be concentrated in Asia, but by then Africa – the least developed continent – will also have made the leap from a rural society to an urban one. Though Greater Tokyo is the only city one that now approaches a population of 30 million, within a few years Mumbai (Bombay), Shanghai, Dhaka, Jakarta, Bangkok and Beijing will be just as crowded. When it comes to the most populous country on the planet, today nearly 100 Chinese cities have populations of more than one million people. With respect to the period just after World War II, when demographic growth began to upset the balance of humankind's prsence on Earth, our means of transportation and our roads have not changed dramatically, and this may negatively affect urban organization in the 21st century. At the same time, however, many of our modes of communication have changed profoundly, and where we socialize has also been transformed. As opposed to just a few decades ago, we now make our purchases at enormous shopping centers, which have replaced markets, and spend our free time at enormous movie theaters and multiplexes. If population forecasts and indexes regarding continued urban growth prove to be correct – and if science and technology keep their promises – tomorrow every aspect of our daily lives will be completely different compared to the generations that preceded us.

This book tells the story of the world's big cities, as they are today and how they were yesterday, with the narrative based on the documentation of their past. We have chosen 60 of them, and they represent all the continents. Some of them, such as Athens, Rome and Cairo, are cloaked in the allure of thousands of years of history: the benchmarks of civilization, they have experienced highs and lows, yet have survived through thousands of years of history. Others, like Mexico City, have seen the birth and death of extraordinary civilizations and have risen again from their ashes. Yet others have a very recent history spanning only a few centuries, like St. Petersburg, built by Peter the Great at the beginning of the 18th century, and Cape Town, Singapore, and Sydney, and the many extraordinary metropolises of the American continent. Some are boundless in size and their populations continue to expand rapidly, and many of them are rushing towards the modern idea of development at an unbridled pace. Others, above all in Europe, number only several hundred thousand residents, and their greatness marks a tribute to an era in which they played a key role in history.

The Great Cities of the World takes a look at human civilization through the places we have chosen as our home, and where we have built stable and enduring communities. This book illustrates their history and architecture, but also their modern atmosphere and dynamics: in a word, the metropolitan "aura" that makes a city a living entity.

---

1 left St. Mark's Square, in Venice, with the basilica and the bell tower.

1 right The Sumitomo Building, in Tokyo's Shinjuku district.

2-3 View of the center of Rome, with Castel Sant'Angelo on the left and the white Vittoriale monument in the background.

4-5 Westminster Bridge crosses the Thames near Houses of Parliament.

6 The fountains at the Arc de Triomphe du Carrousel are visible in front of the Eiffel Tower, along the Champs de Mars, with the École Militaire in the background.

7 The concentric shells of the Sydney Opera House.

9 The Forbidden City and the skyline of modern Beijing, viewed from the historic Beijing Hotel.

10 The basilica-mosque of Hagia Sophia in Istanbul.

11 Mount Corcovado, in Rio de Janeiro, with the statue of Christ the Redeemer.

12-13 Central Park and the urban fabric of Manhattan.

14-15 San Francisco's downtown and the Golden Gate Bridge.

EUROPE

The history of cities is rooted in the history of European culture, so much so that it is inextricably tied to it. This means that, in effect, it is impossible to understand whether the city is a product of culture or vice-versa. One fact is certain, however. The Greek city-states marked the establishment of the first complex forms of government. It was in Athens, in about 500 BC, that one of the founding concepts of modern society was invented: democracy.

At the same time, the urban fabric was developing in what was destined to become the most important power in the history of the Mediterranean area and of Europe itself. Rome had been founded on the banks of the Tiber just a few centuries before, but its rapid ascent had already transformed it into the biggest metropolis of antiquity. In about 600 BC, just 150 years after it was founded, Rome already faced the kinds of problems that would characterize big cities millennia later: hygiene, traffic, overcrowding and the lack of distribution networks. Two of the early rulers, Tarquinius Priscus (ca. 616-579) and Servius Tullius (578-535) undertook the first great public works. Paved roads and sprawling squares were built in Rome. Water mains and water-drainage systems were created.

In the centuries after those early forms of government were created, the oldest and most famous cities in European history went through periods of prosperity and periods of decline. After the fall of the Roman Empire, for example, Rome's population declined: during the early Middle Ages it numbered less than 17,000 people, though just a few centuries before its population had been at least one million. The fate of Athens was even more dramatic. When it was declared the capital of independent Greece in 1832, it was no more than a village of 5,000 people. Indeed, this is one of the constants of the great cities of the Old Continent. The history of Europe has shaped its cities over the centuries, and today their structure is the result of the stratification of different eras, architectural styles and city planning, making these cities – considered both individually and as a whole –

modern places yet also important vestiges of the history of this continent. The historic districts of most European cities flourished at the beginning of the Modern Age, when that era of the great expeditions and trade brought the merchant classes wealth and prosperity.

Though Europe is a continent that has been deeply affected by the history of its cities and their vicissitudes, its urbanization process took place slowly and gradually. As a result, it did not spawn massive metropolises like the ones found in America and Asia. With the exception of Moscow, London and Paris, which with their sprawling metropolitan areas have populations approaching 10 million people, Europe has just 36 cities of more than one million people, and 62 with populations of 500,000 to one million. Out of a total of 727 million Europeans, 212 million live in the continent's 500 cities with populations of more than 150,000: just 29% of the total population. And yet nearly 75% of Europe's population lives in urban settings. Thus, the world's most densely populated continent has undergone a different urbanization process than the other continents, with a prevalence of smaller cities rather than large metropolises.

The changing and intricate history of individual European cities makes each one a complex "laboratory" of urban development. Thus, while the topography of Rome – or at least its historic center, with its magnificent palazzi and dark, narrow streets – still reflects the golden age of the Papal State, spanning the Renaissance and Baroque periods, the layout of Paris can be attributed to the ambitions of Louis XIV, and subsequently to the clever city-planning solutions of Georges Haussmann, the architect of Napoleon III. Instead, St. Petersburg is the outcome of the visionary plans of Peter the Great, who at the beginning of the 18th century wanted to give Russia a European-style capital. The canals of Venice and Amsterdam are the result of hundreds of years of struggles to overcome the violent action of water, with innovative hydraulic concepts and new strongholds built over the old ones. In short, centuries of human toil are embodied in the lively urban center of every European city. Today, respect for

the history of these cities and for preserving their legacy almost always prevails over the needs of modernity.

Viewed from this standpoint, Europe seems irrevocably rooted in its past. And this is the impression that strikes many visitors from other areas around the world, like China, which is driven by an all-consuming enthusiasm for innovation. With their historic legacy, old 18th- and 19th-century quarters, Gothic churches and Baroque buildings, European cities seem hopelessly old – as if time has stood still.

But to understand Europe today and trace the path of its great cities for the decades to come, we need to take a brief look at its recent history and go back to the early 20th century. Unsettled by a highly fragile political equilibrium for hundreds of years, by the beginning of the 20th century the continent that dominated the world with its vast colonial possessions and the power of its technology, the continent that had exploited the force of undisputed military supremacy, backed by the marvels of the Industrial Revolution, was overwhelmed by the thirst for power demonstrated by its surfeit of empires. As the figurative arts and architecture experimented with new ways of expression, the continent was besieged by two world conflicts. Over the course of thirty years, these two wars left profound scars – tangible and intangible – on Europe's infrastructures, social fabric and even the morale of its populations.

The two world wars, coupled with the deadly influenza epidemic of 1918-1919 (commonly referred to as the Spanish flu) claimed the lives of tens of millions of Europeans. There were food shortages and, particularly during World War II, cities were largely abandoned and were bombed by both sides in the conflict. After 1945, with the war over, Europe undertook the difficult task of reconstruction. For several decades, governments and city administrations were mainly involved in urban housing projects. Not only did they have to give homes to the millions of people who had lost everything, but they also had to deal with burgeoning urbanization, due to heavy migration within Europe and from

the outside, and the population boom of the Fifties and Sixties. In terms of urban and architectural growth, Europe had effectively been at a standstill for half a century, greatly slowing down the pace of innovation. When it became necessary to make room for new citizens, it was simply easier for cities to expand outward than to reexamine their layout and functions.

Today, the biggest European cities have essentially stopped growing in terms of population. By 2015, there will not be one European city among the twenty biggest metropolises in the world. Nevertheless, over the past few decades Europe's most important historic districts have been hotbeds of architecture, which is once again shaping the centers of these cities with new concepts and contours. Great architects like Renzo Piano, Santiago Calatrava, I.M. Pei and Frank Gehry have found fertile ground for their creations right in the heart of old Europe. It is through their work that the united Germany has rebuilt the capital city of Berlin, that Paris has successfully linked the classic lines of the Louvre with the glass Pyramid facing the Tuileries Gardens, and that Amsterdam has claimed new land from the sea, creating residential districts with a futuristic look. Elsewhere, the work is less evident – perhaps less courageous or less iconoclastic, depending on one's viewpoint – but the fever for contemporary architecture can be perceived virtually everywhere, from Rome, with the marvelous Auditorium designed by Renzo Piano, to Prague, with Frank Gehry's "Dancing House."

Even Athens has not been spared by these winds of change. With the return of the Olympic Games in 2004, the Greek capital welcomed the world with dazzling sports arenas, as well as a structural makeover that redesigned all its main roadways, the complete reorganization of the port of Piraeus, and the construction of a new subway line. To celebrate this historic rendezvous, Athens also finished renovating the Acropolis, restoring the ancient splendor of the Parthenon, the Erechtheion and all the monuments that once made it the first, extraordinary city of Europe.

17 left I.M. Pei's Pyramid partly conceals a pavilion of the Louvre in Paris.

17 center Big Ben stands elegantly over the Houses of Parliament on the south bank of the Thames.

17 right The Dioscuri face the Senate Building in Piazza del Campidoglio in Rome.

18-19 At Praça do Império the Mosteiro de los Jerónimos, where Vasco da Gama and Luíz Vaz de Camões are buried, is the most striking example of the Manuelino style. This style was named after Dom Manuel I, king of Portugal from 1495 to 1521.

18 bottom left The picturesque Castelo de São Jorge, overlooking the city, was built by the Visigoths in the 5th century and was transformed into a fortress by the Moors in the 9th century. The Christians conquered it in 1147.

18 bottom right Praça de Dom Pedro IV, which dates back to the 13th century, is one of the city's oldest squares. However, 18th- and 19th-century buildings account for its current appearance, attributable to Marquis de Pombal. On top of a column in the middle of the square is the monument to Dom Pedro IV, Emperor of Brazil and King of Portugal.

Lisbon
PORTUGAL

Fernando Pessoa, Portugal's greatest poet, wrote that "each pier is a nostalgia of stone." This is a lovely image that, in Lisbon more than anywhere else in the world, acquires tangible reality. Indeed, the legend whereby Lisbon was founded by Ulysses, the first navigator in history – or rather, mythology – seems almost plausible.

Lisbon is a *finis terrae*, the last European outpost, built along a river, the Tagus, that acts as a gateway to the ocean. The history, economy and imagination associated with the city make it a bridge between the ocean and terra firma, but also between two continents: Europe and America. Over the centuries, the ocean breezes have corroded the façades of its monuments, and they have carried the notes of the *fado*, the poignant music that conveys the dream of faraway worlds and *saudade*, or nostalgia. The designs of the *azulejos*, the Moorish tiles that clad many of its buildings, are the color of the Atlantic. The ocean also played a key role in the capital's renaissance that began on April 25, 1974 – when the bloodless Carnation Revolution overthrew Salazar's dictatorial regime – and culminated in 1998, when Lisbon stepped into the limelight with a dazzling World Expo. This event catapulted Portugal into modernity, and it was the driving force behind the construction of several extraordinary buildings, many of which located in the Parque das Nações, a space that seems to float on water. Some of the most impressive structures are the Pavilhão Atlântico, designed by Regino Cruz in cooperation with the firm of Skidmore, Owings and Merrill, the Pavilhão do Portugal designed by Álvaro Siza Vieira, and Peter Chermayeff's Oceanário. All these designers created works of organic architecture inspired by shells, fish and the ships that set sail for the Indies. The layout of the Estaçao de Oriente is also organic. The majestic hub for city railway transportation, which also dates to 1998, was designed by Santiago Calatrava, and it features roofing supported by slender columns that resemble tropical palm trees.

The most representative symbols of Lisbon, past and

19 top left The Igreja do Carmo, built towards the end of the 14th century, is one of the biggest and oldest churches in Lisbon. The 1755 earthquake destroyed its roof, leaving only the intriguing skeleton of its outside walls.

19 top right The Tower of Belém, built between 1515 and 1521, is one of Lisbon's most famous

monuments. It is a masterpiece of the Manuelino style, a singular blend of Gothic elements with vibrant decorations that show a Moorish influence.

19 bottom Constructed in 1902 using wood and cast iron, the Elevador Santa Justa is an original and spectacular urban elevator that links the Baixa and Chiado districts.

20-21 *The pride of the urban facilities built for Expo 1998, the railway hub of Estaçao de Oriente was designed by Santiago Calatrava. The bearing columns supporting the roof were inspired by palm trees.*

20 bottom left *The Vasco da Gama Bridge, officially inaugurated on March 31, 1998 for the World Expo in Lisbon, makes it possible to circle around the city, greatly alleviating traffic in the downtown area. It is the longest bridge in Europe: 10.7 miles.*

21 center The buildings constructed at the Park of Nations for Expo '98 include museums, auditoriums, skyscrapers, pools, fountains, shopping centers, broad pedestrian areas and the Oceanarium, the largest aquarium in Europe, with 16,000 species.

21 bottom With its height – 475 feet – and its skeletal shape evoking an unfurled sail, the Vasco da Gama Tower dominates the Park of Nations and is the tallest structure in Lisbon.

present, are located along the water. The first one is the splendid Torre di Belém, built between 1515 and 1520 at the mouth of the Tagus, whereas the emblems of the present day are the Vasco da Gama Tower and Bridge, respectively the city's tallest building (475 feet) and the longest bridge in Europe (10.6 miles). In addition to these, a marvelous and dynamic construction was built in 2001. Designed by Gonçalo Byrne, two-thirds of it is clad in copper, and it houses the port authority, underscoring the city's projection toward the world.

Despite ambitious works that have redesigned the urban space – such as the renovation of the dock area of Alcântara and the expansion of museums, planned by famous architects – Lisbon has managed to preserve its decadent and dreamy charm. And its ancient treasures continue to inspire enormous admiration even now. Among these are the Mosteiro de los Jerónimos, a masterpiece of the elaborate Manuelino style (named for Manuel I, who ruled Portugal at the beginning of the 16th century) and the burial place of Vasco da Gama and Luís Vaz de Camões, the mediaeval Castelo de São Jorge, and the Gothic Igreja do Carmo, which lost its roofing during the dramatic earthquake of 1755 and stands out against the skyline like a ghost ship.

Old Lisbon is charming viewed from a quaint tram as it slowly winds its way through the streets of the Alfama quarter, or seen from the Santa Justa elevator in the Chiado area that links the "lower" to the "upper" city, and connects commerce to culture. Tellingly, Pessoa withdrew to "upper" Lisbon when he returned from his long and difficult stay in South Africa, convinced that he would never again abandon that little patch of the city. When he was asked about the "human condition" of his travels, Pessoa –the descendent of a population of seafarers – replied, "Traveling? For me, just existing is enough."

20 bottom right and 21 top right At the mouth of the Tagus, the Monumento dos Descobrimentos, seen here from the front and side (with the crowd of sailors gathered at the prow facing seaward), houses a museum dedicated to the people who discovered the Americas and ruled the seas from the 15th to the 17th century. The memorial was built in 1960 for the 500th anniversary of the death of Henry the Navigator.

21 top left The surprising architectural structure of the Portuguese Bank dominates Avenida da Republica.

22 top *Designed by Helio Piñon and Albert Viaplana, the famous boardwalk of Rambla de Mar, inaugurated in September 1994, connects Passeig de Colom with Moll d'Espanya. The Rambla de Mar has now become one of the city's top attractions.*

Barcelona
SPAIN

Antoni Gaudí, the greatest Catalan architect of all time, left behind no finalized design drawings. For his phantasmagoric constructions, he started with a sketch, a concept that was often barely outlined, and gradually brought it to life in the exhilarating crucible of the work yard. Gaudí would often say that nothing is every truly "completed." Everything is transformed and shaped in space and time. It grows, develops and perhaps even dies, only to be reborn with a new nature.

His madness had just one name: talent. And it was thanks to his talent that, at the turn of the 20th century, Barcelona was embellished with visionary works like the Parque Güell, a lush and colorful park dotted with fantastic animals and a multitude of columns that look animated, and a belvedere, overlooking the city, that is literally enveloped by an undulating bench covered with ceramic chips. However, there are plenty of other examples, like the rippling and colorful Casa Batlló along Passeig de Gràcia, and Casa Milá, referred

to as *La Pedrera*. It was given this name because the architect had unhewn stone blocks brought there so he could cut and shape them on the street where the building was being constructed, transforming the road into a veritable quarry. And, naturally, there is the Church of the Sagrada Família. Still unfinished over a century after it was started, this masterpiece is both a bottomless pit – from a financial standpoint – and a demonstration of pure genius.

Gaudí is a paradigm of Barcelona. This enchanting city, which faces the sea and is blessed with a matchless climate, seems to have a special instinct for "producing" talents. And this is true in all fields. Continuing with architects, two of Gaudí's peers also deserve mention, namely the modernists Josep Puig i Cadafalch and Lluís Domènech i Montaner. Works by the former include the fairytale Casa Amatller, inspired by the Nordic Gothic, whereas the latter designed the extravaganza of styles and colors known as the Palau de la Música Catalana. In our own era, Barcelona is home to

22-23 *The Sagrada Família dominates the city skyline.*

23 bottom left *The Palau Nacional, restored by Gae Aulenti, houses the National Museum of Catalan Art.*

23 bottom right *The famous Rambla boulevard, crowded day and night, is the paradigm of a metropolis that is always on the move and is not afraid to take risks.*

22 center *Lined with elegant porticos, Plaça Real is considered the drawing room of the Catalan capital. The square is embellished with tall palm trees and lampposts designed by Antoni Gaudí.*

22 bottom *The Montjuïc hillside affords breathtaking views of Barcelona, a Mediterranean metropolis with "Nordic" ambitions: it is a city that combines* seny i rauxa, *Catalan for "common sense" and "folly."*

24 top The spires of the Sagrada Família are the universal symbols of Gaudí's art, a world in which everything is transformed into a triumph of forms and figures balanced between reality and fantasy.

24 center The attention Gaudí paid to decoration in all his work is virtually an obsession at Parc Güell, where the Catalan genius shaped his creations using the waste material from ceramics.

Barcelona

representatives of the avant-garde like Josep Lluís Sert, Oscar Tusquets and Ricardo Bofill, who have channeled their creativity toward the city's aesthetic progress. In fact, in 1999 the Royal Institute of British Architects, which generally gives a gold medal to a single artist, decided to award its prestigious prize to all the architects of Barcelona. However, the Catalan capital also boasts painters the caliber of Pablo Picasso, Joan Miró and Antoni Tàpies, and one of its notables in literature is Manuel Vázquez Montalbán. Montalbán was Barcelona's last bard, sketching out the city in his mystery novels.

Perfectly attuned with Gaudí's philosophy, Barcelona refuses to admit being "completed." As perfect as it may appear – so vital, alluring, prosperous, so noble yet also so "familiar" and friendly – Barcelona seems to be on an endless quest to be something more and better. Despite the fact that it has a population of just 1.5 million, it has long taken its rightful place as one of Europe's great metropolises. People were convinced that the city had already astonished the world in 1992 when, for the Olympic Games, it revived the splendid seafront of Barceloneta and Port Vell. At the time, it was the focus of ambitious city-planning and architectural projects that gave the city prestigious residential buildings and entertainment complexes, like the beachfront Hotel Arts skyscraper designed by Bruce Graham of Skidmore, Owings & Merrill, set right next to the incredible metal fish designed by Frank O. Gehry. The city also built new works on the Montjuïc hillside, now the site of the stunning Torre della Telefónica, designed by Santiago Calatrava to represent an athlete carrying the Olympic torch. Nevertheless, the passage of time has made it clear that the "Olympic revolution" was merely a taste of a new series of projects for the 2004 rendezvous, when Barcelona hosted the first Universal Forum of Cultures.

For the occasion, the northeast part of the city was renovated, from the Olympic Village to the Besós area, with the construction of a new seafront promenade stretching nearly five miles, and the upgrade of the Poble Nou district. This area, which was previously strictly the site of modern residential buildings and a futuristic Auditorium designed by Rafael Moneo, is now the location of pavilions for Forum events (the main one was designed by Swiss architects Herzog and De Meuron) and splendid gardens. It also has extraordinary skyscrapers, notably the 472-foot-tall Torre Agbar, designed by Jean Nouvel and clad in a "skin" of colored glass as a tribute to Gaudí.

However, Barcelona, which has always played a key role in Spanish history, owes its charm to its countless architectural layers that dialog in cheerful harmony. Ancient and mediaeval times converge in the central quarter of Barri Gòtic, where the splendid Gothic cathedral, founded in 1298, rises alongside the Roman walls built in the 2nd and 3rd centuries and the ruins of a temple dedicated to Augustus. Nearby is the marvelous Plaça de Sant Jaume, marked off by two of the most important symbols of Catalan self-government, Casa de la Ciutat (1373) and Palau de la Generalitat (1418-1596). Further ahead, Plaça Reial, decorated with palm trees and lampposts designed by Gaudí, projects the area into the 19th century.

24 bottom The polychrome chimneys of Casa Batlló sit on a scaled roof that looks like the backbone of a prehistoric creature. Gaudí restored the house between 1904 and 1906, commissioned by the owner, textile industrialist Josep Batlló i Casanovas.

24-25 According to the final plans, the Sagrada Família is supposed to have 12 towers, symbolizing the Apostles, whereas the 3 façades narrate the mysteries of faith. The immense central tower-spire represents Christ.

25 bottom left The house in Parc Güell is just one of the 60 homes that Gaudí wanted to build here. In his original plans, the area was to be transformed into a garden-city.

25 bottom right Gaudí set a marvelous dragon covered with ceramic scales in the middle of the double stairway at the entrance to "guard" Parc Güell. Doric columns behind it sustain the ceiling of the entrance hall, decorated with stunning mosaics.

Barcelona

26-27 When notes ring out in the lavish hall of the Palau de la Mùsica Catalana, architecture and music merge to form a superior harmony, providing the perfect demonstration of Wagner's theory of the integration of the arts.

26 bottom left Parque de la España Industrial, at Barri de Sants, was designed by Luis Peña Ganchegui in 1984-85. Once a village separated from the city, Barri de Sants became an important textile district and has now been converted into a city park.

26 bottom right The patron saint of Barcelona is the "missing character" in Andrés Nagel's irreverent sculpture The Dragon without St. George, located in the financial district at the foot of the hillside of Montjuïc, dominated by the Torre Cataluña skyscraper.

27 top "The most beautiful ceiling in the world" is how the skylight of the Palau de la Mùsica Catalana has been described. This modernist gem, was built by architect Lluís Domènech i Montaner between 1905 and 1908.

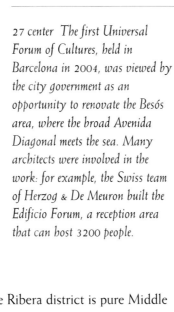

27 center The first Universal Forum of Cultures, held in Barcelona in 2004, was viewed by the city government as an opportunity to renovate the Besós area, where the broad Avenida Diagonal meets the sea. Many architects were involved in the work: for example, the Swiss team of Herzog & De Meuron built the Edificio Forum, a reception area that can host 3200 people.

27 bottom The panorama of the Olympic Village – a splendid area overlooking the sea, created for the 1992 Olympic Games in Barcelona – includes the Hotel Arts skyscraper in the background, designed by Bruce Graham of Skidmore Owings & Merrill, and the extravagant metal fish, visible on the left, designed by the famous and visionary architect Frank O. Gehry.

In contrast, the heart of the Ribera district is pure Middle Ages, with the Neo-Gothic church of Santa Maria del Mar and Carrer de Montcada, the first street in Barcelona to be part of a systematic city-planning project. Nevertheless, Barcelona has plenty of streets that have now become legends, from the Rambla – which is the city promenade and ends near the sea, at the square dominated by the majestic monument to Christopher Columbus – to Passeig de Gràcia. The latter is the dazzling thoroughfare of Eixample, whose name literally means "the extension." During the second half of the 19th century, the city administration appointed engineer Ildefons Cerdà to create the area in order to meet the residential needs of the wealthy bourgeoisie of the era.

The most compelling works of 20th-century Barcelona can be seen in the Montjuïc hillside, a "citadel of culture" with attractions like the Fundaciò Joan Miró and the equally notable but stark exhibition pavilion designed by Mies van der Rohe. The former low-cost district of Raval, which is separated from the Barri Gòtic by the Rambla, has now taken on an air of creativity ever since MACBA opened its doors. This exceptional museum of contemporary art is housed in an airy building designed by Richard Meier.

And yet, who knows what else Barcelona has up its sleeve for the near future? Indeed, work to reorganize its urban fabric continues at a frenetic pace. One example will suffice: with its iron framework, Art Nouveau mosaics, colors and vitality, the Boquería is already considered one of the world's most extraordinary food markets, and it is one of the city's leading tourist attractions. And yet, as if this were not enough, another local market – Santa Catalina – has just been modernized. Santa Catalina is merely where Barcelona housewives go to do their shopping. However, designed by architecture's latest darlings, Enric Miralles and Benedetta Tagliabue, it has an astonishing roof covered with brightly colored majolica tiles. And it certain holds its own alongside Gaudí's inventions.

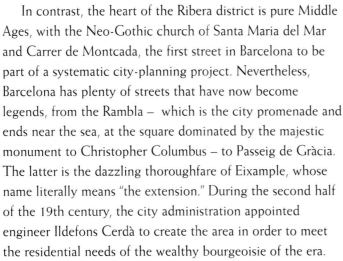

Madrid

SPAIN

At midnight on December 31st, Madrileños gather together under the clock tower at Puerta del Sol and eat grapes as they listen to the clock chime 12 times. This ritual is thought to bring good luck for the New Year. And, indeed, everything in Madrid begins in this lively, sprawling oval plaza. "Mile zero" is marked in the middle of the plaza, and all the streets radiate from this point. It was here that, in 1561, King Philip II decided to make Madrid the capital of Spain. Romantics insist that the king chose the city because its healthy climate – Madrid is located at an altitude of more than 2,100 feet – made it the perfect setting for the convalescence of his beloved third wife, Elizabeth of Valois. In reality, his decision was dictated by geometric reasons: Madrid marks the center of the country. At the time, life in Spain revolved around the sea, promoting trade and the conquest of the New World. Despite its focus beyond its own borders, however,

Spain enjoyed what came to be known as the *Siglo de Oro*, or Golden Century, and the country turned into what poet Pedro Calderón de la Barca would call *el gran teatro del mundo*.

In a certain sense, Madrid is a parvenu among the great capitals of Europe, and it has behaved as such, symbolizing the power of its emperors, kings and the *caudillo* Francisco Franco. As a result, the city is stern and monumental, and one initially perceives solidity rather than elegance. Its squares, from Plaza Mayor to Plaza de Cibeles and Plaza de España, as well as its streets, like Gran Vía, Calle de Alcalá and Paseo del Prado, are broad and magnificent. And its buildings are majestic, first Palacio Real, started by King Philip V in 1723 after a fire destroyed the royal residence of Alcazár. Everything here – from the architecture, which was the work of Italians Filippo Juvara and Giovanni Battista Sacchetti, to Tiepolo's frescoes – was designed to eclipse the magnificence of the other European courts.

28 top The 450-foot-tall Torre Madrid rises over the monument dedicated to Cervantes, Don Quixote and Sancho Panza in Plaza de España.

28 bottom Plaza de Cibeles is named for the 18th-century statue of the fertility goddess on a chariot drawn

by lions. The Palacio de Comunicaciones is visible in the background.

28-29 An enchanting space covering an area of about 400 x 300 feet, Plaza de la Constitutión is the center of Madrid's social life.

29 bottom left The Edificio Metrópolis (1910) is an extravagant combination of Neo-Classic, Neo-Baroque and Art Nouveau styles.

29 bottom right A semicircular colonnade frames the equestrian statue of King Alfonso XII.

30 top *The KIO Towers, or Puerta de Europa, slant upwards to a height of 377 feet in Plaza de Castilla and house the headquarters of Caja Madrid. In the center is the Francoist monument built in 1961 to commemorate the 25th anniversary of the murder of José Calvo Sotelo.*

Its religious buildings, from the Almudena to the Catedral de San Isidro, are extraordinary, and its parks, like the Parque del Buen Retiro, are spectacular. And, of course, there is the marvelous Prado, which boasts over 8000 masterpieces, making it one of the most important museums in the world. For too many years, however, Madrid was little more than a dazzling "container" that left it up to its rival, the maritime city of Barcelona, to test new ideas in everything from social needs to urban planning. Only after the death of Franco did the city come back to life. Thanks also to the economic boom, the city began to value its existing beauty and build stunning new structures. Today, the Prado, which has recenty inaugurated a new pavilion designed by architect Rafael Moneo, vies with the increasingly impressive exhibition venues of the Thyssen-Bornemisza Museum and the Centro de Arte Reína Sofía, to which a dramatic construction by French architect Jean Nouvel was recently added.

Moneo also designed one of the most intriguing works of recent years, the renovation of the 19th-century railway station of Atocha. For the most part, however, contemporary architecture has been relegated beyond the city's center. The Madrilenian equivalent of Manhattan is located in the commercial area of Azca, with the Europe Tower (1975-85) designed by architect Miguel de Oriol e Ybarra, and Minoru Yamasaki's Picasso Tower (1977). More recently, Philip Johnson and John Burgee designed the KIO Towers, twin structures tilted at 14.3 degrees to form a gateway symbolizing Madrid's welcome to Europe. Richard Rogers has instead been commissioned to design the new airport terminal, a futuristic structure that will help make the Spanish capital one of the most important airline hubs on the continent.

At the same time, Madrid has become a kaleidoscope of color and liveliness – but with an unconventional touch – that has transformed it into the trendy capital of fashions and entertainment. This movement, tellingly dubbed *movida*, has had its very own "architect" with film director Pedro Almodóvar.

30 center *The emblem of Bourbon grandeur, the Palacio Real was built in 1723 by Philip V, who ordered architects Juvarra and Sacchetti to build a palace more magnificent than any other palace in Europe.*

30 bottom *The Diego Velázquez monument welcomes visitors at the entrance to the Prado Museum. Inaugurated in 1819, the building houses the priceless royal collection.*

Madrid

31 bottom left *In front of Plaza de Toros de Las Ventas, a bronze monument commemorates matador José Cubero. The inscription under the statue reads, "When a bullfighter dies, an angel is born."*

31 bottom right *Plaza de Toros de Las Ventas, inaugurated in 1931, is a masterpiece of Neo-Mudéjar architecture, which is characterized by the use of bricks and colorful majolica tiles.*

30-31 *It took over a century to complete construction of the Catedral de Nuestra Señora de la Almudena, which stands next to the Palacio Real. Work started in 1879, during the rule of Alfonso XII, but the cathedral was not consecrated until 1993. As a result, the Neo-Classic architecture designed by Fernando Cueca Goitia shows no traces of the original plans, which were based on the Reims Cathedral.*

32 bottom right Baron Haussmann designed Place de l'Opéra, one of the capital's key intersections. The view ends with the Opéra Garnier (1875), which symbolizes the opulence of the Second Empire.

33 top left The Champs Elysées, Paris' most famous boulevard, is lined with enormous chestnut trees, flowerbeds and buildings with luxury hotels, shops and fashionable restaurants.

32-33 An enchanting view of the Seine near Île de la Cité, the seat of the city's secular and religious power (with the Cathedral of Notre-Dame).

32 bottom left The Hôtel des Invalides, topped by the dome over Napoleon's remains, was named after the complex the Sun King built in the late 17th century to shelter his war veterans.

Paris

FRANCE

In 2001 criticism poured in from all sides, above all from motorists, whom the city government "robbed" of 2.5 precious miles of expressway that streamlined urban traffic along the Rive Droite of the Seine. In the years that followed, however, the utopian project of Mayor Bertrand Delanoë turned out to be a remarkable success. All it took was a few tons of sand and some palm trees, beach umbrellas, cabins and recliners to transform the right bank, between the Tuileries tunnel and the Henry IV Bridge, into Paris-Plage, the first metropolitan beach experience – set in the shade of the Louvre. In 2004 this event, which lasted from July 21 to August 20, also involved part of the Rive Gauche, and it attracted over three million people, Parisians and tourists alike. In the end, this initiative was such a runaway success that the municipal council has decided to install two enormous swimming pools along the Seine by 2007, the year its term of office expires. It has also decided to draw up city-planning legislation to ban cars along the Quais – a site inscribed on UNESCO's World Heritage List – by the year 2010.

In short, Paris is just as astonishing as ever. Eccentric, provocative and spirited, the French capital, whose greater metropolitan area now has a population of nearly 12 million, has demonstrated that it is part of the world's cultural vanguard. It is a city prepared to make choices that spark heated debates, which eventually dissolve and become opportunities for innovation. This is what happened several years ago, during the period of the visionary monumental works that left François Mitterrand's mark on the city. And this is how it has been over the centuries whenever architects, be they imperial or republican, redesigned its layout.

In about 250 BC, the Parisii tribe established a modest Celtic settlement in what had been a marshy and inhospitable area during the prehistoric age. It was first

33 top right Built by Louis IX in 1248 to safeguard the alleged crown of Christ and other relics, Sainte-Chapelle is a masterpiece of Gothic architecture. During the Middle Ages it was referred to as the "gate of Paradise" because of its 15 breathtaking stained-glass windows, illustrating over 1000 scenes from the Old and New Testaments.

33 center Designed by I.M. Pei and opened in 1989, the Pyramide (composed of 716 glass diamonds and triangles set on a metal framework) is in the middle of the promenade of Carrousel du Louvre. The superb façade of the Denon Wing, which houses the ancient art and sculpture galleries, is visible in the background.

33 bottom At the Louvre, monumental galleries are devoted to European painting. The immense collection of canvases – covering 5 centuries, from 1400 to 1900 – is an endless succession of masterpieces.

34 bottom right The Eiffel Tower rises above Quai Branly. Built for the 1889 World's Fair, it was supposed to be dismantled shortly after the event but was instead adopted as the symbol of Paris.

35 top Packed with painters and tourists, Place du Tertre is the highest point in Montmartre and thus in Paris. The white Basilica of Sacré-Coeur is visible in the background.

34-35 Started by Henry II in 1578 and inaugurated by Henry IV in 1607, the Pont Neuf is the oldest bridge in Paris – despite its name, which means "New Bridge." Over 900 feet long, it is at the end of Île de la Cité.

34 bottom left The booksellers, or bouquinistes, along the Seine are nothing short of an institution. The first stalls appeared on Quai des Saints Augustins in 1557, during the Wars of Religion.

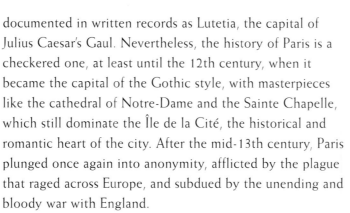

35 center bottom The majestic and aristocratic architectural complex of Place Vendôme rises in the area of the Tuileries. In the center, a spiral of bas-reliefs inspired by imperial Rome decorates the column cast from the bronze of the 1250 cannons Napoleon captured at the Battle of Austerlitz, the most dazzling of his epic victories.

35 bottom Place des Vosges, the heart of the old Marais district, is a perfect quadrilateral. It was built by Henry IV in 1604. The 36 buildings around it, rising above elegant porticos, are surprisingly similar in style. Victor Hugo lived at No. 6 from 1832 to 1848, and wrote Les Miserables *in the rooms of Hôtel Rohan-Guéménée.*

documented in written records as Lutetia, the capital of Julius Caesar's Gaul. Nevertheless, the history of Paris is a checkered one, at least until the 12th century, when it became the capital of the Gothic style, with masterpieces like the cathedral of Notre-Dame and the Sainte Chapelle, which still dominate the Île de la Cité, the historical and romantic heart of the city. After the mid-13th century, Paris plunged once again into anonymity, afflicted by the plague that raged across Europe, and subdued by the unending and bloody war with England.

The capital of a destroyed kingdom in a climate of political instability and internal division, Paris did not rise again until the mid-16th century, when Francis I decided to build a Renaissance-style palace worthy of a great and ambitious capital. It would take three centuries, seven different rulers and a regiment of architects (including Gian Lorenzo Bernini, whose plans were rejected by Louis XIV) to complete construction of the Louvre. Nevertheless, it may well have been this early concept of *grandeur* that spawned the Ville Lumière, or City of Light.

35 center top The richly decorated façade of the Hôtel de Ville overlooks the square named after the building, in the Marais district. The building was constructed at the end of the 19th century, after the previous city hall burned to the ground.

In fact, the 17th century was the first golden age of Paris. Louis XIV, who had moved his court to Versailles in the meantime, built the Hôtel des Invalides, and the powerful Cardinal Mazarin had the Collège des Quatre Nations built. During the 18th century, Louis XV built the Place de la Concorde and the École Militaire, with the open space of the Champs de Mars – the military training grounds dedicated to Mars, the god of war – extending in front of it as far as the Seine. But the heart of the city lay in mediaeval Paris, a labyrinth of dark and seedy alleys that soon became an invaluable ally for insurgents. The year 1789 was one of rebellion. Barricades were set up in the alleys and the king's troops were ambushed. The period that followed was chaos. The republican revolution was suffocated by its own violence, paving the way for a short

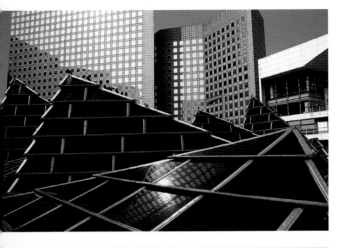

and authoritarian Corsican soldier who seized power, proclaiming himself emperor and challenging the monarchies of Europe. These were the years of the rise and fall of Napoleon Bonaparte who constructed the Église de la Madeleine, restructured the Quais of the Seine by building stone embankments, and constructed the Arc de Triomphe after the victorious Battle of Austerlitz.

But glory was short-lived. Following the French defeat at Waterloo, Paris went through decades of political upheaval. Its population had grown to one million by the mid-19th century when Louis Bonaparte, Napoleon's nephew, restored the empire and proclaimed himself Emperor Napoleon III. Under him, Paris became the capital of Europe through the city-planning revolution implemented by Baron Georges Haussmann. The architect of Napoleon III planned broad straight thoroughfares that cut across Place de l'Étoile and designed majestic boulevards, where new markets were established and the financial, industrial and cultural bourgeoisie constructed lavish buildings. The mediaeval city became a modern metropolis, ready to face the industrial revolution and the advent of the automobile.

This was the Paris where Charles Garnier designed the stylistic tangle of motifs decorating the immortal façade of the Opéra. It is the monumental capital that came alive in the pages of Proust, and at the end of the century it embarked on its latest madness, celebrating its magnificence with the boldest of works: the Eiffel Tower, the iron giant that marked the transition to modernity. In just a few years, Paris became the cradle of Art Nouveau and Art Deco, the home of cinema, which was invented by the Lumière brothers, and the hotbed of artistic movements. From Picasso to Braque, Modigliani, De Chirico, Kandinsky and Duchamp, all the most important artists of the era found inspiration and fertile ground for their ideas in Paris. And perhaps this is also the reason that, even today, the French

Paris

36 top right Oiseau de feu, *the kinetic sculpture created by Jean Tinguely and Niki de Saint-Phalle.*

36 top left and center top Daring *architectural forms and sculptures, like Alexander Calder's* red Stabile *(one of over 50 monumental contemporary artworks that have made the district an extraordinary outdoor museum), distinguish La Défense, the largest business district in Europe.*

36 center bottom The Forum des
Halles, which replaced the historic
covered market of Les Halles in
1979, houses galleries of shops,
exhibition centers and restaurants on
7 floors above and below street level.

36 bottom and 37 bottom
Outdoor escalators, which were
harshly criticized when the building
was inaugurated in 1969, are the
hallmark of the Centre Pompidou.

36-37 Elevators and tensile
structures occupy the "empty cube"
of the 367-foot-tall Grande Arche de
la Défense, which was inaugurated
in 1989 for the bicentennial of the
French Revolution.

Paris

39 top Covering nearly 20 acres, Place de la Concorde was originally dedicated to Louis XV. It was given its current name after the French Revolution to symbolize national reconciliation. In the 19th century the obelisk from Luxor, 2 fountains and 8 statues representing the largest cities in France were added to embellish this octagonal space.

39 center top The façade of Notre-Dame and the Dôme des Invalides – the former a Gothic masterpiece and the latter one of the finest examples of 17th-century French architecture – illuminate this night view of the City of Light.

39 center bottom A river of cars flows towards the Arc de Triomphe, one of the many symbols of Paris:

164 feet tall and 148 feet wide, it is the largest monument of its kind in the world.

39 bottom The fountains at Trocadéro, in front of Palais de Chaillot, are enchantingly illuminated in pale blue. This Neo-Classical building with impressive curved wings was built in 1937 for the Paris World's Fair.

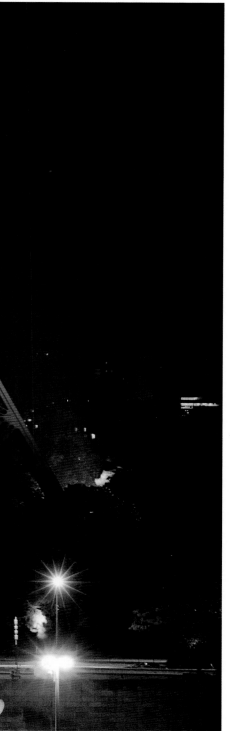

38-39 The arch formed by the base of the Eiffel Tower frames Palais Chaillot, on the Trocadéro hillside. A luxurious restaurant and even a post office are located on the first level of the famous tower, at a height of 122 feet.

38 bottom Pigalle, at the foot of the hill of Montmartre, is no longer the "district of sin." The only historic spot left here is the Moulin Rouge, whose dancers were captured in countless portraits by Toulouse-Lautrec. The venue offers nightly performances of the classic cancan.

capital is home to the most extraordinary array of museums in the world, such as the Louvre, the Musée d'Orsay, the Centre Pompidou and the Musée National de l'Art Moderne.

In fact, the Centre Pompidou launched the renaissance of Paris in our own era. Designed by Richard Rogers and Renzo Piano, the building was completed in 1977. It is a benchmark of contemporary architecture, completely inverting the roles of interior and exterior, and provocatively using ventilation systems and elevators as ornamental elements. In the past 25 years Paris has thus rediscovered its role as a beacon of culture. These efforts started with the restoration of the Gare d'Orsay, which was constructed for the 1900 World's Fair and was redesigned in 1987 by Gae Aulenti to become the showcase for Impressionist masterpieces. The years of François Mitterrand's presidency revived the pomp of late-19th-century Paris. In 1989 I.M. Pei's futuristic Pyramid was inaugurated amidst heated debate, becoming the sensational new entrance to the Louvre. At the same time, the Grande Arche de la Défense was built at the end of the straight line that links the Louvre and Place de l'Étoile through the Tuileries Gardens and the Boulevard des Champs Elysées, immediately becoming the emblem of the largest business district in Europe. In 1989, Dominique Perrault was commissioned to design the Bibliothèque Nationale de France. However, Mitterrand would not live long enough to see the last of the great works commissioned during his two terms of office. He died at the beginning of 1996, and the monumental library that now bears his name was inaugurated on December 20th of that year.

Today, the new Paris is a boundless metropolis that, in order to maintain its human scale, has created beaches on the banks of the Seine in the middle of what is usually an expressway. But perhaps this is also why Paris is Paris.

Dublin

IRELAND

The statue of Oscar Wilde stands across from No. 1, the house where the Wilde family moved when the writer was one year old. The bust of Michael Collins, the revolutionary who "constructed" Irish independence, is just a short distance away. The house of W. B. Yeats is at No. 82, and next door to it is the house in which poet and mystic George Russell lived. In short, Merrion Square is a piece of Dublin history, and of modern culture. The west side of the square is occupied by two of the capital's most elegant buildings, the National Gallery of Ireland, whose construction was funded in part by George Bernard Shaw, and Leinster House, the seat of Parliament. Built between 1745 and 1748, Leinster House was used as a model for the White House in Washington D.C., designed by none other than an Irish architect, James Hoban, who immigrated to the United States.

Merrion Square is also the heart of another "face" of Dublin, which until the Sixties – and thus after gaining its independence from the British Crown in 1949 – was the best example of Georgian architecture of all the cities in the British Isles. Trinity College is also English. Founded by Queen Elizabeth I in 1592, it banned Catholic students until 1793. Immortal figures like Wilde, Jonathan Swift, Bram Stoker and Nobel Laureate Samuel Beckett studied here. Trinity College is an immense campus today. Alongside its historical monuments, such as the Old Library with its dramatic Long Room and a wealth of 200,000 books, including the Book of Kells, one of the most celebrated illuminated manuscripts in the world, the campus features a number of important buildings, such as the Berkeley Library (1967), a masterpiece of modernist architecture designed by Le Corbusier's student Paul Koralek, and the equally functional Ussher Library (2001), with a glass pyramid set into its structure.

The hated English may have given the city its distinctive architectural appearance – they also designed the Grand Canal connecting Dublin to the Shannon River, as well as

41 bottom right Georgian
architecture, which became
popular at the end of the 18th
century, is typically English and
Protestant. Paradoxically,
however, even more than cities in
the British Isles, Dublin is the one
best characterized by this style.
Major figures in Irish history and
culture, such as Michael Collins
and James Joyce, lived in homes
like these.

40-41 The waters of the Liffey
reflect the main historic
buildings in the center of Dublin,
such as the Four Courts, whose
dome rises to the left of the river in
this picture.

41 bottom left The great poet
W.H. Auden considered them gloomy
and uncomfortable, but the city's
Georgian houses now show new
charm, softened by white stuccowork
and brightly painted doors.

42-43 Trinity College is Ireland's most prestigious university. Catholics have been admitted here since 1793, but until 1970 they had to obtain special dispensation from the archbishop in order to enroll here.

42 bottom The outcome of reconstruction work done in 1911, St. Patrick's Cathedral was built over the spot where the patron saint of Ireland baptized the first pagans. Between 1713 and 1745 Jonathan Swift, was dean of the church and wanted to be buried here with the epitaph: "The body of Jonathan Swift, Doctor of Sacred Theology, dean of this cathedral church, is buried here..."

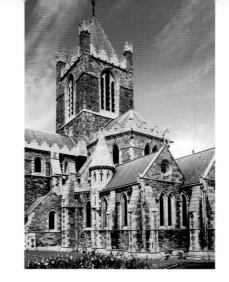

43 top A splendid example of Norman architecture, Christchurch was founded in 1172 by Richard de Clare, the first English invader of Ireland.

43 center The Long Room – 214 feet long – is the most spectacular hall at Trinity Library. It holds 200,000 of the oldest books in the library's vast collection. Since 1801, this institution has had the right to receive a free copy of every book published in Ireland and the United Kingdom.

43 bottom Dublin Castle, on the rise of Cork Hill overlooking the Liffey River near Christchurch, was founded over the ruins of a Viking fortress and was rebuilt several times. Its current appearance dates to the 18th century.

Phoenix Park, the biggest city park in Europe – but even the earliest material evidence of the history of the Irish capital reflects a "foreign" influence. Dublin Castle, the stern symbol of 700 years of British oppression, was built over a Viking settlement, and the city's two most important mediaeval churches, Christchurch and St. Patrick's Cathedral, clearly reflect their Norman origins.

And yet Dublin has a quintessentially Irish soul. Its buildings, its streets and even its pubs echo the pride, imagination and sense of humor of a population whose recovery only commenced fifteen years ago. This recovery began when Dublin found itself in the heart of an economic miracle that, through the success of companies working in the computer hardware and information technology sectors, turned Ireland in the fastest-growing nation in the European Union.

Europe's westernmost capital is a city with a population of one million, and it has remained immune to the problems that afflict metropolises. New wealth has stimulated the renovation of entire urban areas like Temple Bar, once a petit-bourgeois district on the Liffey River's south bank and now a chic and lively cultural center. And there are the docks on the other side of the Liffey, where state-of-the-art residences have been created. And, of course, there is O'Connell Street, the main thoroughfare through the center of town. Its new focal point is a monument that has been named the Dublin Spire, a steel needle rising to a height of nearly 400 feet.

In its path toward modernity, however, Dublin has not forgotten its traditions. In fact, the newest bridge over the Liffey, designed by Santiago Calatrava, is dedicated to the man who truly represents the *genius loci* of Dublin. Located near the house the writer used as the setting for his story *The Dead*, it has been named the James Joyce Bridge.

44 top The population of Ireland has the lowest average age in Europe, and this youthful character is reflected in many areas of Dublin. One of the liveliest is Temple Bar, with an enormous number of pubs as well as an array of contemporary art galleries and centers dedicated to music, photography and cinema.

44 bottom A stop at O'Connell Street to read the latest news. It is no accident that the Irish are the most assiduous newspaper readers in Europe. At least a dozen papers are published in Dublin in English as well as Gaelic, both of which are official languages of Republic of Ireland.

44-45 In the morning, the historic pub "The Temple Bar" in the Temple Bar district stocks up on Guinness. This dark, rich beer is one of the symbols of Ireland. In fact, the 200-year-old brewery was recently renovated and converted into the capital's most popular museum... all about beer, of course.

45 bottom Dubliners traditionally rendezvous on O'Connell Street, under Clerys clock. Located in an elegant building constructed in the 1920s and designed by architect Robert Atkinson, Clerys is a department store that has come to symbolize the Irish style.

London

GREAT BRITAIN

Twenty quid to go in there? I'd rather give the money to my mother-in-law!" This was one of the answers given to interviewers during the survey conducted among Londoners on their opinion of the Millennium Dome. It was the fateful year 2000 and, in order to celebrate it, the British capital spent £839 million (about $1.6 billion) to build a domed fiberglass structure – with a diameter of over 1,000 feet and a height of nearly 100 – on the broad promontory of Greenwich, just east of London. Greenwich is the location of the prime meridian and the place that marks Greenwich Mean Time, where time conventionally "begins." The immense Millennium Dome housed an exhibition about the future, which the city government defined with a brand-new word: *edutainment*, i.e., education-cum-entertainment.

The Millennium Dome was to symbolize the "new" London, but with an influx of visitors that was far less than expected, it has been a resounding flop. Moreover, the idea of earmarking Greenwich for entertainment when London urgently needed new residential areas to cater to a mushrooming population, made Lord Mayor Ken Livingston the target for enormous criticism. In fact, now – well before the year 2025, when the Dome is slated to be dismantled – city planners are already at work to remedy this failed extravaganza.

Apart from the ill-fated Millennium Dome, London has managed to make its triumphal entry to the 21st century thanks to architectural works worthy of its role as one of Europe's most important metropolises. Near Waterloo Bridge is the London Eye, the world's biggest Ferris wheel. Along the Thames, the old Canary Wharf dock area has become a business hub, and new construction has involved notables like Sir Norman Foster, Skidmore Owings & Merrill, Kohn Pedersen Fox, I. M. Pei and Cesar Pelli, who in 1991 designed the Canada Tower, the tallest building in the United Kingdom.

The new City Hall is also located on the riverbank, across from the Tower of London. This imposing building, a crystal bubble that metaphorically represents the transparency of democracy, is the work of Sir Norman Foster, who also left his mark on the City, or London's financial district. Known as the Swiss Re Tower, this cigar-shaped skyscraper is clad with over 258,000 square feet of glass panels, arranged to resemble the facets of a diamond. Until 2010, when Renzo Piano's London Bridge Tower – a 1000-foot giant that will look like a sliver of glass – is completed, the Swiss Re Tower will compete "only" with the Lloyd's Building, designed by Richard Rogers (1986),

46 top Lovely Victorian buildings with boutiques, restaurants and cafés are characteristic of Covent Garden, one of the city's liveliest districts.

46 center top A famous antiques market has been held on Portobello Road, in the heart of Notting Hill, since 1837.

46 center bottom Enormous billboards have been part of the urban furnishings of busy Piccadilly Circus since 1910.

46 bottom This view shows the National Gallery, on the left, and the tall spire of the church of St. Martin-in-the-Fields.

46-47 The Neo-Gothic Parliament Building, with Big Ben next to it, perfectly matches the architecture of nearby Westminster Abbey.

47 bottom left A Guards detachment marches past Buckingham Palace, for the ceremony of the Changing of the Guard.

47 bottom right Designed by Sir Horace Jones and completed in 1894, the Tower Bridge is considered a masterpiece of Victorian engineering, and one of the universally recognized symbols of London. Its Neo-Gothic towers house the mechanisms for raising the two-part span.

51°30'N - 0°007' W

London

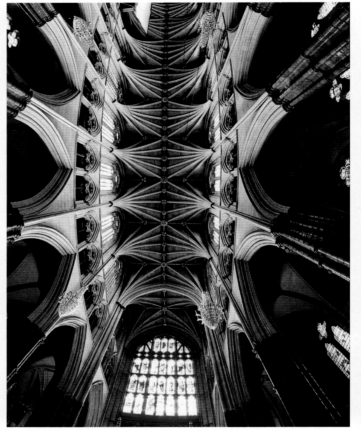

and with two 17th-century masterpieces: the Monument, which is the tallest stone column in the world, and the immense St. Paul's Cathedral, a treasure of the British Baroque style. Both were designed by Christopher Wren, the architect who rebuilt London after the Great Fire of 1666, when 87 churches and 15,000 dwellings burned to the ground.

Though the Great Fire represents a defining moment in the layout of London, the city owes its charm to its many layers of history. Recently, members of the English Heritage Association, influenced by the conservationist ideas of Prince Charles, the heir to the British throne, are moving heaven and earth to fight against new high-rises, which they feel ruin the London skyline. However, the contrast between tradition and the visionary modernity of the most recent architectures is part of what makes this metropolis of eight million people so surprising.

The Romans were the city's true founders. In AD 45, they marked out Londinium as a military camp on the banks of the Thames, exactly where the City (London's financial center) stands today. This small military settlement quickly developed into a prosperous city, which the Romans ruled until 410. This

was followed by a period of decline, but by the 8th century the Germanic Anglo–Saxon tribes – who gave England its name and language, and laid much of the groundwork for its future culture and literature – made London an important city once again. In fact, when the Normans, led by William the Conqueror, arrived in 1066 they found an industrious city they defined as "the market of the world."

William the Conqueror commissioned some magnificent monuments, including the Tower of London. This imposing fortified citadel was the stage for some of the key events in English history (including many state trials and executions) and it now houses the priceless Crown Jewels. The foundations for Westminster Abbey and Westminster Palace were also laid during this period. These two adjacent complexes have had a troubled history. The Abbey, in which the coronation ceremony of English monarchs takes place, was completely devastated by fire in 1298. A later structure was rebuilt in the 16th century in a bold Gothic style and subsequently renovated a number of times. Westminster Palace, which was the royal residence until 1512 and is now where Parliament meets, was

49 bottom left Established following the success of the 1851 World's Fair, the Victoria & Albert Museum boasts nearly 7 miles of galleries set on 4 floors. The museum also houses one of the richest and most eclectic applied arts collections in the world.

49 bottom right Traitors Gate – so called because traitors passed through it – leads to the Tower of London from the river. The complex, founded by William the Conqueror in the 11th century, safeguards the Crown Jewels, the most famous collection of gems in the world.

48 bottom right The nave of Westminster Abbey, which rises to a height of 102 feet, is the tallest one in England. This extraordinary building is both a national church and a memorial, as the country's most illustrious figures are buried here.

48-49 The Baroque masterpiece of St. Paul's Cathedral, in the heart of the City, was designed by Sir Christopher Wren. It was built between 1675 and 1710, after the previous cathedral was completely destroyed in the Great Fire of London in 1666.

50-51 A night view of the City, which has been the financial heart of London ever since the Romans established a trading post here 2000 years ago. The area boasts a number of extraordinary buildings, from St. Paul's Cathedral to the modern headquarters of Lloyd's Insurance Company, designed by Richard Rogers.

50 bottom left Architect Norman Foster designed one of the capital's most spectacular – and controversial – buildings. Known as the Swiss Re Tower, this 585-foot-tall cigar-shaped skyscraper, with 40 floors, is clad with over 258,000 square feet of glass panels, arranged to resemble the facets of a diamond.

50 bottom right For a short time, the London Eye, completed in 1999, held the record as the world's tallest Ferris wheel. The structure, which is 443 feet tall and weighs over 2000 tons, dominates the Waterloo-Westminster area. It is anchored by massive concrete foundations and tie-rods.

51 top left A view of the Embankment from the south bank of the Thames. The pedestrian walkway of Hungerford Bridge, inaugurated in 2002, extends towards the captivating architecture that marks the multipurpose urban complex of Charing Cross Station, designed by Terry Farrell. Built in 1990, it has modernized one of the city's historic districts.

51 top right A classic postcard view of London, with Big Ben, the Houses of Parliament and Westminster Abbey. With a population of 7 million, London is now the 21st largest metropolis on the planet: in Europe, only Paris and Moscow are larger.

51 bottom The venue for an exhibition held in 2000 about future trends, the Millennium Dome is one of the most controversial modern structures in the London area. Nevertheless, its dome – 1050 feet across and 98 feet high – is impressive.

London

ravaged by fires a number of times and was completely rebuilt in the 19th century in a Neo-Gothic style to match Westminster Abbey. Big Ben, the clock tower that was erected in 1859 and has become one of the symbols of London, is part of the Westminster Palace buildings.

In the 16th century, under King Henry VIII (who broke away from the Catholic Church) and then under his daughter Elizabeth I (who laid the foundations for Britain's colonial initiatives) London became the largest city in Europe, with a population exceeding 200,000. At the beginning of the 18th century, following reconstruction after the Great Fire, the city began to attract immigrants and its population grew to over 750,000. It mushroomed to one million by 1801, and then doubled over the following thirty years. With the Industrial Revolution, London became the world's largest and most powerful city. In the 19th century, during the 60-year reign of Queen Victoria, London became the seat of government of one of the most powerful empires in history.

The city's main monuments provide visitors with a glimpse of London's dazzling history. The squares – from Trafalgar Square to Piccadilly Circus – bear witness to military and political triumphs, and the city's elegant Edwardian, Georgian and Victorian homes reflect the substantial wealth of its professional and commercial leadership. London's museums, from the colossal British Museum – one of the oldest public

museums in the world – to the National Gallery, and splendid parks celebrate its citizens' love of learning, art and nature. Marvels of engineering, like the extraordinary Tower Bridge (completed in 1894), the massive docks and the many mechanical treasures of the Science Museum, are a tribute to the British proclivity for the sciences.

While London boasts an astonishing array of treasures – from the royal residence of Buckingham Palace to constantly evolving exhibition venues like the Victoria and Albert Museum (which will soon include the visionary annex designed by Daniel Libeskind) and the Tate Modern, designed by Swiss architects Herzog and De Meuron – justice is not done to the metropolis if we overlook its less-known corners, from its markets to the fashions created here and the distinctive personality of each district. And, above all, by the veritable melting pot of races living here.

The age of the great empire has come to a close, but today's London, with all its contradictions, its inventions and its nostalgic memories, sums it up perfectly. It is telling that in the borough of Neasden, just a short distance from Wembley Stadium, in 1995 London's Indian community inaugurated the Shri Swaminarayan Mandir, the largest Hindu temple built in the 20th century. In effect, this reflects "reverse colonization" by immigrants from what was once the most important British colony of all.

52-53 A dense network of 160 canals winding their way through hundreds of islands makes Amsterdam one of the most charming capitals of continental Europe.

52 bottom left Constructed in 1840, the Magere Brug is the most characteristic bridge in Amsterdam, and it was built in the classic Dutch style of wooden bridges.

52 bottom right Some of Amsterdam's most famous buildings are located along the Oude Turfmarkt, one of the city's innermost basins, and they date as far back as 1642.

53 top Considered the city boundary until the 15th century, in 1586 the Singel was turned into a city canal and became the pride of Amsterdam. This is where the new merchant classes built their homes. Today the 7000 residences built along its banks in the 17th century are considered national treasures.

Amsterdam
THE NETHERLANDS

It is the city of Van Gogh, Rembrandt and Piet Mondrian, but it is also the hometown of Jo Coenen, Sjoerd Soeters and Adrian Geuze, the architects who are redesigning its urban fabric based on a philosophy that brings residential areas to the forefront in both private construction and public works.

Considered one of Europe's most livable capitals, Amsterdam is also one of its smallest in terms of both population and extent, with 700,000 inhabitants crowded around a historic district that was founded in the second half of the 13th century around the Dam, the market square. Over the course of two and a half centuries, the city built at the point where the Amstel flows into the vast inlet formed by the estuary of the IJ grew to a population of 30,000. It was immediately dubbed "the Venice of the North," as it has a dense network of concentric canals (today there are 160) encircling approximately 100 islands. However, it was during the 17th century that Amsterdam became the commercial hub of northern Europe. During this period, a powerful bourgeoisie of traders started to build sumptuous homes on the banks of the Singel, the canal that had once been considered the very edge of the city.

Today the Singel is an internal waterway, and exploring this area means entering a cityscape of buildings with tall narrow façades, steeply pitched roofs, and gilded friezes, images of classical deities and finely crafted frontons. More than 7000 17th-century houses along the canals have been awarded the status of national monument, in a hotbed of styles demonstrating the variety and originality of Dutch architecture. The Royal Palace, which originally served as Amsterdam's city hall, the Renaissance Westerkerk, Holland's most monumental church, which is topped by a 278-foot tower, and the Magere Brug, considered one of the most picturesque of the city's 1280 bridges, were also built during this period. One of the few exceptions is the Beurs van Berlage Building, constructed between 1898 and 1903, and considered the most important Dutch work of the 19th century. The first major work designed

by architect Hendrik Petrus Berlage, this impressive building erected on the banks of the Amstel to house a commercial exchange has now been turned into an important exhibition and conference center. The Singel has effectively become a divide between old Amsterdam – which remains the heart of the city – and modern Amsterdam, which is now undergoing a dynamic renewal process. This process can be seen starting with the point of arrival, Schiphol International Airport. On December 9, 2002, the day the Rijksmuseum Amsterdam Schiphol was inaugurated, it became the only airport in the world incorporating a prestigious cultural institution. In fact, this is a branch of the city's main museum, with paintings by Vermeer, Jan Steen, Frans Hals and, naturally, Rembrandt.

However, the architectural scope that makes Amsterdam virtually an open-air workshop can be perceived above all in the residential quarters that are being built to provide the city's mushrooming population with revolutionary living solutions. For example, KNSM Island, which until 1977 served as the headquarters of the KNSM shipping firm, has become one of the most desirable places to live. Planned by architect Jo Coenen, it showcases buildings like the monumental Piraeus by Hans Kolhoff and Cristian Rapp, as well as the stunning Barcelona condominium designed by the Belgian Bruno Albert in 1993. The most ambitious challenge is still underway. This is the Ijburg, a complex of seven new islands reclaimed from the Ijmeer, and 18,000 homes will be completed there by 2012. For the time being, the most striking work is the bridge linking the first island, Steiger Island, to the city; the bridge, designed by Nicholas Grimshaw, was completed in 2001. Nevertheless, Ijburg is already the sought-after arena of experimentation for dozens of architects committed to striking a new urban balance: living in the city while enjoying a suburban or rural quality of life. And perhaps it is this constant quest for balance and middle ground that holds the secret of a city that is seemingly immobile yet perpetually evolving.

54 top Sint Nicolaaskerk was built between 1874 and 1877, and this enormous, stately church in the heart of the city is the largest Catholic building in Amsterdam. Two square towers crown its façade, and its octagonal dome is topped by a lantern with a crucifix.

54 bottom Leidsestraat, was opened in 1663 to alleviate the traffic of carts transporting goods to and from the port. Its name comes from the fact that it marks the beginning of the road to Leiden.

54-55 Designed in 1889 by Pierre Cuypers, who was also the architect of the Rijksmuseum, the Centraal Station is a monumental Neo-Gothic building constructed on an artificial island. The building, embellished with Victorian-style ornamentation, is located in the heart of the city's mediaeval district.

55 bottom left The Royal Palace, an architecturally well-balanced and richly decorated structure, is built in the Dutch classicist style. The frontons on both the east and west façades are decorated with magnificent marble groups. The one facing the Dam represents peace, commemorating the Peace of Westphalia, which was signed in 1648 and ended the Thirty Years' War.

55 bottom right Just its Neo-Gothic architecture, designed by Pierre Cuypers in 1885, would be enough to make the Rijksmuseum an extraordinary structure, particularly because of the work started in 2005 to renovate the entire museum. Nevertheless, its remarkable art collections, with works by the Dutch masters from the city's golden age, are what make it one of the most important museums in the world.

56 top left *The first Protestant church in Amsterdam, the Zuiderkerk was built between 1603 and 1614, and was designed by Hedrick de Keyser.*

Amsterdam

56 top right *The Zuiderkerk, which was inspired by the layout of Roman basilicas and the proportions of Renaissance churches, is characterized by Tuscan columns and barrel vaults. At the end of World War II it was used temporarily as a shelter for the wounded and a morgue for the countless victims of the conflict.*

56 bottom and 57 bottom left *The Keizersgracht – literally the Emperor's Channel, as it is dedicated to the Holy Roman Emperor, Maximilian I – is one of Amsterdam's three main waterways. The splendid 17th-century residences along its banks make it one of the most popular and exclusives areas in the city.*

56-57 *The Royal Palace in Amsterdam was built in the middle of the 17th century to house City Hall, and Jacob van Campen was commissioned to design a building with great visual impact. In 1808 Louis Bonaparte transformed it into a royal residence. It was restored in 1960 and part of it is open to the public.*

57 bottom right *The Nieuwmarkt, a monumental building that resembles a mediaeval castle, housed the central market of Amsterdam until the 15th century. However, its current structure dates to the 17th century.*

58-59 *The Berliner Fernsehturm television tower marks Alexanderplatz, the heart of the city. In the foreground, the historic Deutsche Oberbaumbrücke crosses the Spree River.*

58 bottom *Nikolaiviertel, along on the Spree, is the city's oldest historical district. Visible beyond the rooftops are the spires of the Nikolaikirche, the oldest church in Berlin.*

59 top *The gilded 26-foot statue of Winged Victory, the work of Friedrich Drake, stands atop the Siegessäule column erected between 1871 and 1873.*

59 center *Built between 1695 and 1699 as the summer residence of Sophia Charlotte, wife of Frederick I, the first Prussian emperor, Schloss Charlottenburg is the city's largest and most elegant palace. Its delightful park, which has been restored in the original French Baroque style, is a favorite Sunday destination for Berliners.*

59 bottom *The red-brick Rotes Rathaus, built between 1861 and 1869, houses City Hall. Inspired by the Italian Renaissance, it is decorated with the "chronicle in stone," a frieze showing scenes and figures from city life. Across from it is Reinhold Begas' Fountain of Neptune, built between 1886 and 1891 and inspired by Bernini's fountain.*

Berlin

GERMANY

Goodbye Lenin, a 2003 film by Wolfgang Becker, is the story of a young man, the son of an ultra-loyal official of the German Democratic Republic, who does everything in his power to prevent his mother – in a coma when the Berlin Wall fell – from discovering upon her awakening that, in the meantime, Germany has been reunified. In a crescendo of hilarious gags, the movie opens a "private" window onto one of the most sensational events of the 20th century. Today, over a decade later, people can joke about the fall of the Berlin Wall, because now that East and West have been "sutured" the new Berlin has become a reality. Not even the *Ossis* and *Wessis*, the "Eastern" and "Western" Berliners, acknowledge any differences between themselves. Naturally, you might still see someone behind the wheel of a Trabant, but in all likelihood it will be a former West Berliner with a passion for collecting old cars. Indeed, the new Berlin is extraordinarily young – at least by European standards. Of its approximately 4 million inhabitants, nearly half are under the age of 35, and 14 percent are under the age of 18. In short, they are people who have no memory of the city's painful past.

Nevertheless, the preservation of memory has been a key item on the agenda of the administrators, city planners and architects responsible for redesigning the capital of the united Germany. This is a project that, between the end of the second millennium and the beginning of the third, turned Berlin into the most extensive, ambitious and stimulating building yard in Europe and, possibly, the world. Although its new architectures have garnered awe and admiration, what makes the city unique is the continuous dialog between past and present, as well as the extraordinarily successful attempt to transpose the "human experience" of Berlin's history into architecture. In fact, the "Berlin model" is already being discussed as a political, city-planning and even philosophical handbook for the metropolis of tomorrow.

Indeed, Berlin has never been a city to take small steps. As the capital of the Prussian empire, it was constructed in a monumental Neo-Classical style by the inspired architect Karl Friedrich Schinkel, who conceived it as an "Athens on the Spree." Today, some of his most magnificent works are part of the extraordinary complex of Museuminsel, the island of museums on the river near Unter den Linden, the boulevard that

starts at the famous Brandenburg Gate. This is the same thoroughfare where the disconcerting military parades of the Third Reich were held – as documented by Leni Riefenstahl's films – when Hitler nurtured his dream of transforming Berlin into a "universal capital." He appointed Albert Speer to construct it and, in his delirium, the city was destined for immortality: Hitler was convinced that 2000 years later its ruins would be as celebrated as those of ancient Rome. Fortunately, that Germany remained a dream, and only a few years later Berlin was reduced to a pile of rubble through ceaseless Allied bombing. With the construction of the Berlin Wall, the two Berlins developed very distinctive and opposite styles, and even now these differences are still respected. A good example can be seen in the plans, still in the implementation phase, for Alexanderplatz, which was the "showcase" of the DDR. This

60-61 The dome of the Reichstag –
considered an architectural
masterpiece – is powerfully
symbolic: through it, Germany's
political life is visible to the entire
country, since it is open to the public
even when the Bundestag is in
session.

60 bottom During the day, a
sophisticated system of 360 mirrors
lets natural light into the hall where
the Bundestag meets.

61 By night, the dome is lit up by a
dozen 1000-watt spotlights that
make it clearly visible over 2 miles
away.

square clearly reflects a formal analogy between the new architectures and the existing "socialist-realistic" buildings, dominated by the Berliner Fernsehturm television tower.

The new Berlin has many symbols – perhaps too many. So many that Berlin is literally overwhelming. Potsdamer Platz is one of the most extraordinary compendia of contemporary architecture, with works by notables like Renzo Piano, Arata Isozaki, Helmut Jahn, Richard Rogers and Rafael Moneo. At the same time, however, due to the fact that it has been built over what was "no man's land" separating two worlds for forty years, it represents a kind of "open-heart surgery" of the entire process of the rebirth of Berlin. Likewise, Friedrichstrasse, located in what was formerly East Berlin, is not merely the most exclusive shopping street (the Galeries Lafayette department store was designed by Frenchman Jean Nouvel), but the "personification" of the triumph of the marketplace. The Reichstag, which in 1999 was chosen as the seat of the Bundestag, the government's

portrayal of the fate of the Jews in Hitler's Germany.

Now that (almost) all the great works have been completed, it is clear that Berlin has gained a sense of self-awareness and has successfully transformed itself into a joyous and optimistic city. Its architects have effectively ushered in a desire for creativity that can be perceived in every street and district. To get an idea, one can enter the DG Bank, with its austere façade on Pariser Platz, next to the Brandenburg Gate, and then move on to the visionary world of Frank O. Gehry's organic architecture. Or you can go to the Hamburger Bahnhof, the old railway station that was restored by Josef Paul Kleihues and has been turned into an extraordinary contemporary art museum, where you'll discover that the latest artistic trends are enthusiastically welcomed by the general population. From the outside, the building looks like an amusement park, as it is decorated with installations by neon-art genius Dan Flavin. Instead, a peek at the building yard (one

highest legislative body, can be admired for the clear dome, designed by Sir Norman Foster, that has restored the former splendor of the building constructed between 1884 and 1894 to house the government of the Empire. Its very monumentality symbolizes Germany's desire to come forward as the "main power" of a continent that wants to play a leading role on the world chessboard.

Daniel Libeskind, one of the leading theoreticians of symbolic architecture, designed the city's most astonishing building, and it is no accident that it is considered the most significant architectural work completed in Berlin between the postwar period and today. It is the Jewish Museum, a zinc-clad structure shaped like a thunderbolt (or a broken Star of David). Oblique slits set across its silvery surface correspond to the lines that, during the design phase, Libeskind marked on the map of Berlin to connect the points where Jewish intellectuals like Heine, Mies van der Rohe, Kleist, Brecht and others once lived. The building is called "Between the Lines" and it is the perfect – and profoundly dramatic –

of the few that is still open) of the Lehrter Bahnhof offers a preview of the future. When the station goes into full operation in 2010, it will handle 800 trains and 240,000 passengers a day, making it the hub of an ever larger and more united Europe.

With all due respect to the French and Italians, today Berlin is a capital that is never dull, a city that spawns cultures, styles and fashions. This is no news to the fanatics of the latest trends, for whom the city's bars, nightspots and boutiques are a must, whereas cinema and theater aficionados have witnessed the renaissance of the great tradition in which Bertolt Brecht played a leading role. Economic experts consider Berlin a fascinating laboratory, given the fact that the capital and its hi-tech companies boast the highest rate of innovation and development in Europe.

And to think that during the Seventies Berlin was considered the haven of idlers. At the time, many people in bustling West Germany gave the city the cynical moniker *Tunis*, a play on the term *Tue Nichts*, which means "doing nothing." Today, one can barely keep up with this city.

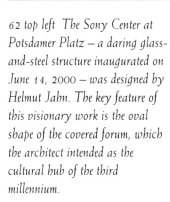

Berlin

62 top left The Sony Center at Potsdamer Platz – a daring glass-and-steel structure inaugurated on June 14, 2000 – was designed by Helmut Jahn. The key feature of this visionary work is the oval shape of the covered forum, which the architect intended as the cultural hub of the third millennium.

62 top right The Berliner Fernsehturm, the gigantic television tower that rises over Alexanderplatz, is one of the tallest structures in Europe. It was completed in 1969 and it has attracted over 37 million visitors, particularly after 1993, when new elevators were installed. They take just 40 seconds to ascend over 650 feet.

62 center Berlin's Neue Nationalgalerie, built between 1965 and 1968, is one of the architectural masterpieces of Mies van der Rohe, one of the leading figures of the rationalist movement and director of the Bauhaus in the Thirties. Têtes et Queues ("Heads and Tails"), a spectacular sculpture by Alexander Calder, is visible on the left in front of the building.

62 bottom The semicircular shape of the Bahn Tower stands out in the middle of the night view of the center of Berlin, illuminated by a phantasmagoria of lights. After the dark decades of the Wall that cut the city in two, Berlin – an extraordinary encounter of history and modernity – now has a population of about 4.5 million and has powerfully come forward as an European capital.

62-63 The sculpture Berlin, created by Martin Matschinsky and Brigitte Denninghoff in 1987 to celebrate the 750th anniversary of the city, creates a startling frame for the Neo-Romanesque Kaiser-Wilhelm-Gedächtnis-Kirche. The church was built between 1891 and 1895 in honor of Kaiser Wilhelm I and was destroyed by Allied bombs on November 3, 1943.

63 bottom Brandenburg Gate is indubitably Berlin's most famous monument. Designed by Karl Gotthard Langhans, the city's first Neo-Classical monument was commissioned by Friedrich Wilhelm II in 1791 to represent peace. In an ironic twist of fate, in the mid-20th century it was incorporated into the Berlin Wall, the terrible emblem of the Cold War.

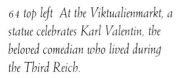

64 top left At the Viktualienmarkt, a statue celebrates Karl Valentin, the beloved comedian who lived during the Third Reich.

64 top right The futuristic 374-foot-tall Hypo-Haus was the tallest building in Munich from 1981 to 2004.

64 center The seat of the Bavarian Parliament, the Maximilianeum was built by Maximilian II between 1857 and 1874. This impressive complex

was originally supposed to copy the style of Greek and Roman buildings. However, with its Neo-Renaissance arches, the building acquired a highly original appearance by the time it was finished.

64 bottom Established in 1810 to celebrate the marriage of Ludwig, the Bavarian crown prince, and Princess Therese von Sachsen-Hildburghausen, Oktoberfest now attracts millions of the visitors to Munich every year.

Munich
GERMANY

For the stern Germans of the north, Munich is a "southern" city in the "philosophical" sense of the word. Much as they might denigrate it, however, a recent survey shows that Munich is where 80 percent of the "other" German citizens would like to live. Munich's fame as a "pleasure-loving" city stems from the fact that it hosts Oktoberfest, the world's biggest beer festival. Despite its name, Oktoberfest starts in September, and the two-week festival attracts 6 million visitors every year.

Set on the banks of the Isar River and protected by the Alps, whose snowy peaks are perfectly visible from the center of town on clear days, Munich enjoys an enviable position. Its geography is an intrinsic part of its history, and in the course of a thousand years – with enormous acceleration in the past century – it has been transformed from a village built around a monastery (*München* means "place of the monks") to the third-largest city in Germany. It now has a population of nearly 1.5 million people and is considered one of Europe's top hi-tech centers.

This friendly and cosmopolitan city is the home of prestigious cultural institutions, including 45 museums. The most recent is the Pinakothek der Moderne, inaugurated in 2002 and designed by architect Stephan Braunfels, who conceived the structure as an "organism of light." In terms of the size of its exhibition area and the value of its collections of modern and contemporary art, in Europe it is rivaled only by the Beaubourg in Paris and the Tate Modern in London. The Pinakothek actually houses four museums under one roof: the Staatsgalerie Moderner Kunst (modern art), the Neue Sammlung (design), the Architekturmuseum (architecture), and the Staatliche Graphische Sammlung (graphics). The 19th-century Alte Pinakothek, located directly across from the Pinakothek der Moderne, is another cultural gem, and it houses works by masters like Dürer, Rubens

65 bottom left Swans and other birds animate the park at Nymphenburg Castle, viewed from an unusual angle in this winter scene.

65 bottom right The Ahnengalerie of the Munich Residenz, displays portraits of the most important members of the Wittelsbach family up to Ludwig III.

64-65 Twin bell towers mark the Munich cathedral. On the right, the Neues Rathaus (new city hall) in the Marienplatz was built in the second half of the 19th century. It is famous for the Glockenspiel, the clock tower with colorful figures that move when the hour strikes.

66 top left Marienplatz, dominated by the bell towers of the Frauenkirche, was the location of the mediaeval market.

66 top right Designed by Viennese architect K. Schwarzer and completed in 1972, the BMW complex is over 330 feet tall. Its four towers are clustered together to evoke the cylinders of an internal-combustion engine.

66 bottom The Feldherrnhalle, inspired by the Loggia dei Lanzi in Florence, was built by Ludwig I in the first half of the 19th century.

66-67 Marienplatz is the true heart of Munich. The square is named after the bronze statue of the Virgin Mary, the patron of Bavaria, which the prince-elector Maximilian I installed on a tall marble column in 1638.

and Altdorfer. Together, they constitute a museum center that is just a short distance from the fascinating Schwabing, Munich's bohemian quarter, and the Altstadt, its elegant historic district.

In addition to being one of the liveliest and most extensive traffic-free pedestrian zones in Europe, the Altstadt boasts monuments of enormous historic and artistic interest. Overlooking Karlsplatz – or Stachus, as the people of Munich call it – is Karlstor, which was the main gate to the city during the 14th century. Just beyond it, the 320-foot-tall towers of the Frauenkirche, the Gothic cathedral, are the picture-postcard symbol of Munich. Nevertheless, the key role in the old city is played by Marienplatz, the square dominated by the spires of the Neues Rathaus, the Neo-Gothic city hall. Its façade has an enormous carillon whose mechanism activates 32 figures representing key persons in the history of the city.

The triumphal Neo-Classical part of Munich, promoted by King Ludwig I during the first half of the 19th century, is also fascinating; the most superb buildings from this period can be seen at Königsplatz and in Ludwigstrasse. Two of the most

intriguing modern buildings are the impressive BMW headquarters (1972), with a form reminiscent of a four-cylinder engine, and the futuristic Herz Jesu Kirche (2000). Designed by architects Allmann, Sattler and Wappner, this ultramodern church is composed of a translucent glass parallelepiped containing another parallelepiped made of wooden slats, which houses the liturgical space. This building is essentially the "offspring" of the citywide construction policy promoting new concepts in contemporary architecture and launched in 1972, the year Munich hosted the Olympics. The Olympic Park was constructed the same year, and it is still an attraction today. The cycle-racing track was recently converted into an electronic game park that simulates the various Olympic sports.

Finally, following the enormous investment made by the city government and approved by a referendum passed by Munich residents, with the 2006 World Soccer Cup matches approaching, the Olympiastadium, the home of the beloved Bavarian soccer team, will be abandoned to make room for a new and even more surprising sports complex.

67 bottom left The Bayerische Staatsoper, the home of the Bavarian State Opera, was designed by François Cuvilliés and inaugurated in 1753. Over the course of more than 250 years, it has staged extraordinary premières.

67 bottom right Inspired by the Arch of Constantine in Rome, the triumphal arch of the Siegestor was built at one end of Ludwigstrasse (the Feldherrnhalle is at the other end) in 1852 to celebrate the victories of the Bavarian army.

68-69 This splendid view of the Neva and of the monumental Palace Embankment was taken from Troitsky Most, or Trinity Bridge. The bridge, which is 1910 feet long, was inaugurated for the bicentennial of St.

Petersburg and is decorated with cast-iron lampposts shaped like candelabra.

68 bottom With the foundation of the Peter-Paul Fortress on the island of Petrograd in 1703, Czar

Peter the Great began to build his city. The original wooden structure was replaced by a stone complex designed by Domenico Trezzini and dominated by the steeple of the Peter-Paul Cathedral.

69 top The Grand Ducal Museum is located next to the Peter-Paul Cathedral. Many of the noblemen killed during the Bolshevik Revolution, which began on the banks of the Neva in 1917, are buried here.

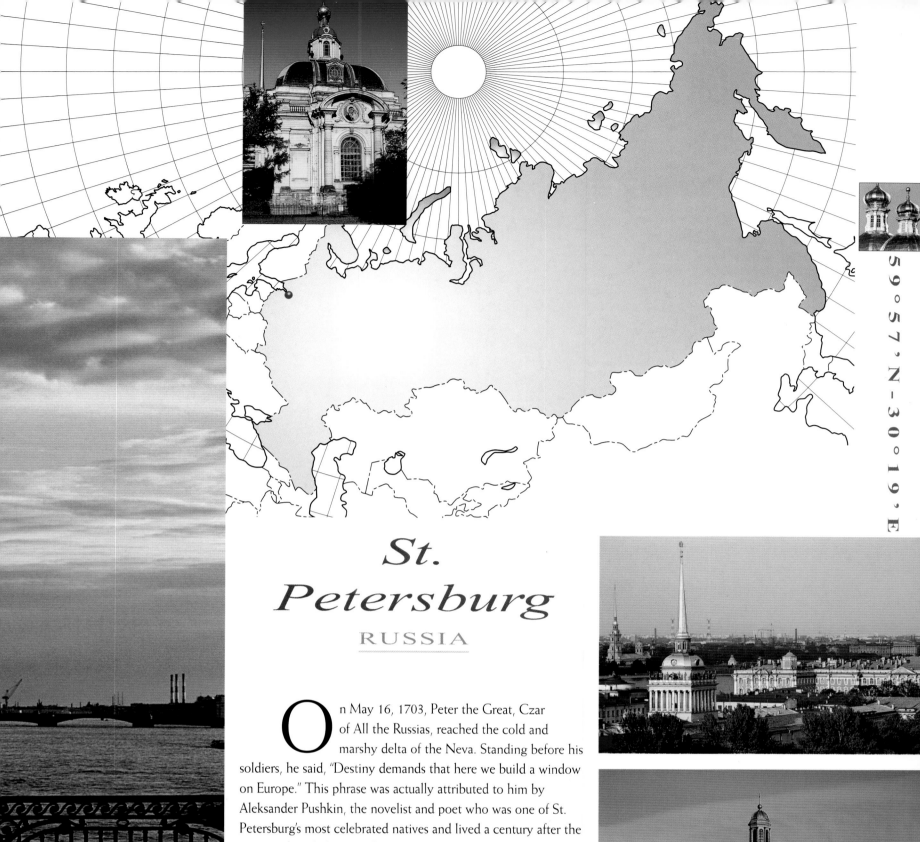

St. Petersburg

RUSSIA

O n May 16, 1703, Peter the Great, Czar of All the Russias, reached the cold and marshy delta of the Neva. Standing before his soldiers, he said, "Destiny demands that here we build a window on Europe." This phrase was actually attributed to him by Aleksander Pushkin, the novelist and poet who was one of St. Petersburg's most celebrated natives and lived a century after the city was founded. As is often the case in literature, Pushkin gave these events legendary importance to lend merit to the extraordinary foundation and destiny of St. Petersburg. It is likely that, at the time, the young sovereign – who had not yet earned the epithet "The Great" – used the royal "we" as befitted his rank. History tells us that the idea of creating a capital that would rival the magnificence of the great European cities, to the detriment of "Asiatic" Moscow, was purely the result of his stubbornness. Moreover, it was a concept that was opposed by the powerful and corrupt Muscovite court.

Peter was a determined man. He loved the sea, had traveled extensively and was willing to get his hands dirty, working as an ordinary laborer at a Dutch shipyard. A man of Spartan habits, in order to oversee construction of the city that would be named after him, he spent two years living in a poor wooden house with just two rooms. This hovel, now protected by a stone structure, can still be visited today on the island of Petrograd, the original settlement of St. Petersburg.

Extending over an area of 540 square miles, St. Petersburg,

69 center *The spire of the stunning Admiralty stands out on the city skyline. The building has housed the Naval Engineering School since 1925. Its Neo-Classic appearance is the work of Andrei Zacharov, who in 1804 expanded a military structure built by Peter the Great.*

69 bottom *Designed in 1818 by French architect Auguste de Montferrand, who was unknown at the time, St. Isaac's Cathedral is one of the largest churches in the world. It took over 200 pounds of gold to finish the cupola alone.*

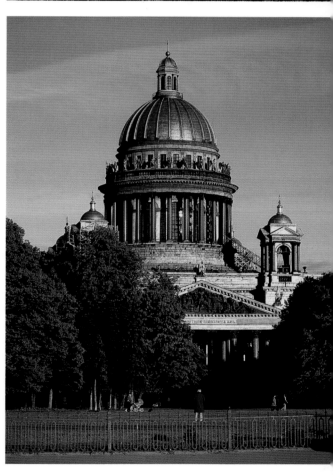

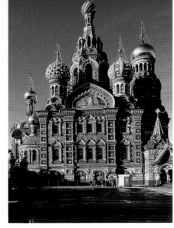

70 top left Gilded domes top the St. Nicholas Cathedral, a Russian Baroque masterpiece built between 1753 and 1762. The building encloses two churches; the bare and almost mystical appearance of the lower one creates a sharp contrast with the liveliness of the upper one, which boasts a superb iconostasis.

70 top right With its 75,000 square feet of mosaics and five enameled domes, the Church of Our Savior of the Spilled Blood is the least European-looking church in the city. Czar Alexander III had it built over the spot where his predecessor was assassinated on March 1, 1881.

which has a population of 5 million, is composed of 44 islands divided by 50 canals and rivers, the most important of which are the Neva and its five tributaries. Just 500 miles from the Arctic circle, it is one of the world's northernmost metropolises on the planet; only Helsinki and Reykjavik are closer. To celebrate the 300th anniversary of its foundation, in 2003 the Russian government – led by Vladimir Putin, a native of St. Petersburg – spent the enormous sum of $1.3 billion to restore its magnificent architecture, bestowing great honors upon Peter the Great and all those after him who helped make it one of the most beautiful and fascinating cities in the world.

It is no accident that St. Petersburg is associated with some of the key figures and episodes in the cultural history of Russia.

Tchaikovsky, Stravinsky and Shostakovich wrote immortal symphonies here, Pushkin, Dostoevsky and Gogol wrote their masterpieces, and Mendeleev and Pavlov made enormous contributions to science. The figures of Peter the Great and his successors, including the equally extraordinary and strong-willed Catherine the Great, "live" here in the magnificent works they commissioned from inspired architects. This is also where Rasputin, the most visionary and controversial figure in Russian history, lived and was assassinated. The first shots attacking the Winter Palace, marking the demise of the Romanovs and leading to the establishment of the Soviet Union, were fired from the cruiser *Aurora*, which is still docked on the bank of the Neva. And during World War II, the city faced the most dramatic siege in history.

Under Communism, the city's name was changed to Leningrad, but Soviet power spared its elegant albeit reactionary architecture: Stalin preferred to "leave a mark" by constructing enormous "socialist-realistic" buildings on the outskirts as well as some of the city's splendid subway stations. With the collapse of the Soviet empire, the city regained its former name of St. Petersburg through a referendum whereby its citizens rewarded the city's capacity to overcome the enormous upheavals of history by remaining faithful to itself and its dreams.

Nicholas II, Russia's last czar, loved to tell foreign guests at his court that "St. Petersburg is in Russia, but remember that it is not Russia." In fact, the only building that reflects Russian tradition is the Church of the Resurrection, which was started in 1882 and modeled after the "Oriental" Cathedral of St. Basil in Moscow. Much of the city's early architecture – a triumph of the Baroque, Rococo and Neo-Classical styles – was produced by illustrious Europeans. Peter the Great relied heavily on Domenico Trezzini, who designed the Peter-Paul Fortress and cathedral (where most of the Romanovs were buried), the Summer Palace, the Twelve Colleges building (which houses twelve ministries) and numerous aristocratic residences.

Following Peter's death, the czarinas Anne and Elizabeth

70 center *The Nevsky Prospekt is the main thoroughfare of the center of St. Petersburg. It is over 2.5 miles long, the Admiralty is situated at one end of this boulevard and the Alexander Nevsky Monastery is at the other.*

70 bottom *A pair of magnificent cast-iron lions decorates the Bank Bridge, an elegant footbridge built in the 1830s by the engineer Pavel Sokolov over the Griboedova Canal.*

70-71 *The Church of Our Savior on the Spilled Blood ends the view of the Griboedova Canal, one of the artificial waterways built by Peter the Great. Inspired by Amsterdam's urban landscape, the czar wanted to "tame" the branches of the River Neva.*

71 bottom *The statue of Alexander Pushkin welcomes visitors to the Russian Museum, located in Mikhailovsky Palace, one of the city's most exquisite examples of Neo-Classic architecture. It was designed by the Italian architect Carlo Rossi in 1819.*

72 top Stuccowork, gilding and priceless furnishings give every room in the private apartments of the Winter Palace a sumptuous air. Most of the furniture dates after 1837, when a fire devastated the building.

72 center A sculptural group portraying the chariot of Victory tops the enormous triumphal arch that connects the two wings of the General Staff Building in the Palace Square. It was designed by Carlo Rossi.

turned to the inventive architect Bartolomeo Francesco Rastrelli, who completed magnificent works such as the unsurpassed Winter Palace and the suburban palace of Tsarskoe Selo. Even the statistics about the two buildings are impressive. The former has 1,800 windows, and the façade of the latter, covered in stuccowork and gilding, is 1,115 feet long. Rastrelli also designed the harmonious Smolny Convent

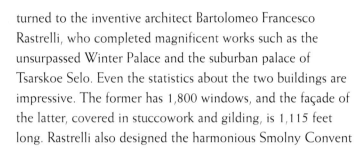

and the austere Admiralty, whose dizzying spire still marks the heart of the city.

Another great czarina, Catherine, also looked to Europe and the Enlightenment to give the city what would later become the Hermitage Museum. With its heritage of 2.7 million works displayed in 400 rooms in six buildings (including the Winter Palace), it is second only to the Louvre. Catherine and her descendents brought other Italian architects to St. Petersburg, such as Giacomo Quarenghi, who worked here from 1779 to 1810 and designed splendid Neo-Classical works (such as the Hermitage Theater), as well as the Frenchman Auguste de Montferrand, who designed St. Isaac's Cathedral. The design of the Kazan Cathedral was also entrusted to Russian architects, though they were required to model it after St. Peter's Basilica in Rome. Another Italian, Carlo Rossi, arrived in 1819 and gave the city's architectural layout – exceptional in and of itself – an air of incomparable harmony. Rossi designed the extraordinary sequence of the three squares in the heart of St. Petersburg: the Winter Palace Square, the center of the empire; the Decembrists Square, the administrative center; St. Isaac's Square, the religious center. A street was named after the architect – ulitsa Rossi – and the façade of his sophisticated Aleksandrinsky Theater can still be seen.

With the exception of several Art Nouveau buildings from the early 20th century, such as the one housing the sumptuous Eliseev department store along the Nevski Prospekt, which is the center's main thoroughfare, St. Petersburg has made very few concessions to modernity, at least from an architectural standpoint.

Whenever the city decides to commission ambitious works, however, plans must also take into account the devout respect the people of St. Petersburg have for the already-perfect landscape of their city. American architect Eric Owen Moss found out the hard way. In 2001 he won the competition to build the new Mariinsky Theater next to the celebrated 19th-century one, but his plans were rejected because, according to the city government, his structure in undulating glass and blue granite would have evoked "creased plastic bags." Thus, the new project was awarded to French architect Dominique Perrault, who has designed a bubble-shaped golden theater. As to Moss, he will have to settle for designing an exhibition and events center on the city island of Novaya Hollandia, the site of the harbor warehouses of Peter the Great. From here, people will be able to observe the eternal spectacle of St. Petersburg's famous White Nights.

73 bottom left The Rotunda, decorated in 1830, connected the private apartments in the west wing of the Winter Palace to the dazzling official rooms.

73 bottom right The Hermitage Museum, founded by Czarina Catherine, boasts 2,700,000 works of art displayed in 400 rooms, for an exhibition route covering more than 15 miles.

72 bottom Massive black granite columns sustain the vaults over the Jordan Staircase in the Winter Palace, the masterpiece of Bartolomeo Francesco Rastrelli.

72-73 On the banks of the Neva, still partly frozen, a hint of sunshine illuminates the sumptuous architecture of the Winter Palace, designed by Bartolomeo Rastrelli for Czarina Elizabeth.

74-75 The Kremlin (from kreml, "fortress") is the most extraordinary building in Moscow. Its walls — over 1.5 miles long — enclose government buildings, palaces and cathedrals.

74 bottom left The czar would receive guests in the Golden Hall, which was added to Terem Palace in the 17th century. The original palace was built between 1499 and 1508.

74 bottom right A central pillar on a square base, from which all the frescoes in the hall seem to originate, is the distinctive feature of

Granovataya Palata's ("Palace of Facets") main hall. The palace, the Kremlin's the oldest civic building, was built between 1487 and 1491.

Moscow
RUSSIA

Careful not to be overheard by the wrong ears, Muscovites once referred to the Vysotniye Zdaniya as "Stalin's Wedding Cakes." In truth, these buildings – known as the "Seven Sisters" – have a somewhat kitsch air, as they boast pseudo-Gothic spires, a profusion of red stars, and symbols of the hammer and sickle rising from bundles of wheat. Conceived by Stalin as a response to the skyscrapers of the American enemy, for years they were the tallest and most impressive structures in Europe. The most famous are the Palace of the Soviets and the University (the other five house ministries, hotels and residences), and their Soviet-style bulk dominates the capital of a Russia that is no longer Soviet. Curiously, however, most of the nearly 500 skyscrapers that delineate the new Moscow skyline, such as the Triumph Palace and the Paveletsky Tower, are nearly perfect replicas of the Vysotniye Zdaniya, almost as if the architects (and Moscow's citizens) were wistful for the past. Indeed, the past – the troubling past of the 20th century – still "weighs" on the city in which the ambitions and contrasts of Russia are more tangible than they are elsewhere.

However, Moscow looks like the set for a colossal movie with its 10 millions inhabitants as actors. Let's consider its center, the majestic Red Square, with the extraordinary St. Basil's Cathedral, Lenin's Mausoleum, Lubyanka Prison (now the headquarters of the Intelligence Agency) and GUM department store. Founded 850 years ago, Moscow was the seat of power of Ivan the Terrible and as well as the Romanov dynasty. It was from here that the Soviet leaders "played out" the Cold War, until the time when – here again – the empire fell apart.

The Kremlin, which has witnessed countless events, is a complex covering about 69 acres on the capital's only hill,

75 top There are four cathedrals, topped by characteristic gilded onion domes, along Sobornaya Square in the heart of the Kremlin. The scene is dominated by the grand Cathedral of the Assumption, built in the 15th century: this is where the czars were crowned, and Orthodox patriarchs and metropolitans are buried here.

75 center Completed in 1849 during the reign of Czar Nicholas I, the Great Palace of the Kremlin was the residence of Russian rulers until the October Revolution of 1917. It later became the seat of the Supreme Soviet, the Parliament of the Soviet Union, and of the representatives of the Russian Federation.

75 bottom Facing the Moscow River, red walls reinforced by mighty towers – each of which has its own unique history and legends – surround the Kremlin, which was fortified as early as the 15th century.

76-77 Red Square (its Russian name comes from the word krasnij, "beautiful") covers an area of nearly 80,000 square feet at the foot of the east wall of the Kremlin. In ancient times it was Moscow's main marketplace, and a wide moat separated it from the Kremlin.

76 bottom Every architectural element of the State Historical Museum – designed by English architect R.O. Sherwood and engineer A.A. Semyonov and built between 1875 and 1881 – represents an artistic interpretation of Russian history.

77 center The current appearance of the Red Square dates back to the early 19th century. The State Historical Museum, opened in 1883, stands out in the background; on the left is the colossal building housing the GUM department store, whose façade is 820 feet long.

77 bottom The nine colorful domes of St. Basil's Cathedral – made entirely of brick, in keeping with Russian tradition – symbolize the main feast days of the Orthodox Christian Church.

bounded by the confluence of the Neglinnaya and Moscow Rivers. It has dozens of magnificent buildings, such as the Great Palace that was the seat of the Romanov court; the Cathedral of the Assumption, where rulers were crowned; the Senate Building, which is now the residence of the president of the Russian Federation; and the Armory Palace, which houses the treasure of the czars. But these are just a few of Moscow's marvels, which are often well concealed amid blocks of gray buildings in the socialist-realist style. Hidden beneath the city is its remarkable subway system, with stations built in the Stalin era, so richly decorated with marble, gilding and crystal that 44 of them have been declared national monuments. And there are places like Gorky Park, the delightful Arbat district that housed the craftsmen who worked for the czars, the Bolshoi Theater, where one of the world's most illustrious ballet companies performs, and Novodevicky Monastery, with the cemetery where Chekhov, Gogol and Eisenstein are buried.

Much has been torn down and much has been built in Moscow. To the dismay of the more nostalgic, symbols like the Hotel Moskva – designed by Aleksei Shchusev, the regime's most celebrated architect – have been demolished by bulldozers to make room for a more modern five-star hotel and a new shopping center. Following heated debate, the sum of $260 million was spent to restore the White House, the seat of Parliament that was built in 1980 and was one of the last works of the Soviet era. However, the palaces of the Kremlin and the enchanting churches that were closed to worshippers for decades have also been restored with maniacal historical rigor, like the Cathedral of the Archangel, the Church of the Assumption and the Cathedral of the Annunciation, which house Russian iconographic treasures. A residential complex will soon be built on the outskirts of the city center, inspired by the forms and colors of the works of Alexandra Ekster, Wassily Kandinsky, Kazimir Malevich, Lyubov Popova and Alexander Rodchenko, the five great names of the Russian avant-garde. The plans have been entrusted to Dutch architect Eric van Egeraat, a foreigner who certainly does not suffer from nostalgia.

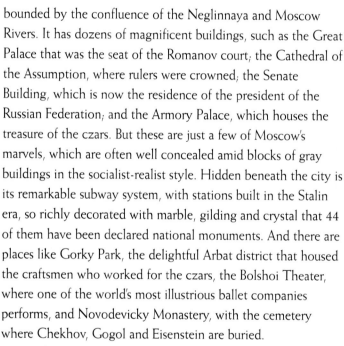

77 top Moscow's most celebrated monument, St. Basil's Cathedral in the Red Square, was built by Ivan the Terrible in 1552 to celebrate his victory over the Tatars. The interior is decorated with splendid 16th-century frescoes.

78 top A gambling house overlooks the Arbat, the favorite street of 19th-century aristocrats and intellectuals: in 1986 it became the city's first pedestrian thoroughfare.

78 center top Close to the Red Square, the Hotel Rossija, one of the most famous in Moscow, contrasts sharply with the domes of one of the splendid cathedrals of the Kremlin.

78 center bottom Advertising has invaded the streets of the city center: the market economy has radically changed the Moscow panorama.

78 bottom A massive portico marks the entrance to the Bolshoi. Destroyed several times in the first half of the 19th century, the current building, designed by Albert Kavos, dates back to 1856.

78-79 The banks of the Moscow River seem to be "crushed" by the enormous building of Moscow State University, built in 1953 and nearly 790 feet tall.

79 bottom left The Eliseev department store, which was founded in 1903, always specialized in groceries, but it was recently renovated and converted in a store offering luxury goods.

79 bottom right Granite, marble, mosaics, glass and wrought iron are the "ingredients" of the incredible stations of the Moscow subway, inaugurated in 1935.

Moscow

80-81 and 81 top *The Rynek, or market square, is the heart of city life. Its buildings, which were seriously damaged during World War II, were restored based on 22 views painted by Venetian artist Bernardo Bellotto in the mid-1700s.*

80 bottom left *The charming old castle square of Plac Zamkowy still seems to be imbued with the spirit of the Swedish conqueror King Sigismund III Vasa, who moved the capital from Kraków to Warsaw in 1596.*

Warsaw

POLAND

Warsaw is composed of symbols. Each brick recounts the struggle for survival, the courage to be reborn, the need to preserve memory. Warsaw is stubborn and rebellious. As a result, time and again it has been oppressed – by Swedes, Czarists, Nazis and Soviets alike – ever since King Sigismund III Vasa proclaimed it the capital city about 200 years after it was founded, moving his court here from Krakow in the south. Again, as far as symbols are concerned, the official emblem of the Polish capital is a warrior mermaid holding a shield and a saber. According to legend, this "aquatic Amazon" appeared to a fisherman, prophesying that an indestructible city would be built there. And she was right. Though 85% of its buildings were razed during World War II and most of its citizens were killed, deported to concentration camps or fled the city, Warsaw rose again. Today it is the capital of a country that has entered the European Union, and it is more prosperous than ever.

The Vistula River divides the city in two, and most of the historic monuments are on the left bank. According to critics, Stare Miasto – the Old Town, which is centered on the market square, the Rynek – is a sensational fake because it has been reconstructed. And yet it is a fake that is "truer than true," because many of the buildings are now more faithful to the ancient original than they were at the time they were bombed. To redo the façades, the architects used the 22 views painted by Venetian Bernardo Bellotto in the mid-18th century, as their model. Between 1971 and 1984, the city reconstructed the Zamek Królewski, the royal castle that overlooks the city, and Katedra Sw. Jana, the Gothic cathedral that is the city's oldest religious edifice and one of the symbols of fervent Polish Catholicism. However, three stretches of wall and three monuments are all that remain to mark the Warsaw Ghetto.

Today the Polish capital has a population of 1.6 million, and it has undergone intense urban development that has nevertheless not forgotten to include new green spaces. The city also has its historic parks, namely Wilanów, which surrounds a Baroque palace, and Łazienki, with a majestic monument to Frédéric

Chopin, who lived in Warsaw for thirty years. The least "invasive" and most intriguing of the new city buildings is annexed to the botanical gardens: the Biblioteka Uniwersytecka (2000). Designed by architects Badowski and Budzyński as a "city in the woods," it engages in a dialog with its natural setting and has a hanging garden that is accessed from a dramatic staircase.

The new skyscrapers, such as the Warsaw Trade Tower and the Warsaw Financial Center are less original in design. Crowding the skyline, they act as a counterpoint to Palac Kultury i Nauki, or the Palace of Culture and Science. The latter rises to a height of over 750 feet, making it the tallest building in Poland. Built in 1955, it was Stalin's gift to the city. The people of Warsaw say that its terrace offers the finest view of the city: because that is the only point from which the building itself is invisible.

80 bottom right *The Monument of the 1944 Uprising (in which 220,000 Polish civilians and 20,000 soldiers died), near Plac Zamkowy and across from the Piarist Church, is a highly emotional site even today.*

81 bottom *Inaugurated in 2000, the Świętokrzyski Bridge immediately became a distinctive feature of Warsaw's cityscape. It connects the city center with the residential district of Praga Pólnoc, on the east bank of the Vistula.*

Warsaw

82-83 The majestic Palace of Culture and Science – is the tallest building in Poland (758 feet), but also the most widely detested. Built in 1955, it was Stalin's gift to the city and it remains the symbol of Soviet oppression.

83 top The 377-foot-tall Fim Tower, which was completed in 1996, is one of the many office buildings. Its gleaming windows reflect the scenes on Aleje Jerozolimskie, or Jerusalem Avenue, the ultramodern street in the city center built over the area that was turned into the Jewish ghetto in the 18th century.

83 center Rondo Dmowskiego, at the intersection of Aleje Jerozolimskie and Marszalkowska, is the lively center of the new Warsaw, the capital of a country that, starting in the mid-1990s, was transformed into the "tiger" of Eastern Europe.

83 bottom Ornate 19th-century palaces and imposing skyscrapers are the backdrop for the liveliest area of Aleje Jerozolimskie.

Warsaw

84 top The Audience Hall in the Royal Palace, the work of Domenico Merlini, was faithfully reconstructed in 1945 after it was damaged during the war.

84 center top The lavish iconography of the stuccowork on the façade of Wilanów Palace combines symbols drawn from classical mythology with representations of the triumph of the Polish monarchy. The oldest part of the palace, designed by Augustyn Locci, is a suburban residence entre cour et jardin, typical of the European Baroque.

84 center bottom Stanislaw August Poniatowski, favored by Czarina Catherine II of Russia, rose to the Polish throne in 1764 and immediately had his summer residence built. Known as Palac na Wyspie, or the Palace on the Water, it was built on a small island in the lake in the center of Lazienki Park and it has now been converted into a museum.

84 bottom The Slasko-Dabrowski Bridge, built in 1949 to replace the one designed by engineer Stanislaw Kierbedz in 1864, connects the old city with the luxuriant Praski Park.

84-85 Wilanów Palace – the "Polish Versailles" – survived World War II unscathed. It was built between 1674 and 1696 by King Jan III Sobieski, who in 1683 headed the Holy Alliance to free Vienna from the Turks.

Prague
CZECH REPUBLIC

86 top The "Dancing House" by Frank O. Gehry and Vlado Milunic bewildered many people when it was inaugurated, but it fits in perfectly with the 19th-century buildings along the Rasinovo Nábrezí riverfront.

86 center The two old districts of Staré Mesto and Malá Strana, overlooking the Vltava River in the heart of town, are the areas with the most fascinating buildings in the city of Franz Kafka.

When the building was completed at the corner of Rasinovo and Resslova Streets, along the Vltava River, a number of people in Prague termed it scandalous. Others welcomed it as the latest gem of city architecture. No matter how one might judge it, however, with its asymmetrical digressions the "Dancing House" – or, as it is more officially known, "Ginger and Fred" (1993-95) – designed by the legendary Frank O. Gehry and his pupil, Bohemian Vlado Milunic, continues a tradition of architectural avant-garde that is typical of Prague.

Prague, labyrinthine and magical, has a taste for paradoxes. And one would be willing to bet that this is the reason it is so fiercely loved by its 1.2 million residents. In a word, it could be described as Kafkaesque. And what better city than Prague for such a moniker? The city's notable 20th-century manifestations, though secondary to some extent, also merit attention. Shortly before it fell under Soviet domination, the capital experienced a brief but intense Cubist period, which saw the development of the *Secese* style – Prague's version of Art Nouveau, but with a functionalist interpretation – and subsequently transposed the paintings of Picasso and Braque into architecture. This came about through the efforts of the architects who studied at Otto Wagner's school and designed the buildings facing lively Wenceslaus Square in the heart of town, to Adolf Loos, who designed an extraordinary villa in the Stresovice quarter, and to Oldrich Tyl and Josef Fuchs, who designed the futuristic Trade Fairs Building. In 1928 this building earned the admiration of Le Corbusier; saved from a fire, it now houses the Museum of Modern and Contemporary Art.

Some might object that Prague – lovely, famous Prague – is a city of the superb Baroque style of Malá Strana, the picturesque bohemian district and the home of the Carolinum, the city's noble university and the site of the extraordinary Klementinum library. Or that Prague is the city of the Gothic style that predominates in Staré Mesto, the "old

87 bottom left The first stone of the castle was laid in 880. Since then, the complex has expanded enormously, with the addition of palaces, churches, towers and fortifications.

87 bottom right The historic and cultural symbol of Czech nationalism, the Národní Muzeum closes off one end of Wenceslaus Square. Built in 1891, it is topped by the dome of the 230-foot-high Pantheon.

86 bottom Eighteen bridges connect the banks of the Vltava. Some of them were designed by Vlatislav Hofman, one of the leaders of the Czech Cubist movement in the early 20th century.

86-87 Splendid buildings along the banks of the Vltava reflect the architectural wealth and melting pot of styles that have made Prague one of the most enchanting cities in Europe.

88 bottom right and 89 top right
Recent studies have dated the
astronomical clock of City Hall to
approximately 1410; it has been
attributed to clockmaker Mikulas of
Kadan and astronomer Jan Sindel.

89 top left Splendid Baroque
buildings line Nerudova Street,
the main thoroughfare in
Malá Strana, the quaint
and romantic district at the foot
of the castle.

88-89 The Church of the Holy
Savior, in the foreground, rises amidst
the roofs and towers of Staré Mesto.
Founded in 1593, it is part of the
Klementinum, the Jesuit college that
now houses the National Library.

88 bottom left The stage
of the most tragic events
in Prague's history but also its most
festive ones, the irregularly shaped
Staromestské Námestí is the heart of
the old city.

city" set around Starometské Námestí, the square dominated by the impressive 14th-century tower of City Hall. Or that Prague and its history are recounted by the splendid statues decorating the Charles Bridge, the city's most ornate. Nevertheless, the architectural harmony that makes Prague one of the most fascinating capitals in Europe (and thus in the world) stems from what can be dubbed "faux acrobatics."

In the early 18th century, Bohemian architect Johann Blasius Santini Aichel marvelously managed to blend Gothic and Rococo, not only in restoration work on older buildings in Staré Mesto but also in the construction of new buildings, earning him the nickname of "the Gaudí of the 18th century" many years after his death. At the end of the 19th century, the city was overwhelmed by an architectural wave that redesigned it in a "patriotic" style. This was the neo-Gothic style that paid tribute to the city's golden age, the period of Charles IV, the Bohemian emperor of the Holy Roman Empire who ruled it between 1346 and 1378. As a result, Prague's most famous church, the theatrical St. Vitus Cathedral rising on a hill on the left bank of the Vltava, is done in a so-called "Gothic" style (most of it was built after 1871). The cathedral is part of Prague Castle (Hradčany), a complex covering an area of 2.8 million square feet that has always been the symbol of the capital city. Hradčany itself, which had 40 owners throughout its history and underwent 30 sackings and fires, was later remodeled between 1928 and 1932. Plying his unparalleled elegance, Slovenian Joze Plecnik merged the most disparate architectural elements, giving the complex its air of grace and completeness.

In short, it seems that its "fraudulent" architects merely helped the great writers of Prague weave the literary and imaginative legend of this city. Indeed, it should come as no surprise that Prague is the capital of a nation that chose a playwright, Vaclav Havel, as its leader.

89 center The 262-foot Gothic towers of the Church of Our Lady before Tyn, founded in 1365, overlook Starometské Námestí, the square with the statue of Jan Hus.

89 bottom The Charles Bridge, build by Charles V in 1357, is nearly 1700 feet long and is decorated with 30 statues of national saints, forming a "spiritual corridor" modeled after the Sant'Angelo Bridge in Rome.

90-91 The imperial court complex of the Hofburg, which took several centuries to complete and has 2600 rooms, is one of the most monumental residences in Europe. In this view, the Neue Burg, the new castle built by Franz Josef between 1881 and 1913, overlooks Heldenplatz, a broad square with equestrian statues of Archduke Charles and of Eugène of Savoy.

90 bottom right The Burgtheater – Austria's national theatre and one of the most important theaters for the German language – was built between 1874 and 1888 by Karl Hasenauer and Gottfried Semper. It is the second oldest theater in Europe, after the Comédie Française in Paris. Frescoes by Gustav and Ernst Klimt, and Franz Matsch decorate the interior staircases.

90 bottom left The building that houses the Austrian Parliament, located on the Ringstrasse, was designed by Theophil Hansen and constructed between 1874 and 1884. It was subsequently reconstructed between 1945 and 1956 as it was damaged during World War II. The edifice is inspired by classical architecture and is decorated with the statues of Greek and Roman military leaders and historians.

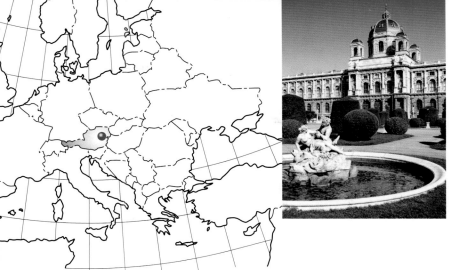

Vienna
AUSTRIA

"In Kakania it was only that a genius was always regarded as a lout, but never, as sometimes happened elsewhere, that a mere lout was regarded as a genius." This quotation is from *The Man Without Qualities*, Robert Musil's novel set in the imaginary philosophical-political macrocosm of the State of Kakania. However, from the opening pages of the book it becomes clear that Kakania is none other than Vienna under the Austro-Hungarian Empire, which the author depicts as a place where people were obsessed with relativism and were always ready to ridicule excess.

Though this empire no longer exists and the dualism between the Western and Eastern "empires" – for which Vienna effectively acted as a cultural linchpin – has likewise disappeared, a penchant for understatement is still inherent in the genetic makeup of the Viennese. Perhaps this is the reason that, in our collective imagination, Vienna remains a nostalgic city whose icons, romantic albeit old-fashioned, include Empress Sissi, Strauss's waltzes, the Danube that crosses it (though the river is no longer blue) and *Sachertorte*. Yet Vienna is a magnificent city that has always been "modern" and ahead of its time in every era, embracing – or probably putting up with – new ideas, regardless of how odd they may have seemed. It was here that the most visionary Baroque style triumphed between the 17th and 18th century. It was here that the Jugendstil movement, or Art Nouveau, literally flourished. And it was here that, just when the Viennese had become accustomed to pretentious "showcase" palaces, in 1908 Adolf Loos proclaimed that "ornamentation is criminal," marking the start of the rationalist movement and ushering in the age of modern architecture. Nevertheless, the locals considered Loos's most important building in Vienna, located in Michaelerplatz just yards from the entrance to the Imperial Palace, "about as charming as a hole in the ground." Even Emperor Franz Josef, who had authorized its construction, was outraged, supposedly lowering the curtains in his carriage to avoid looking at it whenever he passed in front of it. Nevertheless, the "house without eyebrows" (so called at the time because of its unthinkable lack of pediments over the windows) is now considered a masterpiece. More recently, the Viennese have dubbed the "dazzling" Hundertwasser Haus (1985) the work of

91 top left The Kunsthistorisches Museum, inaugurated by Franz Josef in 1891, houses the art collections of the Hapsburgs, starting with the historic core collection of 1400 works amassed by Archduke Leopold Wilhelm, who governed the Netherlands during the Baroque period.

91 top right St. Stephen's Cathedral is the symbol and heart of Vienna. It was constructed in the 12th century in the Romanesque style and rebuilt with Gothic lines after a fire destroyed it in 1258. The building is flanked by two towers that are almost 200 feet tall, and it culminates with the Steffl, the 446-foot-tall bell tower.

91 center Two columns inspired by Trajan's Column in Rome, decorated with scenes from the life of St. Charles Borromeo, are set across from the Karlskirche. Work to construct this masterpiece of the Viennese Baroque, dedicated to the patron saint of the plague-stricken, began in 1714.

91 bottom Schönbrunn palace was built between 1693 and 1749 by Leopold I, who wanted an official residence on a par with Versailles.

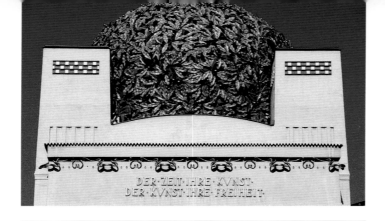

DER·ZEIT·IHRE·KVNST·
DER·KVNST·IHRE·FREI·HEIT·

92 top A dome of bronze laurel leaves covers the Sezession Haus, the work by Joseph Maria Olbrich that was the hotbed of the artistic avant-garde known as the Viennese Sezession movement.

92 center Twelve historical figures rotate throughout the day, moving across the face of the Anker Clock, the Art Deco masterpiece completed between 1911 and 1917.

92 bottom The sculpted figure of an owl characterizes the daring architecture of the library of the Technische Universität, the first technical university in Central Europe. It was established in 1815.

92-93 Apartment Building Gasometer B is the inventive solution for renovating one of the four spectacular gasometers in the industrial area of Semmering.

a madman. This is the building where painter and architect Friedensreich Hundertwasser put into practice his *Moldiness Manifesto against Rationalism in Architecture*, giving the city a "happy space" inspired by the forms of nature. Instead, in the Nineties another building of enormous importance, designed by Günther Domenig, was the target of criticism. This was the Zentralsparkasse Building, which earned the unflattering nickname of "Dented House" because its steel façade purportedly resembles a car after an accident. To be fair, the Viennese have rightly been polemical in some cases, above all starting in the Sixties, when the city government decided to expand the boundaries of Vienna by building a myriad of drab housing projects. In fact, today the capital of Austria owns the largest amount of real estate of any municipality in the world. Luckily, however, the most recent city-planning works have respected the balance between constructed and green areas, something extraordinary for a European city with a population of over 1.5 million. Out of a metropolitan area of 160 square miles, no less than 77 are covered with parks, gardens, woods (including the famous Wienerwald, the "Vienna Woods") and even agricultural areas, which also happen to produce excellent wine. Notably, after the construction of the now-legendary Ringstrasse, the 2.5-mile-long boulevard commissioned by Emperor Franz Josef in 1858 to enclose the monumental center of his capital, plans to overhaul the urban area – such as the ones drawn up in the early 20th century by Otto Wagner, who also built spectacular subway stations – have largely remained on paper. Instead, the goal of other plans, like Roland Reiner's "Step Project" completed in 1994, was to restore existing buildings, meaning an array of inestimable historical buildings bearing witness to the magnificence of the Empire.

The innumerable historical buildings that make Vienna one of the most fascinating capitals in Europe include St. Stephen's Cathedral, a Gothic masterpiece with a wealth of elaborate sculptures and other treasures, and the many age-old buildings commissioned by the emperors. The most important of these is the Hofburg, the heart of the monarchy. This "city within the city" comprises 18 buildings, each more lavish than the last, for

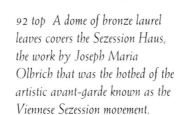

93 bottom left The 453-foot Vienna Twin Towers by Massimiliano Fuksas are two independent buildings whose sides are connected. Completed in 2001, they house offices and conference centers.

93 bottom right The Spittelau incinerator, an ultramodern thermal waste treatment plant that generates heat for the entire district, is Friedensreich Hundertwasser's most surprising work.

94 *The seat of the Municipal and Provincial Assembly, the Neo-Gothic Neues Rathaus was built by Friedrich von Schmidt between 1872 and 1883. Its façade is dominated by the 650-foot central tower and has a tall loggia with delicate tracery.*

95 top *The Riesenrad is the most famous attraction at the Prater, the amusement park inaugurated by Emperor Joseph II in 1766. The enormous Ferris wheel, which was supposed to be a temporary structure, was added by Enperor Franz Josef in 1897.*

95 bottom left *Kartnerstrasse, lined with luxury boutiques and traditional Viennese cafés, is one of the city's most elegant streets. It connects Stephansplatz to the Ringstrasse, the boulevard that circles the entire historic district of Vienna.*

95 bottom right *The monumental entrance to the Hofburg overlooks Michaelerplatz and leads to the imperial apartments that once belonged to Franz Josef and Elizabeth. Construction of the imperial palace began in 1275 by order of Ottokar II of Bohemia.*

a total of 2600 rooms. The complex also includes the Nationalbiblitothek, the Michaelerkirche – the Baroque church of the Hapsburg court – and the Kunsthistorisches Museum, which not only houses a superlative art collection but is also an extraordinary building in its own right. The triumphal entrance to the section on Greek and Egyptian art, with black and white marble columns, a profusion of gilt decorations and dream-like panels depicting the pharaohs, painted by Gustav Klimt, is nothing short of a masterpiece. New exhibition areas were also inaugurated around the Kunsthistorisches Museum in 2001. These areas were created by restoring the immense imperial stables, and today the Museumsquartier is considered one of the world's top ten cultural complexes. The other Hapsburg residences are just as sumptuous, like Schönbrunn Palace, a magnificent example of late Baroque architecture started by Leopold I in 1692 and completed by Maria Theresa in 1749. Surrounded by a park of nearly 300 acres, the palace was inscribed on UNESCO's World Heritage List and is the most visited building in the capital. The palace of Prince Eugène of Savoy, who drove the Ottoman Turks from the gates of Vienna in 1683, is also extraordinary. The residence is composed of three buildings – the Upper Belvedere Palace, the Lower Belvedere Palace and the Orangerie – surrounded by fountains and French gardens, and topped by copper domes that

intentionally evoke Turkish tents. The aristocratic palaces and the theaters for which Vienna has rightly become famous are also of great interest, and as a result, little space has been devoted to contemporary architecture, at least in the center of town. The work reflecting the most evident "break" with tradition is by Hans Hollein, who built the Haas Haus, a commercial building directly across from St. Stephen's Cathedral, about ten years ago. The six-story steel-and-concrete building features blocks of green marble and windows "closed off" by a marquee bent like a sail amidst the rooftops, spires and ancient statues around it. Naturally, the debate over this "foolishness" subsided only recently, once the Viennese finally embraced Hollein's work as the symbol of the new Vienna.

The city of the 21st century is free to expand across the east bank of the Danube, in a quarter – Donau City – housing the United Nations "village" and various buildings that have now become a must-see for fans of contemporary architecture. These include the Church of Christus Hoffnung der Welt, designed by Heinz Tesar, and skyscrapers like Boris Podrecca's Millennium Tower and the Twin Towers by Massimiliano Fuksas.

Despite its new skyscrapers, however, when people in Vienna want to admire the scenery they still prefer a more traditional outing: a romantic ride on the giant Ferris wheel in the Prater, Vienna's world famous pleasure park.

96-97 The Grand Canal curves its way through Venice, intersecting with the Giudecca Canal close to St. Mark's Square, where the bell tower and the basilica's green domes are visible.

96 bottom left The Church of Santa Maria della Salute, near the Punta della Dogana at the beginning of the Grand Canal, was commissioned by Baldassare Longhena to fulfill a vow he made to the Virgin Mary during the 1630 plague.

96 bottom right Beyond the row of gondolas "parked" along the Riva degli Schiavoni, the bell tower stands out near the Church of San Giorgio Maggiore. The church, designed by Andrea Palladio, was completed in 1611.

97 top Established 30 years ago by a group of rowing enthusiasts, the Vogalonga regatta covers an 18-mile route through the city and around the islands in the lagoon. It is held every May to celebrate the traditions of La Serenissima.

Venice

ITALY

Until the early 1900s, the Grand Canal could only be crossed by boat or via the sole walkway over it, the magnificent Rialto Bridge, built in the late 16th century for the astronomical sum of 250,000 ducats. During the 20th century – a different era for *La Serenissima* – the Accademia Bridge and the Scalzi Bridge were added. And soon, a fourth and futuristic bridge – made of glass, steel and Istria stone, and designed by Spanish architect Santiago Calatrava – will link Piazzale Roma and the railway station. Thus, Venice has been transformed from the symbol of trade, with shops lined up along the city's main waterway, to the symbol of tourism, which brings in millions of visitors every year, making it the most important sector in the city economy. Soon Venice will also boast a new airport terminal, designed by the ingenious American architect Frank O. Gehry, from which boats will depart directly for the city.

With a population of 270,000, Venice is a small city by modern standards. In its thousand-year history, however, there were centuries in which it dominated the Mediterranean, conquering islands, ports and cities in the Eastern Roman Empire. The extraordinary profits it earned by trading with the Levant as far back as the 9th century filled the coffers of noblemen, who soon became the patrons of flourishing art schools. Venice's golden age was distinguished by painters like Carpaccio, Giorgione, Paolo Veronese, Titian and Tintoretto, as well as architects, sculptors and decorators who gave *La Serenissima* her eternal charm.

Even today, the city's magical appeal is unparalleled. The heart of historical Venice is St. Mark's Basilica, built to safeguard the saint's remains and completed in 1094. Extending around it are the porticoes of the Procuratie, which housed the offices of the nine Procurators of San Marco. And there is the Ducal Palace, set between St. Mark's Square and the Riva degli Schiavoni. For centuries it was the residence of the Doges and of the institutions governing public life. The city skyline is dominated by the Campanile, which was rebuilt after it collapsed on July 14, 1902.

Nevertheless, what makes the city so breathtaking is not

97 center The Rialto Bridge crosses a wide bight halfway along the Grand Canal. Just to the left of the bridge is the long porticoed building of the Fabbriche Nuove, constructed in the 16th century to house the magistrates in charge of trade. The building is close to Venice's bustling and picturesque marketplace.

97 bottom Designed by Antonio da Ponte and built between 1588 and 1591 for the astronomical cost of 250,000 ducats, the Rialto Bridge is characterized by a single arch that gives it an uncommonly simple and elegant appearance. The Rialto was the only bridge across the Grand Canal until the early 20th century.

98 top right The central arch of the façade of St. Mark's Basilica is decorated with a dazzling gold winged lion set against a starry sky. Over it is a statue of the Evangelist, the patron saint of Venice.

98 top left Statues of saints venerated in Venice and the personifications of virtues embellish the façade of St. Mark's Basilica. The sculptures were done between the 14th and 15th century by Nicolò and Pietro Lamberti, as well as other Tuscan artists.

the beauty of any one work, but the astonishing harmony of Venice's architectural panorama. All it takes is a journey down the Grand Canal to get an idea of this scenario. Starting from Santa Maria della Salute, simply gaze at the silhouettes of the opulent aristocratic residences: from Palazzo Belloni-Battaglia to Palazzo Marcello, where composer Benedetto Marcello was born, and from Palazzo Vendramin Calergi to Ca' Foscari, where the University of Venice is located, and on to Ca' Dario and Palazzo Grassi. And just beyond them, you can discern the outlines of the city's historic churches, among them Santa Maria dei Frari, San Rocco and Sant'Eustachio, with their artistic heritage that includes the works of Donatello, Titian, Tiepolo and Tintoretto.

Even though these glorious years are now part of the past, Venice continues to be a hotbed of culture, with world-famous events like the Cinema Festival, and the Biennial Exhibitions of Art and Architecture. With the magnificent restoration work that has now been completed on La Fenice – the theater was destroyed by fire in 1996 – opera is also back.

Venice is a unique city, and the efforts that have been made to preserve its priceless legacy, restorations and renovations are innumerable. However, today the world is mainly concerned by the fragility of the "Venice Project" as a whole. For decades, the episodes of *acqua alta* – or flood tides – have become increasingly frequent and alarming. If the forecasts about global warming prove to be correct, by the middle of the 21st century flooding could occur up to 100 times a year. As a result, the most ambitious and important of today's architectural works in Venice will be virtually invisible. A massive system of floodgates – the Moses Project – will be anchored to the bottom of the lagoon, along the three inlets of Chioggia, the Lido and Malamocco. When the waters of the Adriatic exceed safety levels, mobile dams will be raised, creating a barrier to defend the lagoon and its priceless treasure.

98 center Statues sculpted by Jacobello and Pier Paolo dalle Masegne at the end of the 14th century rise over an iconostasis that encloses the presbytery in St. Mark's. The statues are considered masterpieces of Venetian Gothic art.

98 bottom The interior of St. Mark's Basilica, with mosaic flooring, walls and vaults, harmoniously unites architectural masses and opulent decoration. One of the most important works of art here is the Pala d'Oro, or Golden Altarpiece, behind the main altar: it is exquisitely decorated with pearls, enamelwork, mosaics and gemstones.

99 bottom right Built over an enchanting colonnaded portico, the Procuratie that lines St. Mark's Square once housed the offices of the Procurators of the Venetian Republic. On the Clock Tower, built in 1493, two statues strike the bell to sound the hour. The statues, which are over 8 feet tall, are referred to as the Two Moors because of the dark patina that covered them almost as soon as they were installed.

98-99 Over the centuries, Byzantine, Romanesque, Gothic and Renaissance works have gradually enriched St. Mark's Basilica. The church was built to safeguard the Evangelist's remains.

99 bottom left More than 86,000 square feet of magnificent mosaics with biblical and evangelical subjects cover the walls, vaults and domes of the basilica, creating intriguing glittering and luminous effects.

Venice

100 top left Aside from their aesthetic value, the reliefs on the façade of the Ducal Palace create a complex allegorical "discourse" composed of men, women, animals, plants, zodiac signs, symbols and legends, grouped into stories and fables, parables and morals.

100 top right In this view, a detail of the sculptural decorations of the loggias of the Ducal Palace can be seen alongside the notorious Bridge of Sighs, so called because prisoners would cross it when they were led before the state inquisitors. Built in 1602, the bridge's interior is composed of two narrow corridors set one over the other.

100 bottom An allegory of The Triumph of Venice by Tintoretto dominates the ceiling of the sumptuous Senate Chamber of the Ducal Palace, where the 60 members of the council of pregadi or senators would meet.

100-101 Aerial view of the center of Venice: on the left is St. Mark's Square, which is 575 feet long and is connected to the seafront by a smaller square. On the right are the domes of the basilica and the Ducal Palace, which overlooks the Riva degli Schiavoni.

101 bottom The residence of the Doges and the seat of the highest magistracy, the Ducal Palace is the symbol of the power and splendor of the ancient Venetian Republic. It was first built in the 9th century, but its current structure – considered the finest expression of Venetian Gothic architecture – dates to the 14th-15th centuries.

102 bottom left A view of the splendid Church of Santa Maria Novella, with the train station behind it. The station, named after the church, is a fine example of the functionalist architecture of the 1930s. Today, it is being modernized by Sir Norman Foster, one of the leading names in high-tech architecture.

102-103 The extraordinary architectural unity of Florence, gently traversed by the Arno River, is evident even from the air. The city has proudly maintained profound ties with its golden age, when it was a driving force of the Renaissance.

Florence

ITALY

The team that is preparing to redesign the urban fabric of Florence includes some of the most prestigious names in contemporary architecture. Sir Norman Foster has been appointed to design the new station for high-speed trains. Enormous steel-and-glass vaults will let light into every corner, reflecting the bywords of this renowned British architect: "space, radiance, visibility, lightness." Jean Nouvel will transform the old FIAT industrial complex on Viale Belfiore, and Richard Rogers will work in the nearby town of Scandicci to renovate the historic district. Santiago Calatrava won the competition to expand the Ponte della Vittoria that spans the Arno and design the extension of the Museo dell'Opera del Duomo, the museum that houses one of the world's most important collections of medieval and Renaissance sculptures. However, he had to relinquish this assignment, which has been turned over to Florentine architect Adolfo Natalini. Thus, Florence is preparing itself for the challenge of the 21st century. Oddly enough, it has long been considered one of Italy's most conservative cities, and it is huddled around its historic center, which flourished between the 13th and the 15th centuries. During the mid-13th century – despite conflicts between the Guelphs and the Ghibellines, who respectively supported the pope and the communal institutions – the Florentine guilds enjoyed unrivalled commercial power. Backed by the wealth of the city's most prominent families, artists' workshops began to thrive in Florence, starting with Cimabue and Gaddo Gaddi, who were followed by Giotto as well architects such as Arnolfo di Cambio and Filippo Brunelleschi. Monumental works like Palazzo Vecchio and the Basilica of Santa Croce were built. The city's most ambitious project was also undertaken: the Duomo (the Cathedral of Santa Maria del Fiore). It would take 150 years to complete this work designed by Arnolfo di Cambio, which is embellished by Giotto's bell tower and crowned by Brunelleschi's remarkable dome. During the 16th century, Giorgio Vasari completed his extraordinary fresco *The Last Judgment* inside the cathedral.

The fragile balance of Florentine power fell apart during the mid-14th century. Banks failed and the plague decimated the population. Protests came to a head with the Revolt of the Ciompi in 1378, but by the middle of the following century the city prospered once again with the rise of the Medici family.

102 bottom right Built in the 12th century, the Baptistery of the Duomo, or cathedral, is one of the city's oldest buildings. In 1401 Lorenzo Ghiberti was commissioned to work on its doors.

103 top The 1322 completion of the Palazzo Vecchio, designed by Arnolfo di Cambio, coincided with the installation of an enormous bell on top of the tower, in order to assemble the Florentines or warn them in case of danger.

103 center The dome of the cathedral, which is virtually in the geographical center of Florence, dominates the panorama not only in height, but also in volume (over 345 feet tall and 167 feet across).

103 bottom The cathedral presents a coherent appearance, but it is actually the outcome of a number of interventions. For example, Giotto designed the bell tower in 1334, whereas Brunelleschi's dome dates to 1420-1446.

104 top *The Fountain of Neptune (1575) in the Piazza della Signoria was designed by Bartolomeo Ammannati. It was commissioned by Cosimo I de' Medici to celebrate the Grand Duchy's seafaring ambitions.*

104 center *Via Giuseppe Verdi, dominated by the bell tower of Santa Croce, is one of the main streets in the historic district. The Bargello Museum and the birthplace of Michelangelo are located nearby.*

104 bottom *Flag-wavers in Renaissance costumes parade in front of Santa Maria Novella, a Gothic masterpiece built between 1279 and 1357 as the seat of the powerful Dominican Order.*

104-105 *In 1504, the David established 29-year-old Michelangelo as the leading sculptor of his day. The original of this colossal nude statue was moved to the Galleria dell'Accademia in 1873.*

The city's leading citizens built marvelous residences, first and foremost Palazzo Medici Riccardi, the residence of the lords of the city, as well as Palazzo Strozzi, Palazzo Rucellai and Palazzo Pucci. However, the most lavish was Palazzo Pitti, with its ashlar façade, designed by Brunelleschi in 1458 for banker Lucio Pitti. When Pitti died, work on the palace stopped for nearly a century, until the Medici ruler Cosimo I took it over as his family's new residence, which overlooked a park covering more than 12 acres: the marvel of Renaissance aesthetics better known as the Boboli Gardens, the work of landscape architect Niccolò Pericoli.

The Medici art collections are displayed inside Palazzo Pitti, with masterpieces by Titian, Tintoretto, Caravaggio and Rubens. Nevertheless, most of the artwork collected by the Florentine seigniory is at the Uffizi, so called because Cosimo I built it to house the offices of the magistracy. Upon his death in 1581, his heirs used the Uffizi to display their artistic wealth. These collections were further expanded with the works brought in by the Austrian house of Lorraine, which succeeded the Medici family in 1737.

Sacked by Napoleon in the late 18th century, Florence subsequently enjoyed another short-lived period of glory between 1865 and 1871, when it became the capital of the Kingdom of Italy. Nonetheless, in its architecture and its common sentiment the city has remained tied to the centuries of its golden age. And this makes the challenge of its new urban-planning project more important than ever.

105 top right The cladding on the façade of Santa Maria Novella, done in black and white marble, is probably the loveliest of all the churches in Florence. The lower portion, up to the first stringcourse, dates to the first half of the 14th century; the upper portion and main entrance are the exquisite Renaissance work of Leon Battista Alberti.

105 center right In a public hall of the Palazzo Vecchio, St. Zenobius, the patron saint of Florence, dominates the central scene of the decoration of the Sala dei Gigli.

105 bottom The splendid Gothic Basilica of Santa Croce houses the tombs and cenotaphs of illustrious Florentines such as Dante, Michelangelo and Galileo, and it is beautifully decorated with frescoes by Giotto and his pupils.

106 top Surrounded by grassy terracing, the Neptune Fountain is one of the most striking spots in the Boboli Gardens. The bronze statue of the god, the work of Stoldo Lorenzi, emerges from a rocky spur adorned with Naiads and Tritons.

106 center The full grandeur of Palazzo Pitti can only be appreciated from a bird's-eye view. The palace was built by Luca Pitti in 1458 with the specific intention of challenging the power of the Medici family. The façade of the building, which has been attributed to Brunelleschi, is over 670 feet long.

106 bottom The Boboli Gardens were designed by landscape architect Niccolò Pericoli. A masterpiece of Renaissance aesthetics, they enclose an outdoor museum with sculptures from various periods and styles that are perfect in these luxuriant surroundings.

106-107 The light of sunset adds to the charm of the Ponte Vecchio, which was designed by Taddeo Gaddi in 1345 and is the oldest in the city. The shops along the bridge were originally occupied by blacksmiths, tanners and butchers, but in 1593 Ferdinand I ordered them to move due to noise and stench produced by these trades.

107 top right The octagonal Sala della Tribuna, the original core of the Uffizi, displayed a collection of paintings and sculptures open to visitors on request as early as the 17th century, making the Uffizi Gallery the first museum in Europe.

107 center right Revolutionary in both color and brushstrokes, Botticelli's paintings represent one of the most valuable treasures of the Uffizi. With his Allegory of Spring (1478), the artist broke away from the tradition of religious painting by reinterpreting a pagan rite.

107 bottom right The Uffizi, seen here in a suggestive nocturnal view, originally housed the "uffizi" or government offices of the Seigniory.

107 bottom left The superbly decorated halls of Palazzo Medici Riccardi contrast with the building's stark exterior. Today the building houses the Prefecture.

107 bottom right The lavish rooms of Palazzo Pitti house the Palatine Gallery, the Silver Museum, and the Gallery of Modern Art and Costumes.

Florence

108 bottom right The famous steps built by Francesco De Sanctis between 1723 and 1726 lead to the Church of Trinità dei Monti, whose façade was designed by Giacomo della Porta in the late 16th century.

109 top Bernini's 16th-century Fountain of the Four Rivers portrays the four continents symbolized by the most important rivers: the Nile, the Ganges, the Río de la Plata (visible in the picture) and the Danube.

108-109 Abundance and Salubrity flank the figure of Ocean (Neptune), in the center. Designed by Nicolò Salvi in the mid-18th century, the Trevi Fountain is considered one of the most beautiful in the world.

108 bottom left Trinità dei Monti — or the Spanish Steps — and Piazza di Spagna stand out in the center of this stunning view of the Pincio, whose slopes were transformed into a public park between 1810 and 1818.

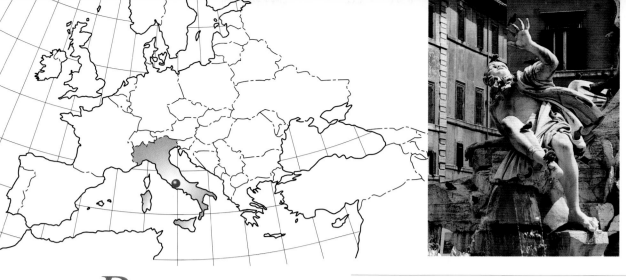

Rome
ITALY

R ome's latest masterpiece was inaugurated on December 21, 2002, with the opening on the largest hall of the futuristic Auditorium designed by Renzo Piano. With a seating capacity of 2,800, it completes the complex, joining the two smaller halls, and the tiered seating for outdoor performances. In the temple of music designed by the famous architect, the three halls are perfect "speaker boxes" designed to enhance acoustics. Here, lead, brick and travertine blend in a harmony of materials and forms, making the Auditorium one of the most elegant and functional structures of its kind.

Thus, at the beginning of the third millennium Rome has returned to the fore on the architectural scene. More than any other city in the world, the Italian capital, which has a population of three million, holds traces of its matchless historic, artistic and architectural heritage in virtually every corner. In the first part of its 2750-year history, it was the center of the one of the most powerful empires ever known, stretching from England to North Africa and across to the Near East. When its political, military and geographical dominion declined, the temporal and spiritual power of the popes acted as a driving force for the city's incredible artistic vitality.

Founded in 753 BC on the Palatine Hill, not far from the mouth of the Tiber, within a matter of decades the nascent city was already one of the leading centers of the Mediterranean. In the centuries that followed, the urban fabric that would ultimately characterize Imperial Rome started to take form. Some of the monuments of the Roman Empire's golden age of the still stand: the Colosseum, the Imperial Forum, the Pantheon, the Circus Maximus, the Baths of Caracalla, the tombs on the old Appian Way (Italy's main thoroughfare, linking Rome with Brindisi), Nero's Domus Aurea, Trajan's Market and the Mausoleum of Augustus. It would be impossible to sum up in just a few words the remarkable remains of a past in which Rome was *Caput Mundi*, the undisputed ruler of the ancient world. Though the most impressive monuments have survived the natural evolution of the urban layout for centuries, much of ancient Rome has changed profoundly. Castel Sant'Angelo is the most striking example of this. Built as a tomb by Emperor Hadrian in the 2nd century AD, during the 5th and 6th centuries it became the city's main stronghold against the attacks of the Visigoths and the Ostrogoths. Powerful aristocratic families transformed it into a residence, and lastly it was annexed to the pontifical estate and converted back into a military stronghold.

109 center Until 1878 the Fountain of Neptune was composed of the upper and lower basins designed by Giacomo Della Porta in the 16th century. Subsequently, Gregorio Zappalà's Nereids, putti and horses, and Antonio della Bitta's statue of Neptune fighting the octopus, were added to balance the Moor's Fountain.

109 bottom An aerial view of Piazza Navona, the Baroque masterpiece built in the 1600s in the area of Domitian's stadium. This picture shows the dome of the Church of Sant'Agnese in Agone (left), designed by Borromini, and the Fountain of Neptune, the Fountain of the Four Rivers and the Moor's Fountain.

110 top left A view of the Pantheon, illuminated only by the 30-foot oculus, the round opening at the top of the 141-foot-high dome. Inside it are the tombs of Raphael and of the Italian royal family.

110 top right Built by Marcus Agrippa in 27 BC and completely reconstructed by the emperor Hadrian at the beginning of the

2nd century BC, the Pantheon was converted into a Christian church in AD 608 when Phocas, Emperor of the East, donated it to Pope Boniface IV. A portico supported by 16 columns, which are 46 feet tall, leads to the large circular hall.

110 bottom The Colosseum – or Flavian Amphitheater – was built by Vespasian and

completed by Titus in AD 80. It rises 158 ft and, could accommodate 50,000 spectators. The first three levels are decorated with Doric, Ionic and Corinthian columns, respectively, whereas the fourth one, made completely of masonry, had a system of posts to support the velarium, a large awning that sheltered the audience from the sun.

Other magical places also conceal their imperial past. For example, this past can be gleaned in the outline of Piazza Navona, one of the most harmonious and distinctive urban complexes of the Roman Baroque. It is lined with buildings that were constructed over the remains of Domitian's Stadium, which was completed in AD 81. What was once the site of the *Circus Agonensis* – horse races and athletic competitions were held there – now boasts splendid *palazzi* and three of the countless spectacular fountains that grace the city: the Moor's Fountain, the Fountain of Neptune, and the enormous Fountain of the Four Rivers, Bernini's magnificent work with travertine statues representing the Nile, the Ganges, the Danube and the Río de la Plata, symbolizing the four parts of the known world at that time.

However, it was during the 16th and 17th centuries, shaped by leading Renaissance and Baroque artists, that the historic center of Rome developed as we know it today. To a significant extent, the rebirth of Rome can be traced to a specific date: April 18, 1506, when Pope Julius II laid the cornerstone for the new Basilica of St. Peter's, which a little over 100 years later would become the center of the Christian faith. Bramante was appointed to oversee the work, and was succeeded by Raphael, Antonio da Sangallo, Michelangelo and, lastly, Carlo Maderno, who completed the façade. Gian Lorenzo Bernini, the symbol of Rome's golden age, also left his mark on St. Peter's, with works like the baldachin over the altar, the Tabernacle, the *Cathedra Petri* (the monument enshrining St. Peter's Chair) and, above all, the extraordinary colonnaded square designed around the Egyptian obelisk that was erected in 1586.

The city's most exquisite monuments and buildings also date to this period: squares, noble *palazzi* and villas surrounded by immense gardens. It would be impossible to detail the astonishing artistic legacy left to the city by those centuries of astounding activity, but we cannot overlook Piazza del

111 bottom right The Tiber River is interrupted halfway along its course through Rome by Tiber Island, which was sacred to the cult of Aesculapius. The island is connected to the riverbanks by two bridges: the Fabricius Bridge, built in 62 BC and still almost perfectly preserved, and the Cestius, built in 46 BC but almost entirely reconstructed in the late 19th century.

110-111 The Imperial Forums, behind the Colosseum at the foot of the Palatine Hill, include the Forum of Caesar, of Augustus, of Nerva, of Trajan, the Temple of Peace, and Trajan's Market.

111 bottom left The Baths of Caracalla, built by this emperor in the early 3rd century, were used extensively until 537, when the Goths cut off the aqueducts that supplied them.

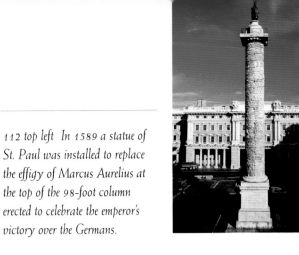

112 top left In 1589 a statue of St. Paul was installed to replace the effigy of Marcus Aurelius at the top of the 98-foot column erected to celebrate the emperor's victory over the Germans.

112 top right Every morning a crowded market animates Campo dei Fiori, one of Rome's most famous squares. In the middle is the monument to Giordano Bruno, who was burnt at the stake here in 1600.

Rome

Campidoglio. This was the first square created as part of a plan assigned to Michelangelo who, to augment its size, gave it a trapezoidal layout that tricks the eye with a unique perspective. Other notable squares include Piazza Colonna, Piazza del Popolo and Piazza di Spagna (dominated by the marvelous church of Trinità dei Monti at the top of the famous Spanish Steps), which were built at the end of the 16th century, prompted by the enthusiasm for city planning that inspired Pope Sixtus V. During this period, the city's leading families competed with each other in the architectural arena, giving the city Palazzo Venezia – the first building of this kind and the work of Leon Battista Alberti – Palazzo Barberini and Palazzo Farnese, Villa Borghese, Villa Doria Pamphilj, Villa Corsini, Villa Sciarra and Villa Ada.

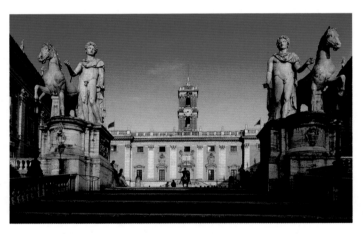

112 center The wide Cordonata staircase leads to Piazza del Campidoglio. At the foot of the Senatorial Palace is a replica of the equestrian statue of Marcus Aurelius.

112 bottom Work to construct the Vittoriano, designed by Giuseppe Sacconi, began in 1885 and was completed in 1935. The monument celebrates Victor Emmanuel II, the first king of a unified Italy.

Baroque Rome essentially remained unchanged until 1870, when it became the capital of the Kingdom of Italy, and into the first decades of the monarchy, with the exception of the Vittoriano. Work on this impressive monument in Piazza Venezia began in 1885; dedicated to Victor Emmanuel II, it was built to symbolize the Unification of Italy. The monument was inaugurated on June 4, 1911 before a crowd of rejoicing veterans and Garibaldi's troops. However, it was with Mussolini's modernist utopia – and with the contribution of architects like Marcello Piacentini and Giuseppe Bottai – that, during the Twenties, Rome once again faced profound upheavals in its urban layout. During the twenty years of Fascism, entire areas of the city were demolished to make room for some of the most significant architectural works built in Rome and its environs in the 20th century. Quarters like Garbatella were constructed, as well as service areas like the Città Universitaria, the Foro Italico and Cinecittà.

However, it was above all with EUR, site of the planned "Esposizione Universale Romana," that the regime expressed its desire to glorify the country's imperialist ideas and celebrated the 20th anniversary of its rise to power. The project was to be completed for the Rome World's Fair of 1942, and it called for constructing an area with impressive buildings, urban infrastructures, public services and green spaces, connected to the center of town by the main thoroughfare of Via Cristoforo Colombo. Though the project was never completed, even today EUR remains one of Rome's most interesting modern areas. After World War II, the city's architectural integrity was threatened by large-scale popular-housing initiatives, which created anonymous suburban quarters designed to accommodate a substantial population boom and the enormous influx of immigrants to the capital. However, its historic center was spared. Today, Rome seems to have become aware of the need to renovate its suburbs, with the contribution of the local governments and, once again, the Church. Thus, this was the concept behind the construction of the church of Tor Tre Teste, built for the Jubilee Year 2000. Shaped like three enormous sails in white concrete, this superb work was designed by Richard Meier. In an era in which many great European capitals have embarked on sensational projects, Rome has just come out of its conservative shell to embrace high-profile contemporary architecture. It is moving cautiously, but is well aware that new technologies and new styles can offer valuable instruments for renewing its immortal beauty.

113 bottom left Constantine had the Basilica of St. John Lateran built in AD 312. The first official see of the papacy, it was destroyed by a fire in 1308 and was rebuilt during the Baroque period.

113 bottom right The 355-foot-long Ponte Vittorio Emanuele II boasts three arches. Inaugurated in 1911, it is considered the most monumental bridge of modern Rome.

112-113 Piazza del Popolo, which is closed off by Porta del Popolo and is dominated by the Pincio, is one of the most picturesque squares in Rome. The Flaminian Obelisk, the 13th-century Egyptian stele that Augustus brought to Rome, is set in the middle of the square. The twin churches of Santa Maria dei Miracoli and Santa Maria di Montesanto, started by Carlo Rainaldi and completed by Bernini, stand on the opposite side of the square.

114-115 From 1508 to 1513, Michelangelo worked on the frescoes of the Sistine Chapel, with scenes from Genesis on the vault and the Last Judgment on the back wall.

115 top The Baldachin of St. Peter, commissioned by Pope Urban VIII was the first major work by Gian Lorenzo Bernini. The artist worked on the baldachin, which is 95 feet tall, from 1624 to 1633.

115 center top Castel Sant'Angelo – in turn Hadrian's mausoleum, a stronghold against the barbarians and a papal fortress – has maintained the cylindrical layout of the original monument.

115 center bottom and bottom St. Peter's Basilica was built in the 16th and early 17th century. Bernini's colonnade, finished in 1656, complements its majestic beauty.

Rome

116 bottom right Built in 1913, the Széchenyi Baths have a magnificent pool. Budapest was built over a network of springs whose waters are renowned for their therapeutic properties.

117 top left An Art Nouveau masterpiece designed by Zsigmond Quittner, Gresham Palace was restored to its original splendor after years of Communism. It was converted into a luxury hotel in 2004.

116-117 The Chain Bridge reaches the riverbank of Pest, with the stately dome of the largest Parliament building in Europe. Completed in 1902, the complex has 691 rooms.

116 bottom left The Central Market in the square of Fövam Tér is a splendid late-19th-century structure that incorporated a covered canal used to transport products.

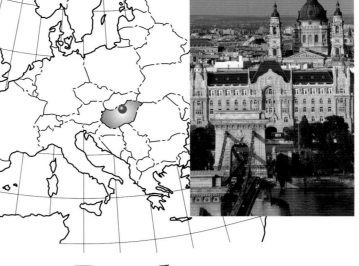

Budapest
HUNGARY

Noble Buda rises on a hill dominating the right bank of the Danube. The commercial city of Pest stretches across the plains on the left bank of the river. Budapest, which has a population of nearly 2 million, comprises not only Buda and Pest but also the original Roman settlement of *Aquincum*, renamed Óbuda, and the city's compound name eloquently reveals its two contrasting souls, which not even globalizing modernity has managed to erase.

Buda and Pest did not "meet" until 1848, when the *Széchenyi Lánchid*, or the Chain Bridge was opened. A few years earlier, Count István Széchenyi was stranded in Pest, unable to cross the Danube to attend his father's funeral on the other side. After this regrettable incident, the count funded construction of the bridge. Designed by William Tierney Clark, a Briton, the *Széchenyi Lánchid* became the symbol of Budapest, as it was the first "step" toward the official union of the two cities, which took place in 1873.

Though the Austro-Hungarian Empire was on the wane by this time, Budapest was instead developing into a dazzling capital. The city was preparing for the year 1896 and the millennial celebration of the founding of the Magyar state by the legendary King Stephen. Teams of architects were involved in restoring the vestiges of the past and designing marvelous new buildings to equip the city with state-of-the-art infrastructures.

At the end of the 19th century, the city inaugurated continental Europe's first subway system, as well as the Parliament Building. Covering an area of 880 feet by nearly 390, with a 315-foot-tall cupola, 691 rooms and over 12 miles of hallways, this building is the largest construction of its kind in Europe. While the urban layout of Pest was reorganized into wide boulevards lined with eclectic buildings designed by Odon Lechner, the architect who ingeniously interpreted the Viennese Jugendstil movement, the monuments of Buda were renovated, including the Fortress, the Royal Palace and the Matthias Church. The Fishermen's Bastion was built on the Danube, with seven towers (one for each of the ancient

117 top right The picturesque Fishermen's Bastion on the Danube has seven towers (one for each of the ancient Magyar tribes) designed in a style blending Neo-Romanesque and Neo-Gothic elements. It was built in 1905 and named in honor of the fishermen's guild that defended this part of the city during the Middle Ages.

117 bottom The Mátyás Templom, or Matthias Church, is the focal point of the hill of Buda, and it bears silent witness to 700 years of city history. In 1541, after the Turks captured Budapest, the church was transformed into a mosque and its frescoes were covered with plaster. Its current appearance is the result of painstaking reconstruction work done in the late 19th century.

118 top A spectacular atrium leads to the Néprajzi Múzeum, located in an eclectic late-19th-century building that housed the Supreme Court until 1973.

118 center In the middle of the elegant columned semicircle that encloses the Heroes' Square, in Pest rises a 390-ft column topped by the statue of the archangel Gabriel. According to legend, Gabriel gave the holy crown to King Stephen, the first ruler of Hungary.

118 bottom Rising nearly 200 feet over banks of the Danube, Castle Hill, or Várhegy, is dominated by the city's most beloved buildings: the Royal Palace and the Matthias Church are located in this ancient district.

119 At night, the Chain Bridge is illuminated by an extravaganza of lights and gleaming gold. Adam Clark, a british engineer, built this impressive structure designed by William Tierney Clark.

Magyar tribes) designed in a style blending Neo-Romanesque and Neo-Gothic elements. This wave of vitality also spawned the construction of theaters and hotels, such as the luxurious Hotel Géllert, as well as the development and upgrading of the area's numerous spas, like the Király Baths, which are another delightful feature of the capital that has appropriately been nicknamed "the pearl of the Danube."

However, this pearl – or rather, the separate cities comprising it – has often been damaged throughout its history. Its most dramatic moments came with the 150-year-long domination of the Turks, who were driven out by the Hapsburgs in 1686 and, more recently, with bombardment during World War II and the failed anti-Soviet revolt in 1956. Nevertheless, Budapest has always managed to find the optimism and imagination to start over again.

Contemporary architecture is also exquisitely represented here, with the eccentric inventions of Hungarian Imre Makovecz, inspired by the forms of nature: his Villa Richter (1983) and Villa Gubsci (1986), both of which in the residential areas of the capital, and the mortuary chapel at Pasaréter Cemetery, enclosed in a wooden structure reminiscent of a ribcage. The restoration work done on the 19th-century building at No. 9 Andrássy utca, the main thoroughfare of Pest, is also fascinating; it was completed in the mid-Nineties by Dutch architect Eric Van Egeraat. The building, the headquarters of the ING Bank, is crowned by an astonishing glass construction that looks like a bubble. The year 2000 also marked the beginning of an ambitious project to upgrade the old Ganz steelworks and, in general, to renovate the old and disused industrial sites along the Danube, which are rapidly being transformed into a fashionable area offering cultural events and entertainment.

Athens

GREECE

38°02'N-23°44'E

120 top The impressive Stoa of Attalus dominates the Agora, the heart of the social, political and commercial life of ancient Athens.

120 center The Church of the Holy Apostles, near the Agora, was built in the 11th century to commemorate the preaching of St. Paul.

120 bottom Consul Herod Atticus built this theater in the 2nd century AD; it is still used today.

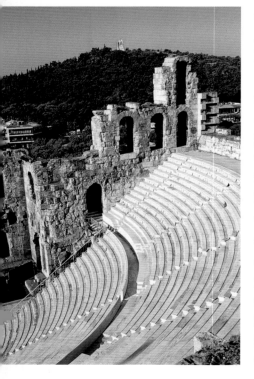

With Homer's masterpieces, the Greeks ushered in the history of literature. With the Acropolis in Athens, they gave architecture its eternal model of balance and harmony. In 508 BC, they gave the world the concept of democracy. And Athens, the cradle of European civilization, gave the best of itself in antiquity, only to decline dramatically in an escalation of warfare. Devastated by the Persians in 408 BC and by the Romans in 86 BC, laid to waste by the Goths in AD 396, occupied by the Turks in the 16th century, bombarded by the Venetians in 1687 and robbed by the British in the early 19th century, Athens was transformed into a humble settlement. However, when Greek independence was proclaimed in 1832, that village of 5000 people was honored with the title of capital, precisely because of its ancient glory.

Both then and now, the Acropolis has rightfully symbolized the grandeur of Athens. Perched atop a rocky hill, this extraordinary complex built by Pericles in the mid-5th century BC boasts a monumental entrance, the Propylaea, leading to the flat open area on which stand the Parthenon and the Erechtheion, with the Loggia of the Caryatids. Architectural gems like the Odeion of Herod Atticus and the Theater of Dionysus are farther away, located behind the Acropolis.

Nevertheless, one must admit that, with the exception of its extraordinary archaeological remains and its Mediterranean atmosphere, Athens is not a pretty city. In just over fifty years, it has grown at a dizzying pace – and without any urban planning – to a population of 4.5 million inhabitants. Anonymous-looking modern buildings have been constructed at random, almost fully concealing the treasures of classical antiquity, Byzantine churches and districts, like Monastiraki, that reflect the soul of eastern Athens, founded under the Turks. The Plaka, the picturesque district that leads to the Acropolis, is now a caricature of itself – a veritable tourist trap. Not even the impressive areas that should celebrate the Greek nation, like Syntagma Square dominated by the Parliament Building, can escape this sense of chaos.

120-121 The view from Lycabettus Hill takes in the center of Athens, with the Parthenon as its dazzling symbol.

121 bottom left The Theater of Dionysus was the birthplace of Greek tragedy during the 5th century BC.

121 bottom right Famous for its harmonious Ionic architecture and the Loggia of the Caryatids, the Erechtheion was built in the Acropolis on the spot most sacred to the ancient Athenians.

The local government in Athens has long felt the need to remedy what is a desperate urban situation, at least by European standards, and glorious tradition has recently come to its aid: the Olympic Games. And 108 years after the first modern Olympics, which were held in Athens, the city has had the honor and burden of hosting the 28th Olympic Games. This major event stimulated work at a feverish pace for a complete makeover of the metropolis.

In addition to colossal sports facilities, which the Spanish architect Santiago Calatrava was commissioned to design, Athens has also finished restoring the Acropolis. The city renovated its deteriorated quarters, reorganized the port of Piraeus and, above all, redesigned the main thoroughfares. The pride of the transport network is the construction of the subway system, which has lightened surface traffic considerably and changed the life of city residents (the subway now carries 530,000 passengers a day). During excavation work, 30,000 archaeological artifacts were uncovered and are now displayed at the stations, creating an expressive dialog between ancient and modern history.

With substantial investments – and against all forecasts by critics – Athens has brilliantly met the challenge that hosting the Olympic imposed. Though it has not been fully transformed into a model city, Athens has made enormous advances. A telling example is the construction of the ultramodern Olympic Village, about 14 miles from the center. It will now become the headquarters for the Ministry of the Interior and a university research center, and the 2,500 apartments used by the athletes will now be turned into urban housing. The fortunate tenants will be picked by lottery: a tribute to the ancient democratic tradition of Athens.

122 top left The House of Parliament (Voulí) was built between 1836 and 1840 by architect Friedrich von Gartner as the residence of Otto of Bavaria, the first king of Greece after the Turks were driven out.

122 top right Outdoor cafés and a colorful flea market with trinkets, fabrics and jewelry give the Monastiraki district, once the heart of Muslim Athens, an "Oriental" air.

122 center The complex designed by Santiago Calatrava to host the 2004 Olympic Games is the pride of modern Athens. The games were also an opportunity to undertake other major works, such as the reorganization of the port of Piraeus and the construction of a futuristic subway system.

122 bottom For over 100 years Plateia Syntagmatos, or Constitution Square, has been the country's main social and political stage. The Parliament and a number of modern buildings line the square, and the new Syntagma subway station is considered a masterpiece of contemporary architecture.

122-123 Rising to a height of 745 feet, Lycabettus Hill is the tallest in the city. The name of the hill reflects an ancient popular belief, according to which dangerous packs of wolves (lykoi in Greek) lived here. On top the hill is the little white 19th-century chapel dedicated to Agios Georgios.

123 bottom The Ceremony of the Changing the Guard is held every Sunday morning at 11 a.m., at the foot of the staircase leading to the Parliament Building near the Tomb of the Unknown Soldier. The Evzones, members of the National Guard, wear traditional kilts and clogs.

AFRICA

For millions of years, Africa was the only continent trod by the forerunners of modern man. It was here that the line of human evolution diverged from that of the anthropomorphic great apes about seven million years ago. And it was here that our most remote ancestors, the Australopithecines, first began to walk in an upright position. Over one million years ago, groups of *Homo erectus* left Africa and colonized Asia and then Europe. Africa was also the starting point for the first groups of *Homo sapiens* who, over 100,000 years ago, reached the Middle East. The history of the evolution of our species is one of migration, and all these migrations started in the heart of Africa.

In Africa, man began to model the first stone tools, learned how to use fire, and started to live in caves and cliff shelters. It is also likely that Africa is where the first large communities developed complex languages. Nevertheless, in more recent periods as well – around 10,000 years ago – Africa played a significant role in the development of human society. Though the first documented cities of the historic age arose in the Middle East, and specifically in Mesopotamia, recent archaeological excavations have shown that about 10,000 years ago, *Homo sapiens* had already started to establish complex social structures and settlements in the once-fertile plains of the Sahara. Evidence of this comes from studies done in Nabta Playa, an Egyptian town not far from Abu Simbel, where traces of human occupation have been discovered: the remains of tombs and stone dwellings, ceramic and terracotta vessels, and – dating back to 9,000 years ago – water wells.

Egypt is also the place where one of the most extraordinary civilizations of all time flourished. Three thousand years before the Common Era, this culture founded large cities, and created marvelous artwork and immortal architecture like the pyramids of Giza, and the temples at Abu Simbel and Luxor. As early as 2000 BC, Memphis and Thebes, the ancient capitals of the Egyptian kingdom – when the planet was largely inhabited by small organized groups of people living in modest villages – must have numbered at least 50,000 people, most of whom engaged in farming activities that flourished in the fertile Nile Valley. Centuries later, it was the turn of Alexandria, the capital of Alexander the Great's empire. This was one of the most important cities of the Greek empire and one of the biggest metropolises in the ancient world, second only to Rome in size and wealth, and celebrated for its legendary library and the magnificent port on the Mediterranean.

However, the recent history of the continent that was the cradle of humanity is a troubled one. Falling into oblivion when the technological evolution shifted the hub of human culture to Europe, Africa virtually disappeared from the main trade routes. As a result, with the exception of the areas north of the Sahara and the lands on the Red Sea, like the empire of Ethiopia, for over 1,500 years it was untouched by the cultural progress that developed in Europe and Asia. It was not until the end of the 15th century that the Portuguese began to establish trade settlements along the west coast of Africa. In the 17th century, the Dutch, French and British followed their lead and embarked on the extended colonization of a continent for which the Latin motto *hic sunt leones*, long seen on maps, was still appropriate.

Black Africa and the innermost regions were not explored until the 19th century, when the continent was still inhabited by tribes who lived chiefly by hunting, farming and raising livestock, according to the customs of the populations of the early Neolithic Age. The Europeans were attracted to Africa above all by the continent's wealth of raw materials, and by the prospect of making money through the worst and most inhuman of enterprises: the slave trade. Accepted estimates suggest that between the 16th and 19th centuries, 10 to 15 million slaves were deported from Africa – particularly the inland areas near the Atlantic coast – and were brought mainly to Brazil, the Caribbean, and North America.

Though most countries had formally abolished the slave

trade by the mid-19th century, European interests continued to ravage the continent until far more recently. The Berlin Conference of 1884-1885 played a key role in carving up the continent into bits and pieces, proffering colonies to all the European countries that declared imperialistic ambitions. Thus, Britain, France, Germany, Belgium, Portugal and Italy claimed their share. The only African states to maintain their independence were Liberia, the land of freed slaves on which slavery had taken such a heavy toll, and Ethiopia, which lost its independence only between 1936 and 1941 when it was invaded by Italy.

After the end of World War II, the African countries slowly gained their independence, sometimes at the price of bloody rebellions against the colonial forces, as was the case in Algeria. In other areas, the artificial division of boundaries created internal conflicts between ethnic groups, in several cases leading to terrible civil wars in countries whose ruling classes were often ill-prepared to govern the transition to independence.

Therefore, it is not surprising that most African cities – with the exception of those on the Mediterranean and Adis Abeba, which has developed without any major interruptions – are relatively young. Notably, the urbanization process here has been limited mainly to the past thirty years, although it is now moving at an extremely fast pace.

Africa is the wildest of continents, as immense areas are dominated by unspoiled natural settings that have sparked the imagination of people everywhere. It covers an area of over 11.5 million square miles, but vast stretches are inhospitable, like the Sahara, Namib and Kalahari Deserts, and – for just the opposite reason – the enormous equatorial forests of the Congo. Until the middle of the 20th century, the continent's total population was less than 200 million. According to reliable estimates, however, the population growth could reach two billion by 2050.

Today, of the continent's 820 million inhabitants, just over one-third currently live in urban areas. Many of them arrived

there in the last 20 years, pioneers in a process that, according to the United Nations, is expected to continue at an astonishing pace until 2030. According to a report published by the United Nations in October 2003, however, 71% of the new immigrants in the cities in Sub-Saharan Africa – from Lagos to Nairobi, Adis Abeba and Lusaka – will populate the immense poverty-stricken suburbs. Few of these 190 million outcasts will find a job or a decent place to live, and for the most part there are no utilities like running water or electricity available.

Urbanization has also gained new impetus due to population growth, which tops 3% a year in many countries. According to official figures, Cairo, which has a population of about 16 million, is the only true metropolis on the continent. Nevertheless, in many other cities, such as Kinshasa, Lagos and Johannesburg, it is difficult to estimate the size of these constantly growing populations.

Moreover, evident differences exist among the people of a continent that is cut in two by the immense Sahara Desert. For thousands of years, the great desert acted as a virtually impenetrable barrier separating the societies developing along its edges. Today, the continent largely reflects the legacy of this division. Lying to the north is Mediterranean Africa, with its civilization and traditions, tied to Roman rule followed by the triumph of Islam. Here, cities like Cairo, Algiers, Marrakech and Casablanca have developed gradually around historic centers that are thousands of years old. To the south is the part of Africa that has faced enormous difficulties in order to overcome colonial rule. It is facing the challenge of modernity without having gone through all its phases at a gradual pace. Thus, this is a continent for which it is often a struggle to reconcile the tribal concept of society – a concept that is still very much alive in many of its countries – with the legitimate ambitions for development felt by the new ruling classes. The road ahead is still a long one, and to follow the path of more advanced societies the continent's major urban areas must inevitably mature.

125 left A view of modern Johannesburg, with the Museum Africa in the foreground.

125 center View of the center of Tunis from the top of the Great Mosque.

125 right The Cairo Citadel, with the Muhammad Ali Mosque towering over it.

Casablanca
MOROCCO

126 Completed in 1993, the Hassan II Mosque is the third-largest religious building in the world. It can hold 25,000 worshippers inside and 80,000 in the outside esplanade. At night, a laser beam on top of the 689-foot-tall minaret points to Mecca.

127 top Inaugurated in 1999, the architectural complex of the Twin Towers best symbolizes the modern entrepreneurial soul of Casablanca. The Towers, which are 377 feet tall, were designed by Spanish architect Ricardo Bofill, who gave Moorish architect a contemporary interpretation in this work.

127 bottom Muhammad V Square is the heart of the Ville Nouvelle district, which developed between 1918 and 1930. It is surrounded by a monumental complex of administrative buildings, including the Grande Poste, the Palais de Justice and the Ancienne Préfecture, dominated by a modernist clock tower.

Say the word "Casablanca" and the most famous movie in the history of Hollywood immediately comes to mind, as well as screen icons Humphrey Bogart and Ingrid Bergman. But then when you arrive at Morocco's only metropolis – whose film depiction is quite different from reality – you discover a city that has very little in common with its "sisters" Fès and Marrakech and, instead, has an atmosphere much more like that of Marseille. That's Casablanca: a foreign city even in its homeland. This "foreignness" starts with its old name, Casa Branca, which the Portuguese gave it during the 16th century and which the Spanish merchants who settled here in about 1830 altered slightly to its modern form. Casablanca's Arabic name, Dar el-Baida, never took hold; Moroccans refer to the city affectionately as Casà. The only reminders that one is indeed in Morocco are the people's faces (though none of the men don the traditional *djellaba* and very few women wear the veil, which is common elsewhere in the country) and an unpretentious fortified medina enclosing a souk. As to the rest, Casablanca is simply itself. The city is Morocco's main port, and 90 percent of the nation's industrial activities are concentrated here.

According to the official census, Casablanca has a population of 3 million, but this figure would undoubtedly double if the fluctuating numbers of those who come to the city seeking work and fortune were to be counted. And yet, this part of a country that prides itself on its long and glorious history was virtually overlooked in history books until 1907, when King Moulay Abdelaziz commissioned France to build a modern port here, modeled after Marseille. The ruler's decision triggered enormous friction with the leaders of the Berber tribes from the interior, who fomented a rebellion in which several French workmen were killed. In turn, the French used this unrest as a pretext for occupying Morocco militarily and expanding their colonial empire. In 1912 the entire kingdom became a French protectorate led by General Hubert Lyautey. Though the forty-year occupation, which lasted until 1956, is a very painful chapter in Moroccan history, Casablanca flourished during this period, becoming a splendid city. The French designed Ville Nouvelle, launching into a city-planning adventure that led to the construction of elegant buildings in a style that gave Arab architecture a modernist and Art Deco interpretation. The most extraordinary buildings are near the square now dedicated to King Mohammed V. They include the Grande Poste (1918), whose façade is decorated with columns and mosaics, the Palais de Justice (1925) and the Cathédrale du Sacré Coeur, designed in 1930 by Paul Tornon (it is now no longer open for services).

The Quartier Habous also deserves special mention. Built in the suburbs southeast of Casablanca during the Forties, it boasts intriguing collective housing solutions designed by architects Bodiansky and Candilis, who were followers of Le Corbusier. Even after Morocco gained its independence, Casablanca was determined to keep its international vocation, and foreign architects continued to be chosen to build ambitious public works. The most extraordinary example is the Hassan II Mosque. It is the second-largest Muslim religious building in the world after the mosque complex in Mecca: it can hold 25,000 worshippers inside and 80,000 in the outside atrium. Inaugurated in 1993, it is the perfect blend of tradition and technology. This structure, designed by French architect Michel Pinseau, rests partially on piers rising from the sea. Its roof opens electrically and the floor is heated by exploiting the hot air of the *hammam* beneath it. A laser beam on top of the 689-foot-tall minaret points to Mecca. And the interior is a paean to the skill of Moroccan craftsmen, who created precious "embroidery" with polychrome marble. The financial center is more recent, and its hub is marked by the Twin Towers, done in a postmodern style and rising to a height of 377 feet. The designer of these towers was the Spanish architect Ricardo Bofill.

128 Tunisian flag pennants circle the obelisk commemorating the country's independence from France, proclaimed on March 20, 1956.

129 top The French built St. Vincent de Paul Cathedral in 1882, in an odd blend of Romanesque, Byzantine and Moorish styles.

Tunis

TUNISIA

129 center top A modern building houses the Hotel Africa.

wide avenues, European-style buildings and public parks.

129 center bottom In Ville Nouvelle, the university area has

129 bottom A monumental clock rises over Avenue Bourguiba.

Tunis harbor is one of the main commercial ports of North Africa, and yet Tunis, which is separated from the sea by a brackish lake, is not a port city. It is the capital of Tunisia, and 50 percent of the country's industrial activities occur there. Nevertheless, with a population of just under 700,000, it maintains the peaceful appearance of a provincial city. From the 12th to the 16th century, under the Hafsid dynasty, Tunis was considered one of the most magnificent cities of Islam, and it boasted a prestigious university second only to al-Azhar, in Cairo. Today, however, it is not a typical Arab city. Though its Ville Nouvelle, built during the period of French colonization, has over 700 "European" buildings, Tunis does not mimic a Western city. The allure of Tunis lies in this sense of "being and not being." The city has an aura of tolerance and openness toward the world, both Western and Muslim, but without being overwhelmed by it. In fact, though its inhabitants are devout believers, they are untouched by any form of fundamentalism. And the women of Tunis rarely wear the Muslim veil.

Naturally, not even Tunis has escaped the recent fate of unbridled suburban expansion, but its suburbs do not show signs of deterioration. And in the center of town, restoration has been chosen over reconstruction. The Association de Sauvegarde de la Médina has been active for several decades, and the Old City is inscribed on UNESCO's World Heritage List because of the enormous historical and artistic value of its monuments.

Jemaa Zitouna, the Olive Mosque, is in the heart of the Medina. It was built in the 9th century by the Aghlabid dynasty over an extant religious structure, using 200 columns from the ruins of nearby Carthage. Over the centuries, the building was adorned with majolica decorations, and a portico was added during the 17th century under the Ottomans. Extending around it are the alleys of the lively souk, which is rigidly divided based on the goods for sale, with everything from perfumes at the Souk el Attarine to colorful Berber carpets displayed at the Souk el Kachachine, jewelry at the Souk des Orfèvres and traditional red felt hats at the Souk des Chechias. Silence reigns in other areas of the Medina, with noble palaces,

130 top right An elegant octagonal minaret marks the Mosque of Hamuda Pasha, in the Medina, which was built in the Ottoman style in the mid-17th century.

130 top left The typical doors of the houses in the Medina are mainly painted light blue, and are decorated with studs and nails forming designs linked with Islamic symbolism.

130 center Located in the former residence of the Ottoman bey, the Bardo Museum boasts one important mosaic collections in the world.

130 bottom Jewelry glitters in the display cases of the Souk des Orfèvres. In the Islamic world, women are the main buyers of silver and gold.

caravanserais and mosques, and here it is easier to appreciate the details of the doors of these buildings. Painted chiefly in light blue – though there are also ones in red, white and green, designating the *hammam* and *zaouia*, or sacred places – they are decorated with nails (*hilia*) forming geometric motifs or designs like the Hand of Fatima, the symbol of the Punic goddess Tanit or the fisheye, which are considered talismans. The doors are also a distinctive feature of the Halfaouine quarter, located next to the Medina, and this area is also known for its mosques and picturesque views.

Bab el Bahr, the Gate to the Sea, separates the Medina from the Ville Nouvelle. The layout of the Ville Nouvelle resembles a checkerboard split in half by the broad Avenue Bourguiba, which is lined with elegant buildings designed in a style referred to as "pompous colonial." Two of the most noteworthy are the French Theater, which is finished in white stucco and has fascinating high-relief female figures decorating the upper part of the balcony, and the cathedral, built in 1882 in a quirky mélange of Romanesque, Byzantine and Moorish styles.

Parc Belvedere, the city's only park, is set on a hill overlooking the Ville Nouvelle and is the location of the Museum of Modern Art. When it comes to museums, however, the treasure of the capital of Tunisia is located 2.5 miles from the center in Beylical Palace, which was once the residence of the Ottoman governors. This is the Bardo Museum, which displays exquisite mosaics from the Roman and Early Christian eras, executed by African workers between the 2nd and 6th centuries AD, when Carthage declined and Tunis rose in its stead.

130-131 The Jemaa Zitouna, or Olive Mosque, was founded in 732 and was enlarged and decorated over the centuries until 1894, the year the minaret was built. Located in the heart of the Medina, it is the largest and most venerated religious building in the city.

131 bottom The traditional terraces on the rooftops of the buildings in the Medina, protected by railings and arches covered with eccentric combinations of traditional majolica tiles, offer a marvelous view of the roofs and alleyways of old Tunis.

Cairo

EGYPT

132 top left In Cairo, the feluccas – typical boats with a triangular sail – now sail the Nile strictly for the enjoyment of tourists. The port of the capital city is in Bulaq, a populous suburb north of Cairo.

132 top right The Ramesses Station was built in 1856 but was reconstructed to give the architecture a more Arabic appearance. A colossus of the famous pharaoh was named was erected in the large square in front of the station in 1955.

One could easily define it as pharaonic – in the true sense of the word – or Muslim. Or African, Roman, Greek, Turkish, Arab, Coptic, European. Each and every time, Cairo opens up to reveal its countless souls, escaping all definition. There are infinite scenarios in a seamless sequence, blending marvelous architecture with building horrors, ancestral remains with modernity, ostentatious wealth with misery. Pyramids, mosques, churches, Art Deco buildings, hovels, alleys and elevated highways: all these elements "are" Cairo. And the Nile – the great river that crosses it – is like a paradigm of the artlessness with which the city has elaborated and absorbed all the moments in its history, showing its vocation for eternity. Indeed, its Arabic name – given to it as "late" as 969 by the sultans of the Fatimid dynasty – is *al-Qahira,* "the victorious."

When the blanket of smog happens to lift, from the top of the Tower of Cairo one can glance down at the agglomerate of 16 million residents forming the capital of Egypt. The brick tower, which was built in 1961 and rises to a height of 607 feet, is located in Zamalek, the quarter built on the Nile island of Gezira. From here, Giza extends to the left with its jungle of buildings and satellite dishes, and the Ancient Egyptian pyramids of Khufu, Khafre, and Menkaure (also known as Cheops, Chephren, and Mycerinus) in the background. To the right is the lively heart of Islamic Cairo, dominated by the Citadel built in 1169 by the Seljuk ruler Salah el-Din, better known as the fierce Saladin. Beyond that is the old city, which safeguards the memory of Coptic Christianity in Egypt. This is the location of El-Mu'allaqa (7th century), which is also known as the "Hanging Church" because it is set atop a Roman wall, Abu Serga (the 4th-century church of St. Sergius), which is said to have been built over the place where the Holy Family rested after fleeing to Egypt, and here too is Ben Ezra, the first synagogue in the country.

Cairo's breathtaking monuments, built by the Arab dynasties that ruled the city, rival the pyramids at Giza. One of the most striking is the Mosque of al-Azhar, in the heart of

132 center Cairo's appeal lies in the surprising continuity between the remains of Egypt's millenary civilization and modernity. This aspect is evident in the picture of the majestic pyramids of Khufu, Khafre and Menkaure, located at the edge of the populous Giza district.

132 bottom In contrast with the rest of the city, Gezira has three parks, and they have become popular Sunday destinations. One of them is the Youth Club garden, shown here, with the national government buildings in the background.

132-133 The garden district of Zamalek is on the island of Gezira, in the middle of this view. It is the location of the Opera House, a masterpiece of modern Islamic architecture, as well as the Tower of Cairo, and various ministry buildings and embassies.

133 bottom left Elegant Neo-Classical, Neo-Baroque and Art Nouveau buildings line Talaat Harb Square in the heart of town. The modern and European city that developed when the Suez Canal was inaugurated has a fairytale atmosphere.

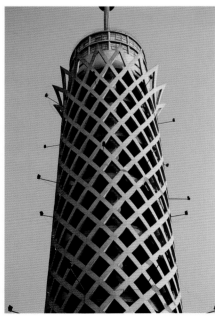

133 bottom right The 607-foot-tall Tower of Cairo is the world's tallest building made entirely of bricks. Its structure resembles the stem of the papyrus plant, whereas the top "opens" like a lotus blossom, thus symbolizing the two plants sacred to the ancient Egyptians.

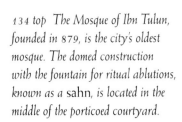

134 top *The Mosque of Ibn Tulun, founded in 879, is the city's oldest mosque. The domed construction with the fountain for ritual ablutions, known as a* sahn, *is located in the middle of the porticoed courtyard.*

134 center top *The portico of the al-Azhar Mosque is filled with worshippers for Friday prayers. The building houses the mosque's archives and the offices of the muftis, the highest religious authorities.*

**30°00'N
31°17'E**

Islamic Cairo. Built in 972 by the Fatimid ruler Gawhar, it houses what is considered the oldest university in the world and, even today, it is the most important religious institution for Sunni Muslims. From an architectural standpoint, it is a stunning palimpsest of the styles and cultural influences that have crossed Egypt. It has five minarets and six entrances, and each room is decorated with intricate bas-reliefs. Other fascinating sights include the oldest mosque in the city, devoted to the Abbasid ruler Ibn Tulun, the Mosque of Aqsunqur (14th century), decorated with majolica tiles from the Turkish city of Iznik, and the Mosque of El-Mu'ayyad (15th century). In addition to its religious buildings, Islamic Cairo shows off its timeless allure at Khan el-Khalili, the city's labyrinthine bazaar. Carried away by the scents and colors of the wares, one can easily get lost here amid caravansaries, hammams and cafés crowded with men busily negotiating business and smoking a *shisha*, the traditional water pipe.

Despite its skyscrapers and traffic, modern Cairo also maintains a fairytale Eastern atmosphere. This part of the city was established with the inauguration of the Suez Canal and the advent of French and British rule. At the turn of the 20th century, Cairo's European masters were determined to give the city an orderly appearance reminiscent of Napoleonic Paris. But they too were spellbound by Cairo, and instead of "taming" it, they were captivated by it. Even Heliopolis, Cairo's most European quarter (now the home of Egypt's upper classes) has an incongruous appearance. A serious Belgian industrialist, Édouard Louis Joseph Empain (1852-1929), decided to build his Baron's Palace here, a surprising residence that evokes the Hindu architectures of Angkor Wat, in Cambodia. Because Cairo caters to every whim. . . .

134 center bottom *The city's profusion of mosques, built over the course of ten centuries and filled with priceless treasures, has earned Cairo the name of "The City of the Thousand Minarets." One of the most striking of these tall and elegant towers is the one of the Sayyida Zeinab Mosque, built in the Mamluk style and decorated with arabesques and inscriptions.*

134 bottom *Two of the most extraordinary mosques in Cairo stand side by side. One is dedicated to the Sultan Hassan, and it is considered the most important example of Mamluk architecture in the country. The other is the Rif'i Mosque, which was completed in 1912 to house the royal crypt of the last Egyptian dynasty.*

134-135 *The immense al-Azhar Mosque, built in the 10th century by the Fatimid ruler Gawhar and dedicated to Mohammed's daughter Fatima al-Zahraa, is the most important religious institution for Sunnite Muslims. It also houses the oldest university in the world: jurist Abou al-Hassan Ibn al-Noaman held the first lesson here in 972.*

135 bottom *The pale domes of the Muhammad Ali Mosque tower over the Cairo Citadel. The building, completed in 1857, is not an architectural masterpiece like many of the other mosques in Cairo, but it enjoys the most scenic setting.*

136-137 The Central Business District of Johannesburg underwent a major urban renewal project in the late Nineties, and has 11 skyscrapers that are over 300 feet tall.

136 bottom Orlando, the "wealthy" area of Soweto Township, is where Nelson Mandela – who was a young attorney and civil rights activist at the time – and Archbishop Tutu once lived.

137 top The Africa Museum is the main attraction of Newbury, the quarter west of the center of town. Since the end of apartheid, it has been transformed into a cultural hub.

137 bottom Soweto, a stretch of houses with tin roofs, is the most famous township of South Africa. Even the local government is unable to estimate its exact population, which may well be about four million.

Johannesburg

SOUTH AFRICA

Let's start with its world records. Johannesburg is one of the world's most sprawling cities, covering an area of 965 square miles on a plateau with an altitude of 5577 feet. It is the heart of the South African economy, and this makes it the richest city on the continent. It is also the city that has grown the fastest, given that in the space of just one year –1889, when inexhaustible gold deposits were discovered here – it was transformed from a forlorn village with a handful of hovels to a bustling city teeming with people. For the record, however, it must also be noted that, sadly, Johannesburg also happens to be the most violent city in the world, with about 5000 homicides reported every year and an inestimable number of rapes, thefts and robberies.

Then there are several odd and, frankly, troubling facts. No one knows how many people live in Johannesburg. According to official figures, the city has a population of five million, but administrators, who are far from being able to manage the entire territory, admit that it would be more realistic to add at least double that amount to this number. Moreover, Johannesburg looks like anything but a city. It is composed of various areas – they cannot be defined as quarters – divided by wide stretches of uncultivated land and gold-mine craters. What is even more amazing (for visitors, but not for South Africans) is that these areas do not communicate with each other. Apartheid has officially been over for several years, but now another form of separation has arisen, and this time it discriminates based on wealth. The rich areas – first and foremost among them is Rosebank, a residential area with villas built from the early 20th century on – are protected by armies of private security guards. In contrast, in the poor areas, which are mainly populated by blacks, people take justice into their own hands. Among the former districts, Sandton is the new financial center of Johannesburg. In 2001, this area of luxurious skyscrapers, five-star hotels and shopping centers hosted 7000 international delegates for the World Summit. Then there are Melville, Jeppestown and Newtown. Newtown was designed as a center for the development of art and culture, and Museum Africa and the Market Theatre are located here.

In contrast, Hillbrow was the center of Johannesburg during the 1970s and 1980s; it was constructed vertically and designed with the concept of an "African Manhattan" in mind. Today, however, its once-modern office buildings and apartments are rapidly being taken over by illegal immigrants from all over Africa. The locals refer to it as "little Lagos" because the Nigerian "mafia" rule it and its economy "thrives" on the sale of drugs and weapons. The city's tallest tower, JG Strijdom Tower (882 feet) neighbors on Hillbrow, but admiring the view from this vantage point means venturing into an urban jungle. Nevertheless, the city government is making investments in order to "clean out" the nearby retail district of Braamfontein as well as the area of the Old Fort (1895), where the Constitutional Court Building is being constructed.

Paradoxically, Soweto – or at least some of its areas – is more inviting: this "city within a city" houses an estimated population of 4 million. Its name is an acronym for South Western Township, and it is the largest, most famous and most dynamic of Johannesburg's six black ghettos. This is where South Africa's first great anti-apartheid revolt began in 1976, and this is where the African National Congress, the party headed by the beloved Nelson Mandela, was established. Aside from its sea of shanties with sheet-metal roofs, Soweto also has a museum, a touching monument dedicated to the long path to freedom of black South Africans, and areas devoted to art, music and theater. It even has a "rich" neighborhood, Orlando, which has been nicknamed Beverly Hills. Soweto also boasts another one of Johannesburg's world records. Vilikazi Street is the only street in the world to have been the address of two Nobel laureates: Nelson Mandela and Archbishop Desmond Tutu.

Cape Town

SOUTH AFRICA

The southern seas have their very own Pillars of Hercules, described in 1580 as "the most stately thing and the fairest Cape we saw in the whole circumference of the earth" by Sir Francis Drake when he rounded the Cape of Good Hope a little more than 100 years after its Portuguese discoverer, Bartholomew Diaz. Little does it matter that the exact point where the Atlantic meets the Indian Ocean, down below Africa, is instead the less poetic Cape Agulhas, about 90 miles south. That promontory had the right kind of intrigue to enter the pages of history, and to become the site of the first "European" city of southern Africa: Cape Town. Cape Town's setting makes it one of the world's most beautiful cities. Bordered by splendid beaches and rocky little islands with whales swimming nearby, it is dominated by Table Mountain, the 3200-ft flat-topped mountain always swathed by clouds (which the locals refer to as "the tablecloth"). It boasts over 5000 indigenous plant species, including the protea, the flower South Africa has adopted as its symbol. The historic right of founding Cape Town goes to the Dutch, who arrived at Table Bay on April 6, 1652, bringing construction materials with them. However, credit for its cultural heritage can be divided equally among its Portuguese, English, French, Malaysian and Indian immigrants,

without overlooking the populations that already lived here, the San and the various Bantu groups. Even during the dark years of apartheid, it was this age-old "melting pot" that helped preserve at least part of the city from the tension and bloodshed that was so common in other South African cities. The townships, the shantytowns populated largely by blacks and extending north of the center for miles, here have become a peaceful tourist attraction. And the whole city seems to have found a balance between Old Europe and Africa, with the ambition of achieving American-style modernity. The most obvious sign of the "Americanization" of Cape Town is the Victoria & Alfred Waterfront, the city's most important urban-planning work. This project transformed the harbor built in 1882 by the British during the rule of their most powerful and long-reigning queen into a dazzling venue for shopping and entertainment. Directly across from the old port authority building – constructed in the Neo-Gothic style and now painted red – catamarans leave for nearby Robben Island, the location of the prison where Nelson Mandela was held for nearly twenty years; it has now been protected by UNESCO as a World Heritage Site.

The visitor must pass by the city's most recent buildings before finding evidence of its old history, such as the Fort of Good Hope, built by the Dutch between 1666 and 1679 according to the principles of the famous French military engineer and architect Marshal Vauban (1633-1707), and the remains of the 18th-century Groote Kerk, the first Dutch Reformed Church in South Africa. The British influence is even more evident, and there are numerous public buildings that date back to the late 19th century, such as the Neoclassic-style City Hall, built to celebrate the jubilee of Queen Victoria, and the Anglican cathedral (1902), which is more famous for the fact that Nobel Laureate Archbishop Desmond Tutu gave his sermons there than it is for its architecture. The residential quarters retain an old-time flavor. One of the most intriguing is Bo-Kaap, where Malaysian Muslims live in Dutch-style houses painted in pastel colors. Nearby is one of the most poignant places in the city, the District Six Museum. It is a place that tells the story of a quarter where whites, blacks, Asians, Jews and Muslims coexisted in harmony. This kind of a place is typical of Cape Town, and it was so embarrassing for the white rulers that in 1966 they sent in bulldozers to level it. Now that the nightmare of segregation is over, the testimony of District Six represents a word of warning on how to construct the future of South Africa.

138 top Long Street is one of the city's most historic streets – and also its liveliest. It extends for about 2.5 miles, linking the ocean with the old district of Tamboerskloof, and is lined with Victorian homes that have elegant verandas and cast-iron decorations.

138 center A view of the Victoria & Alfred Waterfront. The port buildings including the Port Captain's Office, the Time Ball Tower and the Union Castle House, all of which were built at the turn of the 20th century – have been renovated, and the entire area is now an entertainment and shopping district.

138 bottom The University of Cape Town was founded in 1829, making it the oldest university in South Africa. Located in the suburbs of Rondebosch, on the slopes of Devil's Peak, it has a student body of 20,000. Eminent faculty members include heart surgeon Christian Barnard and J. M. Coetzee, who won the Nobel Prize in Literature.

138-139 The natural setting of Cape Town is considered one of the most beautiful in the world. Its urban areas extend from the ocean to the slopes of Table Mountain, the sandstone massif that rises to an altitude of nearly 3500 feet and has extraordinarily rich flora, with 2200 species.

139 bottom With its Dutch-style houses painted in pastel colors, Bo-Kaap is one of the city's quaintest districts. Malaysian Muslims live in here, and it is also the location of the city's oldest mosque, which was built in 1798.

ASIA

Rice, honey and fruit. These were the ingredients of the fermented beverage found in a receptacle during the archaeological excavation underway at the village of Jiahu, in the province of Henan in East-Central China. Dating back 9000 years, this is the oldest terracotta object ever found in China, and it testifies to the first known fermented beverage. In the same village, archaeologists also discovered some of the first musical instruments in the history of civilization, as well as the oldest forms of cultivated rice. Toward the mid-1990s, Mary M. Voigt, from the College of William and Mary in Virginia, made another equally extraordinary discovery at the other end of Asia, in Hajji Firuz Tepe, Iran. This was the oldest documented wine, found there inside a pair of jars dating back to 5400 BC.

This evidence testifies to the fact that since the beginning of the Neolithic period, complex and intricate human societies developed in Asia, and they discovered ways of settling in groups in the fertile lands of the largest continent on the planet. Today Asia – which covers an area of over 17 million square miles, or a little less than one-third of the world's dry land – has 3.7 billion inhabitants, or 61% of the world population. And, naturally, it is also the continent with the largest number of metropolises: 6 of the top 10, and 28 of the top 50. According to the latest surveys, Tokyo is the biggest city in the world, with a population of nearly 30 million.

With its astonishing growth, which started after World War II, and its incredible blend of futuristic modernity and tradition, the capital of Japan is probably the very prototype of the great metropolises that developed during the 20th century, and it indubitably represents the vanguard of the immense urban agglomerations that will dominate the 21st century. Tokyo had barely two million inhabitants at the turn of the 20th century, and less than four million at the end of World War II, when the city emerged from the conflict virtually destroyed by the Allied bombings. Nevertheless, through a formidable reconstruction process, by 1970 – just twenty-five years after the end of the war – Tokyo's population had already

risen to 15 million. Two factors promoted this growth. First, the worldwide demographic boom resulting in large part from generally improved living conditions, particularly with regard to diet and health, which particularly accentuated by Japan's remarkable development. Second, the sweeping industrialization of the capital of Japan, which attracted much of the rural population in search of job opportunities and good salaries – a phenomenon that has characterized urban growth on every continent throughout the 20th century.

According to a report published by the United Nations in 2002, Tokyo will still be the most populated city in the world in 2015, but other enormous urban areas, nearly all of which Asian, are rapidly catching up with it. Within a decade, the list of the world's ten largest cities will include Dhaka, the capital of Bangladesh, the Indian cities of Bombay, Delhi and Calcutta, and Jakarta and Karachi – all of which will have more than 15 million people. These forecasts do not even consider the great Chinese metropolises, which have developed exponentially in the past twenty years and are expected to do so through the first half of this century. Moreover, official estimates vary according to the geographical boundaries used by each country to define the metropolitan areas.

In any event, Asia – with China leading the way – is the continent that will probably lend new thrust to the urbanization process. Giants like Shanghai and Chongqing, the metropolis created through the forced relocation of millions of people who lived in the area where the Three Gorges Dam was built on the Yangtze River, will be the ones to project the cities of the 21st century into the future, delineating not only the infrastructures where millions and millions of people will live, work and shop, but also means of transportation, streets, and entertainment venues. This is not only because China is the most populous country in the world, but also because the rapid concentration of its population in urban centers has been accompanied by unparalleled economic growth, guaranteeing opportunities that would be impossible for many other countries. The city of tomorrow is already being created in Shanghai, the city of a thousand skyscrapers, with innovations like the magnetic levitation train, the fastest

train in the world. It links Pudong Airport to the city and covers 18 miles in just eight minutes, traveling at a top speed of over 265 miles per hour. And the city of tomorrow is also being created through the futuristic plans drawn up by the world's finest architects, who are redesigning Beijing and other major urban centers in China.

In fact, Chinese cities are moving toward the future by wiping out much of their history. In the center of Beijing, close to Tiananmen Square, there is still a district dotted with *siheyuan*, traditional single-story houses, some of which were built as far back as eight centuries ago. But this is a microcosm besieged by modernity, and it runs the risk of succumbing at any moment, just like the historic districts of many other Chinese cities.

The new China looks ahead to the future by revolutionizing its cities' historic districts and replacing the heritage of the past with avant-garde architecture. This trend is shared by much of the Far East, from South Korea, where Seoul embarked on a modernization process years ago, to Southeast Asia, where metropolises like Singapore, Bangkok, Kuala Lumpur and Jakarta are thriving, and other important urban centers like Ho Chi Minh City and Manila are burgeoning.

The pace – and perhaps also the philosophy – of modernity changes as one travels westward. India, the second most populous nation on earth, is also undergoing a phase of important economic growth, and this is reflected by the urbanization process that has involved Delhi, Bombay, Calcutta, Bangalore, Madras (now Chennai) and 30 other Indian cities with a population of over one million. Despite the fact that the metropolitan landscape is taking on new contours, the situation in Indian cities differs profoundly from the one in China. First, India has started out with less prosperous general conditions. Second, the centuries-old caste system of Indian society has prevented the rapid development of a middle class, and this in turn has kept much of the population from accessing more modern infrastructures. Finally, as opposed to the countries of the Far East, India seems less inclined to draw inspiration from Western models,

European cities and, above all, the great American skyscraper cities. This makes the cities of the subcontinent a unique testing ground for an alternative kind of modernity, in which metropolises expand confusedly from the center toward the suburbs without a cogent plan. As a result, their historic legacy is not being overridden by colossal urban planning.

But urban Asia does not end here. In its extraordinary historic and cultural diversity, this record-breaking continent has dozens of other cities worth mentioning, even though many of them are not described in these pages.

Two examples are the sprawling Pakistani port of Karachi, and Teheran, the capital of Iran, which respectively have populations of ten million and seven million. And there are cities like two great capitals of the past, Istanbul and Jerusalem, which have left their indelible mark on the history of civilization. Today, they continue to attract attention, though for different reasons. Istanbul is taking crucial steps to give Turkey the impetus it needs to join the European Union. Jerusalem, in contrast, is the strategic crossroads for the difficult process of peace in the Middle East, as it represents the Holy City of the world's three great monotheistic religions, and a symbol that is hotly contested by Israelis and Palestinians.

At the beginning of the Neolithic Age, the first stable settlements were established at the two ends of Asia, and many centuries later, in Mesopotamia, these settlements spawned the first known cities in history: Babylonia, Ur, Ebla, Uruk, Kish and Akkad. The first written languages and the first laws arose here. A short time later, the two settlements that now claim the title of the world's oldest cities were founded in Asia, and specifically in Syria: Damascus and Aleppo. More than five thousand years have come and gone, and the sense of human coexistence and of the social contract that brings us together in increasingly crowded and structured communities – in which even personal relationships are subject to new rules that are often dictated by the urban fabric – has changed profoundly. And yet, once again, we must turn to Asia to seek the seeds of the radical transformations that the cohabitation of our species will face in the years to come.

141 left The north bank of the Golden Horn is outlined beyond the domes of the Topkapi Saray.

141 center A view of Shibuya, a trendy district that is very popular among Tokyo's young people.

141 right The building of the People's Assembly stands out starkly in Tiananmen Square.

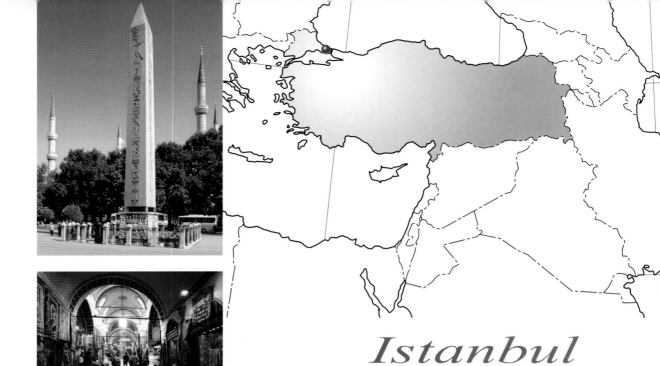

Istanbul

TURKEY

142 top Once a cultural center of the Byzantine Empire, the hippodrome is now a public park known as At Meydam. An Egyptian obelisk brought here in the 6th century stands at its northern end. The scenes around the base commemorate its installation in Constantinople under Theodosius I.

142 center top A maze of 66 streets and alleys with over 5000 shops, warehouses, banks and tearooms, along with a mosque, post office and police station, Kapali Çarsi – better known as the Grand Bazaar of Istanbul – is the largest covered market in the world.

At first it was Byzantium, a Greek colony founded in the 7th century BC. Then it was Constantinople, named after Constantine, the emperor who in 303 declared Christianity to be the official religion of the Roman Empire and made the city its capital. In 1453 – the year it was conquered by Mehmet II – it became Istanbul, the third and last capital of the Ottoman Empire, though its name was not officially changed until 1930. Today, the only city in the world that straddles two continents still goes by this name. In 1923, with the establishment of the Republic of Turkey, Kemal Atatürk moved the capital to Ankara. Nevertheless, Istanbul remains the symbol of a country suspended between one shore of the Mediterranean and the other, between Europe and Asia. And it is the most important city in Turkey, with a population of 12 million that continues to grow at the rate of 500,000 people a year, fueled by massive immigration from the rural areas of Anatolia.

The capital of two empires – one Christian and the other Muslim – for more than a thousand years, today Istanbul is a dynamic metropolis. Nevertheless, it has proudly preserved its historical and architectural heritage, above all in the city's cultural center, which overlooks the open space that was once the site of the Hippodrome built by Emperor Constantine in 330. Facing each other here are the Hagia Sophia, the majestic basilica built between 532 and 538 during the reign of Justinian, and the harmonious Sultan Ahmet Camii, constructed at the beginning of the 12th century and better known as the Blue Mosque, because of the 20,000 blue majolica tiles from the city of Iznik covering its interior. Hagia Sophia, which the conqueror Mehmet II converted into a mosque, has now been turned into a state museum and historical monument, was the model that inspired some of the Ottomans' most impressive and sumptuous Islamic architectures. One example is Suleymaniye Camii, the mosque built between 1550 and 1557 by the renowned architect Sinan for Suleyman the Magnificent. And there is Topkapi Palace, which was the residence of the Ottoman sultans for four centuries, starting in 1465. The allure of the city's monumental architecture, the surreal tranquility of the yali, the historical residences lining the banks of the Bosporus, and the ancient bazaars (such as Kapali Çarsi, the largest

142 center bottom The conical roof of Galata Tower rises in the heart of Beyoglü, on the north shore of the Golden Horn. The tower, which was built in 1348 but is now just 220 feet tall, was the donjon of the stronghold built by the Genoese.

142 bottom Every year about 80,000 cargo ships, tankers and ferries cross the strait of the Bosporus, the arm of the sea that is one of Istanbul's most important — and picturesque — arteries.

142-143 Slender minarets rise above Stanbul, as the oldest part of the city is sometimes called: it corresponds to the area once occupied by Constantinople. In the background, Üsküdar extends on the Asian side, separated by the Bosporus.

143 bottom Rumeli Hisari, built in about 1450, is the larger of the two fortresses built on opposite banks to protect the narrowest point of the Bosporus. Visible behind it is the Fatih Sultan Mehmet Bridge, which is over 3500 feet long. It was inaugurated in 1988 and is located at the point where King Darius of Persia crossed the strait on a bridge of boats in 512 BC.

144-145 Topkapi Palace, the symbolic and political center of the Ottoman Empire for nearly 4 centuries, was built between 1459 and 1465 as the seat of government, but it was not originally set up as a residence.

144 bottom left Ciragan Palace (now a luxury hotel) was destroyed and rebuilt several times. It was not actually completed until 1857, but even in the early 1700s it was greatly admired by European travelers.

144 bottom right Küçüksu Kasri, in the Çengelköy district on the Bosporus, is a splendid residence designed in the mid-1800s by Nikogos Balyan. Its intricate Rococo façade faces the river.

145 top The Ortaköy Mosque, built on the Bosporus in 1854 and designed by Nikogos Balyan, is a blend of the architectures of the era, though the influence of European

classicism is evident. Its minarets are slender columns decorated with Corinthian capitals.

145 center Hünkar Sofrasi, where the sultan would entertain visitors, is one of the most opulent rooms of the Topkapi Palace harem. The palace has over 400 rooms, with the apartments of the sultan and his mother, the Valide Sultan, in the center.

145 bottom Built between 1843 and 1856 by Armenian architect Karabet Balyan and his son Nikogos, Dolmabahçe Palace is the most opulent residence on the Bosporus. Sultan Abdülmecid had it built to replace Topkapi Palace as the imperial residence. Magnificent as it was, Abdülmecid's successors did not like it and almost never stayed there.

covered market in the world, with over 5000 shops), which have maintained their age-old traditions, are offset by the 21st-century city and the pace of a noisy, bustling metropolis. The modern city snakes around Taksim Square, the enormous plaza that offers a sudden sense of liberation to those who enter it after wandering through the alleys of the historic districts on the other side of the Haliç, or Golden Horn, the estuary that cuts the city's European area in half. It is on this bank, between the Galata and Taksim quarters, that by day Istanbul shows off its ultramodern office buildings, teeming with white-collar workers. And by night it shows off its vitality, with cultural offerings that range from the most exclusive theaters to shows sure to dazzle thrill-seekers.

Istanbul has grown disproportionately from its 1950 population of one million. Over the past several decades, however, the city has not erected any noteworthy architectural structures capable of relaunching its role as a national symbol and the beacon of Turkish modernity. Perhaps this is due in part to the lack of interest shown by the various governments in Ankara, which have preferred to promote colossal plans to develop agriculture and energy production in the nation's eastern regions. The projects include the ambitious Southeastern Anatolia Project that calls for 22 dams on upper reaches of the Euphrates and Tigris rivers. Thus, during the second half of the 20th century only two major projects have been completed in Istanbul, but their symbolic importance is inestimable. With the Bosporus Bridge (1974) and the Fatih Sultan Mehmet Bridge (1988), both of which are a little over half a mile long and stretch over a narrow arm of the sea, the two shores of the Bosporus have finally been linked. Indeed, these bridges physically unite the city's dual European and Asian soul.

Istanbul

146 top The splendid mosaics that decorate the ceiling and walls of Hagia Sophia originally covered a surface of 3.7 acres. They were made of glass and gold tiles, and of the ones remaining today the most interesting are the figurative ones done between 726 and after iconoclasm ceased.

146 bottom A sensation of timeless tranquility pervades as soon as you enter the magnificent Süleymaniye Camii, with its lofty dome rising to a height of nearly 175 feet. Light filters into the prayer room through more than 200 splendidly decorated stained-glass windows.

146-147 *In this spectacular aerial view, the Basilica of Hagia Sophia and the Sultan Ahmet Camii, commonly known as the Blue Mosque, face each other across a broad park area. The modern districts of Istanbul, overlooking the Golden Horn, are visible in the background.*

147 top *The Basilica of Hagia Sophia was commissioned by Emperor Justinian in AD 532 to express the power of the Byzantine Empire. It was turned into a mosque in 1453 and continued to be used as a place of worship until 1932, when it was converted into a museum.*

147 bottom *Founded between 1550 and 1557 by architect Sinan for Suleyman the Magnificent, Süleymaniye Camii is almost square in its layout and is covered by a central dome that rests on a drum with windows. As a whole, the mosque replicates the design of the Basilica of Hagia Sophia.*

149 Three views of the Mount of Olives summarize the faiths for which Jerusalem is a spiritual center. Above, the Dome of the Rock gleams beyond the crest, dominated by the bell tower of the Russian Church of the Ascension. In the center, the Church of All Nations was built in 1924 on the spot where Jesus ascended into heaven. Below, the largest Jewish cemetery in the world, dating back to the biblical era and still in use.

148-149 and 148 bottom left
There are 7 gates in the walls of the Old City, which were built by Suleyman. The most impressive one is Damascus Gate, shown in this picture.

148 bottom right Now the site of the Museum of the History of Jerusalem, the Tower of David was given this name by the Crusaders. It is actually the minaret of a mosque built in the early 14th century.

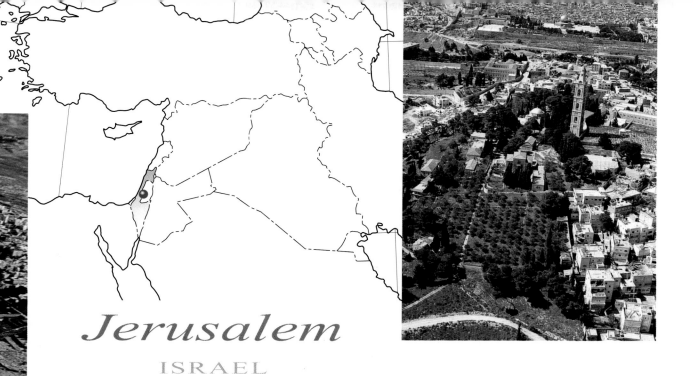

Jerusalem

ISRAEL

Muslims call it *al-Quds*, "the Holy One," Islam's most sacred place after Mecca and Medina. They say that "dying in Jerusalem is like dying in heaven" because, according to the Koran, the prophet Mohammed commenced his journey to Eternity by ascending from the rock upon which the *Qubbat as-Sakhra* (Dome of the Rock) was built. Jews call it *Yerushalaim*, the "City of Peace," and Mount Moriah, corresponding to the western section of its walls, is the center of their universe. This is where Abraham, the patriarch of the people of Israel, prepared to sacrifice his son Isaac and where Solomon built the Bet-El, the Temple to house the Tables of the Law. The *shekhinah* – the presence of God – hovers here in eternity. Finally, Christians know it as the holy place that was the scene of the death and resurrection of Christ.

Consequently, Jerusalem belongs to everyone, and for this very reason it should belong to no one. However, the reality of things is quite different, for the "City of Peace" has always been a theater of war. The first plan for the internationalization of Jerusalem, drawn up by the United Nations, dates back to 1947, but just one year later the Arab-Israeli War divided the city into West Jerusalem, occupied by Israel, and East Jerusalem (including the holy Old City), occupied by Jordan. The Israelis reunified the city in 1967 with the Six-Day War, and in 1980 they ratified the status of Jerusalem as the "eternal and indivisible capital of the State of Israel" with an official deed, thus provoking a UN resolution denying annexation and inviting its member states to withdraw diplomatic representation from the city as a sign of protest. Even today, the only countries in the world to acknowledge Jerusalem as the capital of Israel are the United States, Costa Rica and El Salvador. However, the "Chosen People" – confident of the support of their powerful American ally – still refuse to listen to reason.

Regardless of how one wishes to view it, if anything the complex conflict that Jerusalem symbolizes somehow seems to add to the intriguing beauty of an immortal city. The battle of the Palestinians to announce it as the capital of their independent state, the fierce determination of the Israelis for it to remain part of their country, and the concern of all Christians to protect the holy sites are an integral part of Jerusalem's destiny, life, and very scope. And a sense of profound spirituality pervades every corner of the city.

These factors mean that the city cannot simply be described as a collection of monuments, however extraordinary they may be from both a historical and artistic standpoint. Each one of them, from the oldest to the most recent, embodies a symbol or an ambition, a warning or a promise. Indeed, it is no coincidence that modern medicine has diagnosed the "Jerusalem syndrome," a temporary mental disorder that affects around 200 visitors each year, who are overwhelmed by the "burden" of the Holy City.

Three thousand years of history and the supreme shrines of

150-151 The last fragment of the Temple of Israel destroyed by the Romans in 70 BC, the Wailing Wall is dominated by the massive Dome of the Rock. The al-Aqsa Mosque, on the lower right, is the oldest and most important Islamic place of worship in Israel.

150 bottom HaKotel HaMa'aravi, or the "Western Wall," is also known as the Wailing Wall because this is where the Jewish population comes to commemorate the destruction of the second temple. The faithful tuck papers containing their prayers between its stones.

151 top left The Dome of the Rock was built by Caliph Abd al-Malik between 687 and 691, but its splendid cupola, which is regilded periodically, dates to the 11th century. The Knights Templar, convinced that the place marked the ruins of the Temple, made it their headquarters.

151 top right The Dome of the Rock encloses the sacred rock thought to be where Abraham prepared to sacrifice his son Isaac. Moreover, the Muslims believe that the prophet Mohammed ascended into heaven from this spot.

151 center Just beyond the entrance to the Church of the Holy Sepulcher and across from the Chapel of Golgotha, a clergyman kneels in prayer in front of the Rock of the Anointing, the stone slab where, according to tradition, the Messiah's body was covered with ointment and prepared for burial. This relic, which has been venerated for centuries, is imbued with profound spirituality.

151 bottom The present-day Church of the Holy Sepulcher was built during the Crusade of 1194. It can be accessed through a courtyard with other places of worship: the Chapel of the Forty Martyrs, the Greek-Orthodox Church of St. John, and the Church of St. James. The bell tower, on the left in this picture, was partly destroyed during an earthquake and was never rebuilt, hence its squat appearance.

Jerusalem

the three great monotheistic religions are concentrated in the Old City alone, an area of approximately half a square mile divided into three quarters – Jewish, Muslim and Christian – and enclosed by the 16th-century Ottoman walls. Here, in front of the *HaKotel HaMa'aravi* – the last fragment of the Temple of Israel, destroyed by the Romans in AD 70 – the Jews lament the fate of the shrine and leave between its stones their folded petitions containing their most intimate prayers to God.

The Wailing Wall is dominated by the massive Dome of the Rock, with its gleaming golden dome. This masterpiece of Islamic art was built between AD 685 and 691 around the stone bearing Mohammed's footprint, and was subsequently embellished with decorations during the 16th century. However, not far away is the Church of the Holy Sepulcher, at the end of the street known to Christians as the Via Dolorosa, the theater of Christ's Passion. Although considered quite modest by art experts, this building dating back to the times of the Crusaders is of extraordinary importance to followers of the Christian faith. All of the Old City's 100 streets are lined with an alternating succession of monasteries and churches of six Christian confessions – including the Romanesque church of St. Anne built on the spot in which the Virgin Mary received the Annunciation – and synagogues, mosques and civic buildings constructed by the Mamluks and Romans.

Outside the old walls lies a city of 700,000 inhabitants, where the places of biblical episodes – such as Mount Zion and the Mount of Olives – contrast with those in which today's various communities exhibit and magnify their differences. Jerusalem combines the liveliness and gaudy colors of the Arab bazaars with the anachronistic austerity of Mea She'arim, the quarter inhabited by the city's ultra-orthodox community of Hasidic Jews from Eastern Europe, which constitutes the only "living" example of a *shtetl*, the ghettos that were destroyed by the Holocaust. Other contrasting aspects of the city include the European elegance of the early 20th-century buildings constructed by leading figures at the time of the British Mandate of Palestine, and the untidiness and

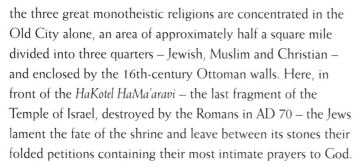

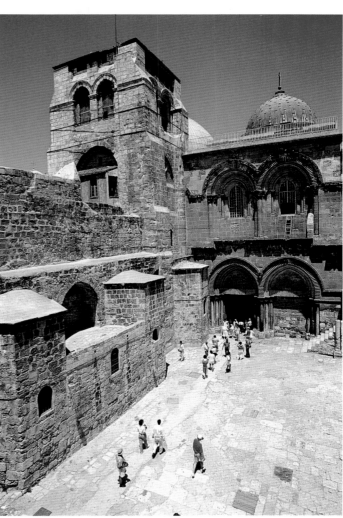

Jerusalem

152 bottom right The most
moving symbol of modern
Jerusalem is Yad Vashem (literally,
"A Place, A Name"). The complex
commemorates the victims of the

Holocaust. Its monuments include
the Hall of Remembrance, in which
the names of the various death
camps have been inscribed in the
stone floor in Hebrew and English.

152-153 Work to construct the
Knesset, the seat of the Israeli
Parliament, began in West Jerusalem
in 1958. The complex, which was
funded by the Rothschild family,
was inaugurated on August 31, 1966.

152 bottom left One of the
distinctive features of Hurva Square
is the large brick arch. This is all
that remains of the Hurva
Synagogue built by the Ashkenazic
community in 1864.

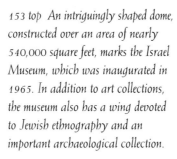

153 top An intriguingly shaped dome, constructed over an area of nearly 540,000 square feet, marks the Israel Museum, which was inaugurated in 1965. In addition to art collections, the museum also has a wing devoted to Jewish ethnography and an important archaeological collection.

153 bottom The Israeli Supreme Court Building, designed by Ada Karmi-Melamede and Ram Karmi, is one of the country's most important contemporary works. Inaugurated in 1992, it is characterized by arches and domes that evoke the motifs of Middle-Eastern architecture.

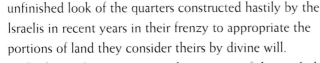

unfinished look of the quarters constructed hastily by the Israelis in recent years in their frenzy to appropriate the portions of land they consider theirs by divine will.

In the modern city center, the triteness of the symbols of Israel's Western affluence – composed of fashionable restaurants, large hotels, fast-food outlets and chain stores, clones of those found throughout the "rich" world" – is also apparent. Similarly, the Knesset building, housing the Israeli parliament (built in 1966 with funds donated by the Rothschild family and embellished with works of art by Marc Chagall, Danny Karavan and others), is more than just an institutional seat, precisely because it is situated in "international" Jerusalem.

The strongest and most moving of the city's modern symbols in undoubtedly Yad Vashem, which literally signifies "A Place, A Name." The complex commemorates the victims of the Holocaust with a series of monuments, including the

Hall of Remembrance, in which the names of the various death camps have been inscribed in the stone floor in Hebrew and English, and the Children's Memorial, dedicated to the 1.5 million children killed by the Nazis. Entering this building designed by the architect Moshe Safdie is an extremely poignant experience. The dark interior is pervaded by a recorded voice reciting an endless litany of the victims' names, while images of their faces impressed on glass panels seem to hover in the air. The flame of a candle, reflected hundreds of times in a system of mirrors, symbolizes their immortal souls.

It is impossible not to experience a sense of horror over what was the greatest tragedy of the 20th century, and compassion for the people who suffered it. Once outside in the streets of Jerusalem, it becomes even more impossible to grasp why peace cannot be established in a Holy City that truly belongs to everyone.

154 *The changing of the guard at Rashtrapati Bhavan, the residence of the Indian president. It was designed by Sir Edwin Lutyens and completed in 1929 as the Viceroy's residence.*

155 top *Another work by Lutyens: the monumental India Gate was built in 1931 as a tribute to the 90,000 Indians killed during the Great War.*

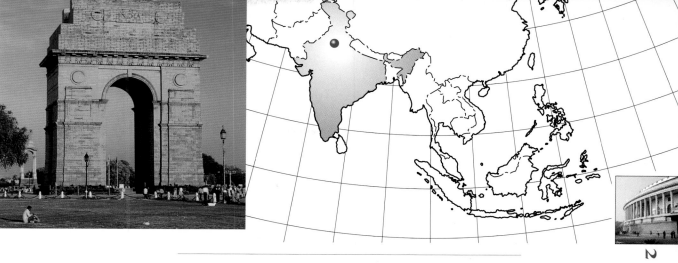

Delhi
INDIA

155 center top *A Mogul-style garden extends in front of the north façade of the presidential palace.*

155 center bottom *The circular building of the Indian Parliament has a diameter of 561 feet.*

155 bottom *An enormous plaza surrounded by buildings with colonnades and colonial architecture, Connaught Place became the commercial heart of Delhi when King George V decided to move the capital here from Calcutta in 1911.*

Khushwant Singh, India's most famous and controversial journalist, devoted a novel to Delhi. The odd-numbered chapters, which are autobiographical, are set in the present – troubled but terribly fascinating – of the Indian capital, while the even ones recount its past, from the Middle Ages to Gandhi's assassination, through the lives of ordinary characters who would never otherwise have found a place in history with a capital H. British journalist William Dalrymple sketched a tableau of the city entitled *The City of Djinns*, in which the *djinns* are the prankish spirits of the Islamic epic. Dalrymple is convinced that these magical figures "live" in Delhi and should even be counted in the census of its 12 million inhabitants.

Delhi is a literary city encompassing worlds that constantly overlap, in a precarious balance between the real and the imaginary. And here reality is often more incredible than fantasy. But this is its destiny: Hindu mythology indicates it as the city of the Pandavas, the heroes of the sacred text of *The Maharabata*, and material remains testify that it is composed of seven cities established starting in the first millennium BC. However, Delhi's oldest extant monuments date back to the end of the 12th century. One example is the astonishing Qutb Minar, the 240-foot-tall minaret that was built by Qutb-ud-din, the sultan who ushered in Muslim domination, which lasted for nearly 700 years. This structure and the buildings connected with it replaced the Lal Kot, the defensive posts of the Hindu sovereigns who until then had ruled over the territory.

In 1398 Tamerlane (Timur) sacked the city, and his successors left other masterpieces of Islamic architecture, such as the Lodi Gardens. A century later, the family of sultans, the Moguls, broke away from that dynasty and would later turn the city in the center of an empire. Nonetheless, the long and prosperous era of the Moguls did not always coincide with Delhi's good fortune. Several rulers moved the capital to Agra, albeit for a short period of time, while others instead worked to make Delhi the magical place it still is today. The most inventive of these was Shah Jahan, who can be credited with legendary works like the monument to love and folly known

156-157 The Jami Masjid, the enormous Friday Mosque, is the largest Islamic place of worship on the Indian subcontinent. The Mogul emperor, Shah Jahan, built it in 1644.

156 bottom left Every day in the Diwan-i-Am, the Hall of Public Audience at Lal Qila, the emperor would sit on a massive marble throne covered with gem-studded panels.

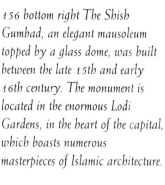

156 bottom right The Shish Gumbad, an elegant mausoleum topped by a glass dome, was built between the late 15th and early 16th century. The monument is located in the enormous Lodi Gardens, in the heart of the capital, which boasts numerous masterpieces of Islamic architecture.

157 top Nearly 240 feet tall, the spectacular sandstone minaret of Qutb Minar was built by Qutb ud-din in 1193 to indicate the southernmost point reached by Islam, and as a portent for new conquests. The intricate bas-relief work covering it has inscriptions with verses from the Koran.

157 bottom When he moved the capital of the Mogul empire from Agra to Delhi in 1638, Shah Jahan decided to build a magnificent royal palace, the Lal Qila, now known as the Red Fort because of the color of the sandstone used to construct it. The fortified walls, which are between 59 and 108 feet high, extend for over 1 miles.

as the Taj Mahal, located in Agra. Shah Jahan, who succeeded to the throne in Delhi in 1638, designed the Lal Qila, better known as the Red Fort, the lavish complex enclosed by a perimeter over one mile long; today it is the most visited place in the capital. In 1644 the ruler also built the Jami Masijd, the largest mosque on the Indian subcontinent. Its main entrance opens onto Old Delhi, a maze of alleys with a highly colorful bazaar.

The city that was built starting in 1911, when George V of Great Britain, the King-Emperor, decided to move the capital of his Indian realm from Calcutta to Delhi, is the exact opposite of Old Delhi. The commercial heart of New Delhi is Connaught Place, an enormous square surrounded by colonnaded buildings. However, its institutional center is entered through India Gate, a triumphal arch built to commemorate the soldiers who died in World War I and in

the Third Anglo-Afghan War of 1919. From here, the Rajpath, a broad avenue that is now the setting for the Republic Day Parade, leads to Parliament and Rashtrapati Bhavan, the official residence of the Indian president. These monuments were designed by the English architect Sir Edwin Lutyens to celebrate the power of the empire, and in 1947 Nehru, the country's future president, disparaged them using the words "vulgar ostentation."

Nevertheless, during the Mogul era, under the British and even today, the capital of the largest democracy in the world has always loved ostentation: the beautiful and the ugly. And in every corner of this tentacular metropolis, where ancient and modern clash constantly, what bonds the city as a whole is the teeming mass of humanity that inhabits it. And the odor mixing spices, incense, exhaust fumes and rot, which goes by just one name: the smell of India.

Bangkok
THAILAND

158 top The 40-floor Peninsula Bangkok Hotel rises to a height of nearly 500 feet tall, making it the tallest hotel in the capital.

158 center Inaugurated in 1999 to alleviate Bangkok's chaotic traffic, the Sky Train – Rot ai Fah in Thai or, according to its official name, the Bangkok Mass Transit System – has also become a tourist attraction.

His Majesty King Bhumibol Adulyadej, who at the age of just 18 ascended the throne of Thailand in 1946, taking the name Rama IX, was born in Cambridge, Massachusetts. An expert in agricultural policy and a fervent Buddhist, he has always had a boundless passion for jazz. By way of contrast, Jim Thompson was born in Delaware in 1902 and became a CIA agent, moving to Bangkok in 1955. He started working in the silk business, living in a traditional teak residence full of antiques and surrounded by a garden of orchids until his mysterious death in the Malaysian jungle in 1967. An "American" Thai king and a "Thai" American adventurer. The two figures could not be more different, and yet together they could be the perfect testimonials of Asia's most exotic and contradictory capital: Bangkok, a city that looks to the West yet remains profoundly Oriental.

Rama I, founder of the Chakri dynasty, to which the current sovereign pertains, was the monarch who laid the cornerstone of Bangkok in 1782. Located on the right bank of the Chao Phraya, the original settlement developed as an "amphibian" city, with most of its population living on boats or in pile-dwellings along the canals branching from the river. In the late 19th century, to stem the plague of malaria many waterways were filled in or covered over and modern-day Bangkok began to take shape.

With nearly 8 million inhabitants, Bangkok is not only the largest urban agglomeration in Thailand – it has almost 50 times the population of Chiang Mai, the country's second-largest city – but it is also the main hub of tourism in Southeast Asia. The fact that the tourist industry is a key part of the economy is evident. Aside from the brand-new World Trade Center, the tallest and most dazzling buildings host luxury hotels and shopping centers, and entire districts are allocated to shopping and entertainment. The fast – and schizophrenic – race for well-being and modernity has recently attracted a multitude of people from all over the country, and in Bangkok traffic and pollution (as well as social problems like child labor and prostitution) have reached record levels. Work to alleviate traffic has done little to help. The elevated roads that now crisscross it everywhere are always congested with cars and tuk-tuks, the characteristic three-wheeled taxis. The only thing that has

158 bottom Damnoen Saduak is the famous floating market of Ratchaburi, 68 miles south of Bangkok.

158-159 Bangkok, which is cut in two by the Chao Phraya River, is the modern capital of a country that embarked on the path of industrial and technological development years ago. It is one of the "Asian tigers" that underwent astonishing economic growth between the 1960s and the 1990s.

159 bottom Just around the corner from the city's financial district, amidst the canals that wind their way through Bangkok's traditional districts, it is easy to find little food markets, modest pile-dwellings and small Buddhist temples. They are traces of a culture that, despite ongoing development, has not lost its identity.

160-161 Work to construct the Royal Palace in Bangkok began in 1782, when King Rama I founded the city and made it the capital of the Kingdom of Siam.

160 bottom left The Emerald Buddha is preserved inside Wat Phra Kaeo, in the Royal Palace. For the Thais, the statue, which was discovered in 1434, symbolizes the country's good fortune.

160 bottom right There are three remarkable structures on the upper terrace of Wat Phra Kaeo: the Golden Stupa, or Phra Sri Ratana Chedi, which holds Buddha's relics; the Phra Mondhob, which holds the Tripitaka, a Buddhist scripture; the Royal Pantheon, or Prasat Phra Dhepbidorn, the pavilion where the statues of all the rulers in the Chakri dynasty are kept.

161 top left *Wat Phra Kaeo is surrounded by splendid sculptures of mythological animals.*

161 top right *There is a pair of demon-guardians, erected during the reign of Rama III (1824-1851), in front of each of the six entrances to Wat Phra Kaeo.*

161 bottom *Chakri Maha Prasat, one of the most impressive residential buildings of the Royal Palace, was built by King Rama V between 1876 and 1882 to commemorate the centennial of the Chakri dynasty. The ashes of the dead rulers are preserved on the top floor of the central block.*

alleviated the chaos to a small extent is that the subway will be completed: it is the only public underground transportation system in the world funded entirely by private capital.

However, in Bangkok there still survive poignant places where the stench of exhaust fumes blends with the heady scent of tropical fruits and flowers, and where – like Chinatown – one can easily happen upon an elephant plodding slowly between cars. And where the hustle and bustle of white-collar workers is contrasted by the disarming peacefulness of the monks, dressed in saffron robes, on their way to bring offerings to the city's numerous beautiful Buddhist temples. In fact, for the people of Bangkok, Krung Thep, which means "City of Angels," is still the capital of Thailand. These are the temples built by the Thai rulers on the Chao Phraya to safeguard the essence of the capital: from Wat Arun, the phenomenal belvedere on the left bank of the river, to Wat Pho, housing a statute of the reclining Buddha, which is 150 feet long and nearly 50 feet high, to Wat Phra Kaeo on the right bank. The latter is a complex that covers approximately 1 square mile and houses the old Royal Palace as well as various shrines, including the one with the Emerald Buddha, the nation's sacred symbol. With their elaborate architecture, the roofs made of orange and green ceramic tiles, the profusion of gold and the countless representations of the deities, these temples could be part of a Hollywood set – precisely what a Westerner would expect to find on a postcard of Asia. And yet it is in here, just a stone's throw from the noisy metropolis, that the visitor can understand why Thailand is known as the "Land of Smiles."

Bangkok

162-163 The Temple of the Reclining Buddha or Wat Pho (also called Wat Phra Chetuphon in Thai) is the largest temple in Bangkok. It was built in 1688 under King Petraja, long before the city became the capital of the country. However, nothing is left of the original structure: the temple was completely restructured during the reigns of Rama I and Rama III.

162 bottom left Located on the west bank of the Chao Praya, Wat Arun has safeguarded the Emerald Buddha for several centuries.

162 bottom right The Erawan Shrine – Samrong Tai – is a mystical oasis in the heart of Bangkok. Its four-headed bronze statue of Brahma is devoutly worshiped by the people of Bangkok.

163 top left Over 150 feet long and about 50 feet tall, the gigantic statue of the Reclining Buddha was erected in 1832, during the reign of Rama III.

163 top right There are over 1000 portrayals of Buddha on the vast surface of Wat Pho. Most of them come from the previous capitals of the Kingdom of Siam, Ayutthaya and Sukhothai.

163 bottom Wat Arun or Temple of the Dawn – is one of the most striking religious buildings in Bangkok. It was built when Ayutthaya was the capital city and it was considered the favorite temple of Rama II, who decided to restore it. It has a 262-foot tower, or Phra Prang, built by Rama III in the Khmer style and covered with sculptures of mythological figures.

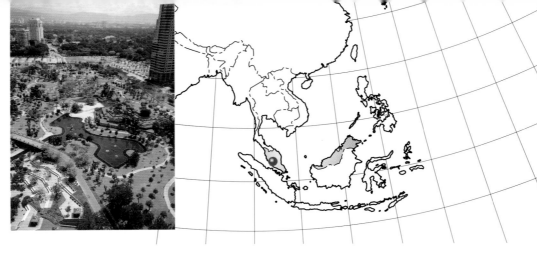

Kuala Lumpur

MALAYSIA

164 top Kuala Lumpur was founded as a small mining site in 1857 and became the capital of the Federation of Malaya in 1896, when the country was still a British colony. Today, the city has a population of 1.8 million and covers an area of over 77 square miles.

164 bottom The dazzling Petronas Towers, the headquarters of the national oil company, rise to a height of 1483 feet and were the tallest buildings in the world until 2004. It took 899,000 square feet of steel and 592,000 of laminated glass to clad the structure.

With a height of 1,483 feet, they were the world's tallest buildings for seven years. More importantly, however, since their completion in 1997 the Petronas Towers have been the symbol of Kuala Lumpur and of Malaysia. According to the vision of rheir designer, the American architect Cesar Pelli, they were to look like a "multi-faceted diamond sparkling in the sun." This image is not far from the truth, as it took 899,000 sq. ft of steel and 592,000 sq. ft of laminated glass to clad the structure. The Petronas Towers are also dazzling in terms of sheer wealth: they cost $1.2 billion to build and were financed by the national oil company for which they are named, which is now headquartered here.

The Petronas Towers are the heart of a city that is expanding at a dizzying pace. Its population has grown exponentially over the past twenty years and now tops 1.8 million people. Today Kuala Lumpur is a urban area extending for a radius of 15.5 miles from the original nucleus of the city, encompassing Putrajaya, the seat of government and since 2001 Malaysia's administrative capital; Cyberjaya, an "intelligent city" where the headquarters of the most important international high-tech industries and a multimedia university have "grown" in place of coconut plantations; and KL International Airport, the biggest hub in Asia. Everything is connected by an innovative transportation network and communications are supported by thousands of miles of optic-fiber cables. The future already lives here, and it is the intention of its government that Malaysia will be off the list of developing countries by 2020. And to think that in 1857 Kuala Lumpur was merely a "muddy confluence," the meaning of its name in the Malay language. This was the year that 87 Chinese settlers came to the marshes between the Klang and Gombek Rivers, driven by their quest for tin, as the area's subsoil conceals the planet's richest deposit of this lightweight but vital metal. Only 17 of these pioneers survived malaria and few of them became wealthy. Nevertheless, that mining center attracted the attention of four sultans on the Malay Peninsula. In fact, in 1896 the British arrived to settle the disputes that had arisen and took control of the region, choosing Kuala Lumpur as the capital of the Federation of Malaya.

164-165 Silhouetted against the futuristic cityscape, the Moorish architecture of the Masjid Jamek Mosque, or Friday Mosque, is emblematic of the different facets of a burgeoning capital. An ethnic and religious melting pot, Kuala Lumpur is also one of the most important trade centers in Southeast Asia and is gaining a reputation as a major technological hub.

165 bottom left The Islamic center of Kuala Lumpur is an important point of reference for the Muslim community. The minaret of Masjid Negara, the national mosque, rises in the background amidst the skyscrapers. The mosque was built in 1965.

165 bottom right Near Lake Gardens Park in Kuala Lumpur, the Malaysian Parliament – the seat of the Chamber of Deputies and the Senate – was inaugurated in 1963, six years after the country gained its independence.

166-167 Built in 1909 at the confluence of the Gombak and Klang rivers, the spectacular Masjid Jamek Mosque was built over the site of the first settlement in the area, which later became the Malaysian capital.

166 bottom left Kuala Lumpur has developed into the capital city of a highly advanced country, yet there are still areas that have maintained the festive atmosphere of the traditional markets of Southeast Asia.

Kuala Lumpur

166 bottom right Spires, towers and arches make the Kuala Lumpur railway station – which travel writer Paul Theroux described as "the grandest station in South East Asia" – one of the city's most fascinating buildings. Completed in 1901, it was designed by A.B. Hubbock, a Briton who was captivated by Mogul architecture; Hubbock also designed the Masjid Jamek Mosque.

167 top The colorful Raja Gopuram was added in 1968 to the city's oldest Hindu temple, Sri Maha Mariamman, which was built in 1873.

167 bottom A 141-foot clock tower on the Sultan Abdul Samad Building (built between 1894 and 1897) marks the traditional center of Kuala Lumpur in Dataran Merdeka (Freedom Square).

From then on, Kuala Lumpur developed as the perfect model of a British colonial city. Among the period's most representative monuments, constructed in a style blending Moorish and Mogul elements with Neo-Classic ones, we can cite the Masjid Mosque, built at the confluence of the two rivers; St. Mary's Cathedral; the Sultan Abdul Samad Building, topped by a copper dome and flanked by a 426-foot-tall clock tower; and the Selangor Club, an exclusive rendezvous overlooking the lush expanse of a cricket field. The symbol of colonial oppression, that field – renamed Dataran Merdeka, or Freedom Square – marks the spot where, on 31 August 1957, the Union Jack was lowered and the Malaysian flag was hoisted in its stead.

Today the city of Kuala Lumpur reflects the country's varied ethnic and religious composition. Located within just a short distance of each other are mosques, Buddhist temples and lavish Hindu temples, such as Sri Mahalariaman, which is the starting point for pilgrimages to the nearby Batu Caves. Nevertheless, the "temples of commerce" are what predominate everywhere, from colorful Petaling Street, the main thoroughfare of Chinatown where a nighttime market is held, to the futuristic shopping, office and residential complex of Plaza Rakyat designed by the architectural firm of Skidmore, Owings & Merrill, which also designed the famous Sears Tower in Chicago. Regardless of whether the focus is on small traditional shops or high-tech shopping centers, however, the "masters" here in Kuala Lumpur are the Chinese, who represent 30 percent of Malaysia's population but hold virtually all of its economic power.

168-169 The Singapore River separates the two faces of Singapore: the Colonial District in the foreground, and the Business District.

168 bottom left The Merlion – half lion, half fish – is the symbol of Singapore. Singa-pura means "City of the Lion" in Malay.

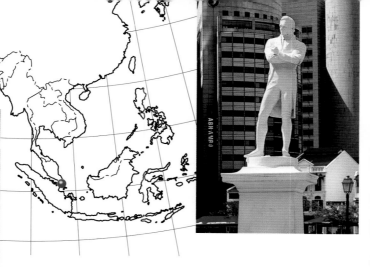

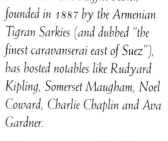

Singapore
SINGAPORE

On January 28, 1819, Sir Thomas Stamford Raffles, explorer and agent of the British Crown's East India Company, landed in Singapore, a little island off the Malacca Peninsula. There to welcome him were about 100 Malaysian fishermen, about 30 Chinese merchants and pirates, and several million mosquitoes. Nonetheless, Raffles refused to be discouraged, relaying a message to England to say he had found the perfect place to establish the greatest trade emporium in Asia. Back in London, he was considered a madman. In reality, however, Raffles had perceived the full potential of this location.

A little more than ten years later, Singapore – which already had 10,000 inhabitants from India, China and the Middle East – became a British colony. The inauguration of the Suez Canal in 1869 did the rest, because at this point the port of Singapore lay exactly halfway between East and West. Thus, the city developed and prospered at an astonishing pace, governed more by sound pragmatism than by the Crown.

This marvelous fairytale was interrupted in 1941 with Japan's entry into World War II. Though the British were convinced that Singapore was impregnable, they were unable to hold off the attacking Japanese, who occupied it and held it for three years. It was an economic catastrophe and, more importantly, a psychological one. The myth of the invincibility of the white man was dashed miserably in the minds of the Asiatic population. This awareness paved the way for independence, which came in 1959.

It took the inspired insight of someone like Raffles to allow the city-state – which covers an area of 263 square miles, currently has a population of 4 million but is devoid of natural resources, including drinking water, which must be imported from Malaysia – to continue to prosper. With the motto "government knows best," the country's charismatic leader Lee Kuan Kew, a Singaporean of Chinese descent, has transformed the city into an industrial and financial center,

168 bottom right Inaugurated in 2002, the Esplanade Performing Arts Centre includes an auditorium, areas for open-air shows, and an array of shops and restaurants.

169 top left A white monument honoring Sir Thomas Raffles stands at the point where the city's first stone was laid. In 1819 Raffles became the first European to land on the island.

169 top right A majestic dome, a replica of the one at Saint Paul's Cathedral in London, crowns the Neo-Classical Supreme Court Building, built in 1939.

169 center The Raffles Hotel, founded in 1887 by the Armenian Tigran Sarkies (and dubbed "the finest caravanserai east of Suez"), has hosted notables like Rudyard Kipling, Somerset Maugham, Noel Coward, Charlie Chaplin and Ava Gardner.

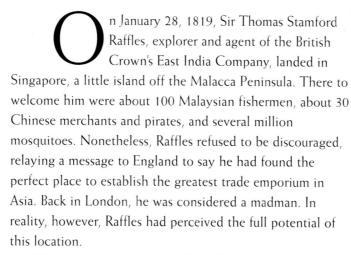

169 bottom The Victoria Theatre, founded as City Hall in 1862, was expanded in 1905 to house Memorial Hall, in honor of Queen Victoria; four years later it was converted into a theater.

attracting foreign capital in exchange for tax and customs breaks, political stability and qualified labor. Today Singapore is home to 200 banks, its port rivals Rotterdam as the most heavily trafficked in the world, most of the planet's crude oil is refined here, and there are countless chemical, electronic and pharmaceutical industries.

Pragmatism and authority have made Singapore the cleanest and most orderly city in the world. Nevertheless, Singapore has its own unique charm, due not only to its multitude of ethnic groups, which have recreated colorful little homelands in the city districts, but also to its spectacular sprawling green spaces (such as the world's largest Orchid Garden) and the Colonial District. The heart of the Colonial District is Padang, a broad field surrounded by dazzling Neo-Classical buildings, such as the one that houses the Supreme Court, City Hall, St. Andrew's Cathedral, the Victoria Theatre and the Boat Quay, the walkway along the natural canal leading to the sea. Here, the statue of Sir Thomas Stamford Raffles marks the Singapore Landing Site.

Rising above these historical places are countless skyscrapers, the tallest of which – the United Overseas Bank Plaza, the Republic Plaza and the Overseas Union Bank Centre – rise to a height of over 900 feet, and the city's myriad of shopping centers has made it a veritable consumers' mecca. However, the building that best symbolizes Singapore is the Raffles Hotel, the most famous luxury hotel in Asia. Since its inauguration in 1887, it has hosted adventurers, writers, politicians and financial magnates: in other words, all those who helped make Singapore a legend. Tellingly, it is also the only place named after the equally legendary Sir Thomas, who could rightfully have given the city his own name. But perhaps it was Sir Thomas himself who decided otherwise. When he landed, Singapore already had a name that promised a roaring future: Singa-pura, the City of the Lion.

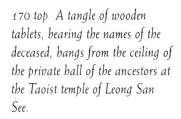

170 top A tangle of wooden tablets, bearing the names of the deceased, hangs from the ceiling of the private hall of the ancestors at the Taoist temple of Leong San See.

170 center top With its precious pagodas, the Chinese Garden – or Yu Hwa Yuan, "Garden of Beauty" – is a modern and somewhat kitsch replica of the Summer Palace Garden in Beijing.

170 center bottom Once the dwellings of Chinese merchants, the colorful little houses at Boat Quay, overlooking a curve in the Singapore River, now add a lively note to one of the city's top entertainment areas.

170 bottom When the Chinese New Year is celebrated, Chinatown is dotted with typical red lanterns. Chinese immigrants account for 75% of the population of this city-state.

170-171 Recent conservative renovation work restored the 19th-century shophouses of Chinatown merchants to their former splendor. The brightly painted buildings had shops on the ground floor and homes on the top floors. Today they house boutiques and trendy restaurants.

171 bottom left The 177-foot Clock Tower, which was completed in 1902, is part of the Victoria Theatre complex. In front of the building, a statue by Thomas Woolner commemorates Sir Thomas Raffles.

171 bottom right St. Andrew's Cathedral, dedicated to the patron saint of Scotland, was the colony's first Anglican church. The original building, constructed in 1839, was damaged by lightning and was demolished in 1860 in order to build a more solid structure modeled after Salisbury Cathedral.

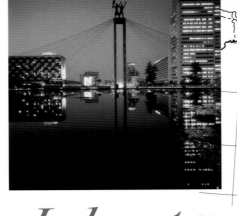

6°08'S - 106°45' E

Jakarta

INDONESIA

The marble obelisk, rising to a height of about 440 feet, is crowned by a flame forged from 77 pounds of pure gold, and its base conceals two large rooms. In the first one, a series of dioramas relates the story of Indonesia's path to freedom. The second one, the Hall of Contemplation, displays the original Declaration of Independence of Indonesia, promulgated in 1945 and ratified by the international community in 1949. The National Monument, referred to simply as *Monas*, dominates Lapangan Merdeka, or Freedom Square, which is officially considered the center of Jakarta. In reality, however, this city on the northwest coast of the island of Java has no center. In fact, it has recently been given the status of province, and a governor now works alongside the mayor in administrating it. This is due not only to its dimensions, covering 250 square miles, but also to the size of its population, which now exceeds 9 million people. As a result of its recent economic revival, which has gone hand in hand with efforts to undertake a series of urban-planning works, Jakarta now has a massive network of elevated highways as well as a financial district, known as the Golden Triangle, full of skyscrapers housing luxury hotels, banks and multinationals. At the same time, however, there has been a dizzying increase in the number of temporary dwellings to house the people who, in search of fortune, continue to flock here from the most remote corners of the Sonda archipelago. Jakarta embodies Indonesia's betrayal of the national motto "Unity in Diversity," coined by Sukarno, the father of the Indonesian nation. Indeed, in recent years it has been afflicted by ethnic tension and protest movements that have also left behind obvious damage to city buildings. Today, crossing its quarters means taking in its different cultures and its contradictions. For example, the picturesque chaos of Javanese markets is countered by the rigid "socialist-realist" monumentality of the public buildings Sukarno constructed when he nurtured the ambition of being *primus inter pares* in an axis of Afro-Asian countries unaligned with any major power. And yet Jakarta has an extraordinary past. As early as the 6th century, its original settlement, Sunda Kelapa, was the port of the kingdom founded in Java by the peoples that came from India. Ten centuries later, the Portuguese arrived, only to be driven out by a Javanese prince in 1527. On that occasion, the liberator baptized the port Jakarta, meaning "Glorious Victory." This victory was as glorious as it was short-lived: In 1619 the efficient forces from the Dutch East India Company arrived and destroyed Jakarta, establishing Batavia in its stead.

At the height of its splendor, Batavia was surrounded by defensive walls and crisscrossed by a network of canals reminiscent of those of Amsterdam. Jembatan Pasar Ayam is the only one of the ancient bridges that has survived to our day and it is now a tourist attraction, together with the buildings that were carefully restored in the Seventies and now comprise the area known as Old Batavia. The buildings that house City Hall and the Supreme Court have been transformed into museums, and the old port of Sunda Kelapa has also been revitalized.

In effect, even the name Jakarta is the result of "restoration" work. The Japanese, who occupied it during World War II, can be credited with giving the city back its memory of "Glorious Victory" as a way of currying favor with the local population. At the time, the residence of the supreme commander of the Japanese forces was located in the heart of the city, in a place now marked by a monument in honor of President Sukarno and Vice President Muhammad Hatta. But even this is merely a place of memory. Today, Jakarta's most animated and increasingly crowded venues are its countless mosques, the most important of which is Istiqlal, which can accommodate 10,000 people. In fact, today Jakarta is proud to be the capital of the most populous Islamic nation in the world.

172-173 and 173 bottom right The Golden Triangle, the business center of Jakarta, is full of skyscrapers, but American-style gigantism is merely a façade: the city has maintained a profoundly Oriental spirit.

173 bottom left The Mesjid Istiqlal is crowded with worshipers for Friday prayers.
One of the largest mosques in Southeast Asia, it can hold 10,000 people.

172 top The 443-foot-tall National Monument, commonly referred to as the Monas, is the symbol of Jakarta. Two museums at the base of the monument illustrate Indonesia's path to independence.

172 bottom The statue of Arjuna Wijaya is at the southwest end of Lapangan Merdeka. The archer of the Indian poem Ramayana is portrayed aboard a lavish chariot drawn by six galloping horses.

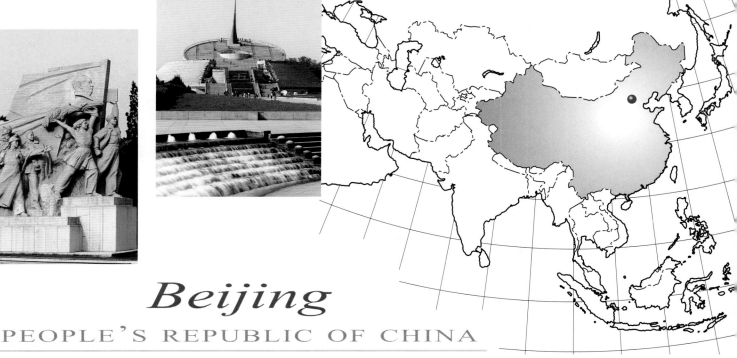

Beijing

PEOPLE'S REPUBLIC OF CHINA

174 top left An impressive sculpture portraying those who participated in the Long March stands in front of Mao's Mausoleum.

174 top right The China Millennium Monument occupies an area of over 322,000 square feet.

174 center In 1959, for the 10th anniversary of the Communist Revolution, Mao had the Great Hall of the People built in Tiananmen Square, with an auditorium that can accommodate 10,000 people. This is the seat of the National People's Congress and the Chinese Parliament.

174 bottom Beijing, which has been the capital of China since 1272, is now a metropolis of 8 million people. This picture shows one of the city's commercial streets.

175 Tiananmen Square covers an area of nearly 100 acres and Mao's Mausoleum is located here. It was built in 1976-77 to commemorate the founder of the People's Republic of China.

Aboard pedal-operated rickshaws, tourists start out at the *siheyuan* – the traditional low dwelling made of gray bricks and set around a courtyard – that once belonged to Guo Moruo, one of the most famous Chinese intellectuals of the 20th century, for a fascinating itinerary through a *hutong*, one of the "memory districts" of Beijing. From there, they skirt the north shore of Lake Qinghai, crossing Yinding Bridge to the Bell Tower and Coal Hill, for a breathtaking view of the city. Along the way, there are picturesque images of everyday life: men hawking *baozi* (steamed dumplings), children playing in the alleys and women doing the laundry outside their front doors. The tour ends in the garden of Prince Gong's Palace, where there is a performance by the Beijing Opera, and visitors are offered tea and snacks.

But in Beijing, the *hutong* are now merely the legacy of bygone days, and only 25 of them have been preserved to cater to tourists. All the rest have been leveled (and their residents were given small sums as compensation) as part of the massive urban reconstruction plan for which the city government has budgeted the fabulous sum of about $3.8 billion – of which only $55 million will go to safeguarding the capital's historic sites. Beijing is preparing for the 2008 Olympics, and by then – indeed, long before that, as the deadline for completing the new buildings is 2006 – it will present itself to the world as "the" city of the 21st century, astonishing everyone with its grandeur and its magnificent innovative architectural concepts.

The quintessential competition has begun, and Beijing, which considers European and American metropolises far too outdated, is vying with the equally dynamic city of Shanghai. According to the people of Beijing, however, the architecture of its Chinese "cousin" is boringly vertical, mimicking America. The capital city, which will take the forms and symbols of a millenary culture as its starting point, is convinced it can do better.

In essence, Beijing has always been a record-breaking city with great ambitions. It is so old that traces of human life dating back 500,000 years were discovered in the cave of Zhoukoudian, not far from the city, as proven by the famous

华人民共和国万岁　世界人民大

177 top In addition to the apartments of the emperor and of the royal family, the Hall of Mental Cultivation (left) and the concubines' pavilions (right) are also located inside the Forbidden City.

177 bottom The third emperor of the Ming Dynasty, began to construct the imperial residence of the Ming and Qing dynasties in 1407. Known as Zijin Cheng, or the Forbidden City, it is the largest residential complex in the world.

skull of *Homo erectus*, more commonly referred to as "Peking Man." Marco Polo wrote that medieval Beijing had "so many houses and people that no man would ever be able to count them." In 1407, the rulers of the Ming Dynasty began construction of the Forbidden City, an imperial palace worthy of the "Children of Heaven." Upon completion, the palace covered an area of 183 acres and had 9,999 magnificent buildings. But there is more: the 168-acre Beihai Park next to it, dotted with artificial hills and elegant pavilions, the Temple of Heaven, whose roof is covered with tiles the color of lapis lazuli, and the enchanting Summer Palace favored by Ci Xi, the mother of Pu Yi, the last emperor. Following the establishment of the People's Republic of China, Mao Zedong had Tiananmen Square built directly across from the Forbidden City. This square, which is still the largest one in the world, is lined with the stern and imposing buildings that house the offices of the Chinese government, and it is also the site of the mausoleum that holds the remains of the Great Helmsman.

The architect who has now been commissioned to redesign the layout of Beijing is Albert Speer, Jr. (he is the son of Hitler's leading architect, Albert Speer, who was commissioned to turn Berlin into the "universal metropolis" of Nazi Germany). According to some, Speer's plans – envisaging the creation of a 15.5-mile thoroughfare to link Tiananmen Square to the Olympic Park, monumental squares, housing complexes adjoining factories, a gargantuan railroad junction to connect the capital with every city in China, over 185 miles of urban highways and about 87 miles of subway lines – bear a notable resemblance to the colossal works that Speer's father designed for Hitler. This has inevitably led to comparisons and bitter controversy. The architect has defended his position, affirming that there is nothing megalomaniac about his plans, as they are commensurate with a capital city of 12 million people, set in the heart of a country – the largest and most populous in the world – whose economy is expanding at a feverish pace. Moreover, the plans provide a number of solutions to the problems faced by the

178-179 The Summer Palace, built by Empress Ci Xi between 1888 and 1898, covers an area of over 740 acres.

178 bottom left There are numerous colossal statues along the road leading to the tombs of the Ming emperors.

178 bottom right The Temple of Heaven, which was built in 1420, extends over an area of almost 670 acres. Qiniandian, the Hall of Prayer for Good Harvests, is a three-story pagoda.

179 top The 17-Arch Bridge, in the garden of the Summer Palace, was given this name because of the number of bays reflected in the water of Lake Kunming. It was built in 1750 during the reign of Qian Long. The balustrades on the 492-foot-long bridge are decorated with 544 white marble lions.

179 center *Like all the works of the Chinese empire, every aspect of the Summer Palace is lavishly decorated with lions, dragons and marvelous mythological figures.*

179 bottom *The Hall of Benevolence and Longevity, reconstructed in 1890 after a fire destroyed the original building, is where the emperors administered affairs of state. This sumptuously decorated room is frescoed with the classic dragon and cloud motifs of imperial China.*

city, first and foremost its high pollution level, which has been addressed with systems for recycling rainwater, alternative energy sources and eco-sustainable factories.

Together with Speer, many of the world's most famous and visionary architects have also been invited to Beijing, and they have been given just one categorical imperative: be daring. Thus, the National Theater, designed by Frenchman Paul Andreu, has just been completed near Tiananmen Square. The building, which covers an area of 1,280,000 square feet, has been nicknamed the "duck egg" because of its shape, enveloped in an ovoid structure made of glass and titanium, and illuminated so that it will change color according to the time of day. Similarly, Sir Norman Foster has been commissioned to design the new airport terminal. The architect's concept alludes to the sinuous form and colors (red, yellow and green) of a dragon, the fantastic creature of Chinese mythology. As to the facilities for the Olympics, one of the most notable is the 80,000-seat National Stadium; architects Herzog and De Meuron designed the stadium as a "swallow's nest" and turned to the colors of Ming vases for inspiration. Next to it is the National Swimming Center, designed by the Australian firm PTW Architects. Known as "The Water Cube," it is shaped like a simple parallelepiped and looks like a "liquid" volume evoking the transparency of water bubbles. This effect has been achieved by using EFTE, an innovative polymer, for the cladding.

One of the most ambitious projects in central Beijing is the extension of the National Museum (which increases the museum's exhibition space from 700,000 to 1,600,000 square feet), but there is also the Media Park, the general headquarters of Chinese broadcasting giant CCTV, in the heart of the financial district. The Media Park is probably the most surprising of the great new works of Beijing. At the same time, however, private industry is also vying to transform the face of the capital city. An extraordinary space devoted to the artistic vanguard was recently opened: it is the outcome of the highly imaginative restoration of the Bauhaus-style Factory No. 798, which once made electronic components. And entrepreneur Zhang Yongduo commissioned Raimund

Abraham to build a restaurant complex. The Austrian architect responded to the request that his design evoke the ocean by creating a 12-story building resembling "a cliff at the edge of a raging sea."

Lastly, to respond to the need for residential space in an increasingly wealthy city, the SOHO Company built dozens of buildings that have gained international acclaim for their aesthetics and functional features. In fact, SOHO owners Zhang Xin and Pan Shiyi called on famous and unconventional figures like Iraqi architect Zaha Hadid. They have also commissioned what will be one of the most elegant residential complexes in the world: the Commune by the Great Wall, an array of homes perfectly camouflaged in the landscape, with a view of that mighty structure: the most daunting work ever achieved by human effort.

180-181 and 180 bottom left When you admire the skyscrapers of Pudong, it is hard to imagine that this area on the east bank of the Huangpu was an enormous plain covered with rice paddies until the early 1990s.

180 bottom right Together with Bund, Bingjiang Da Dao – Pudong's riverside promenade – is one of the city's most popular recreation spots. Even early in the morning, this broad sidewalk is an outdoor practice area for tai chi.

181 top A picturesque bridge leads to the historic Hu Xin Ting tearoom. This wooden building with a pagoda roof is located in the middle of a little lake in the old city, across from the delightful Yu Yuan Gardens.

Shanghai
PEOPLE'S
REPUBLIC OF CHINA

"It doesn't matter if a cat is black or white, as long as it catches mice." With these words, Deng Xiaoping, leader of the People's Republic of China, inaugurated the epochal transition of Chinese Communism in the early Nineties, reinterpreting it in a capitalist vein. And in his speech, rich in imaginative but effective similes, he added that "If China is a dragon, then Shanghai is its head," thereby confirming the rebirth of the city that would become the driving force behind this economic boom. At the time, Deng also set the goal of bringing Shanghai up to the level of Hong Kong (the British colony that would be returned to China shortly thereafter) by 2010.

His deadline is still a few years away, but it is clear that Shanghai has already conquered the position of "dragon's head." In fact, it is demolishing all records, coming to the fore as the "global metropolis" of the 21st century. This is a century in which China will clearly play a leading role.

In no other part of this immense country, and probably nowhere else on the planet, can one sense the enthusiasm and dynamism evident in Shanghai. It is situated on the delta of the Chang, precisely at the point where the river ends its 3,400-mile journey to the Pacific Ocean, and it has 16 million inhabitants, to which we must add its "fluctuating population" of three million commuters. Within just three years, the city inaugurated three subway lines and a brand-new ultramodern airport that is connected to the city center by the world's first magnetic levitation train. Most of its inhabitants were evicted from the low houses of the *lilong* (the alleys of old Shanghai) and were relocated in skyscrapers, in apartments at dizzying heights. Statistics lovers have calculated that in 1990 there were just 150 of these vertical buildings, but today there are approximately 2500, and this figure continues to grow at an astonishing pace. Moreover, the city's breathtaking skyline is crisscrossed by one-fifth of all the cranes operating at building sites around the world today.

Just ten years ago Shanghai lay within the boundaries of Puxi, an area on the west bank of the Huangpu, the river that meets the Chang near the northern outskirts of the city; Pudong, on the east bank, was an immense plateau of rice

181 center The 935-foot Tomorrow Square, a skyscraper that ends in a dramatic pyramid, towers over one of the new areas of the Puxi riverfront.

181 bottom Thousands of shops line Nanjing Xi Lu, the main commercial thoroughfare in the Puxi area, extending for nearly 5 miles.

182 left Designed by the famous Chicago architectural firm of Skidmore, Owings & Merrill, the Jin Mao Tower is a sensational 1575-foot-tall building that perfectly blends postmodernism with the classic style of a Buddhist pagoda.

182-183 An "extraterrestrial" structure rises at the base of the Oriental Pearl Tower, the tallest television tower on the continent (over 1500 feet). The spherical glass-and-steel building next to it houses the Space City entertainment center.

182 bottom A spectacular view of the interior of the Grand Hyatt Hotel, with balconies leading to its 555 luxurious rooms. Listed in the **Guinness Book of World Records** as the world's highest hotel, it occupies the 53rd to the 87th floor of the famous Jin Mao Tower.

183 top The 656-foot Golden Bell Mansion, completed in 1998, towers over the Luwan district. It is named for the enormous bronze bell installed as a "lucky charm" in the conical structure that covers it.

183 bottom Though its official name is now Wai Tan, everyone still calls the breathtaking Puxi riverfront "the Bund." The name comes from an Anglo-Indian word for "muddy embankment," which is what it must have looked like in the early 1900s, before the European and American built stately Art Nouveau and Art Deco buildings here.

is composed of the ideograms *jin*, which means "gold" or "economy," and *mao*, which stands for "commerce" or "success." However, this record-breaking construction is already eclipsed by the project of the Kohn Pedersen Fox Architectural Studio for the Shanghai World Financial Center, with 101 floors and rise to a height of over 1,600 feet.

Extraordinary as it may be – and this is demonstrated by the forward-looking architectures of Pudong – the renaissance of Shanghai was faithful to its traditions. In a nation that boasts thousands of years of history, this city is actually a modern invention. It was a sleepy fishing village until 1842 when, at the end of the First Opium War, the British set up a commercial port here, thus forcing China to open its doors to foreigners. Within a short time, Shanghai blossomed into a city divided into concessions administered

paddies. Today, absolutely nothing is left of that rural world, and the Pudong New Area has become the financial center of China. Its countless giants include the Oriental Pearl Tower, a structure with a space-age look, with three spheres made of steel and iridescent glass. Rising to a height of over 1500 feet, it is the tallest television tower on the continent. And there is the Jin Mao Tower, one of the world's most spectacular skyscrapers. Designed by the famous Chicago architectural firm of Skidmore, Owings & Merrill, the building perfectly blends Western postmodernism with the classic architectural dictates of a Buddhist pagoda. This office building is 1,400 feet tall and has 88 floors (this is not a random number: for the Chinese, 8 represents prosperity), and the luxurious Grand Hyatt Hotel occupies all the floors from the 53rd to the top. Trivia lovers will be delighted to discover that it is the tallest hotel in the world. The very name of the skyscraper expands its symbolic meaning, as it

by the British, French and Americans, all of which were independent of Chinese law, and each Western community brought in its experiences, culture and architecture. As a result, it earned the title of "the Paris of Asia" as well as the less flattering one of "Whore of the Orient." During the 1920s, it was a hotbed of wealth, legal and less-than-legal business, with people from every corner of the world (after the 1917 Revolution, many White Russians also fled there), and it was cloaked in an atmosphere so magical that it was often used as a Hollywood set.

That part of Shanghai – crushed by the Japanese invasion during World War II and then by the "hard and pure" years of the Maoist Revolution, which considered it the symbol of the wicked and decadent West – has now been revived, and is more beautiful than ever. The majestic European buildings that line the Bund, the spectacular Puxi riverfront, have been restored, first and foremost the sophisticated Peace Hotel

184 bottom left The Customs Building and its Clock Tower stand on the Bund, evoking the sophisticated atmosphere of the Twenties, when Shanghai was considered the "Paris of Asia."

184 bottom right The single arch of the 1800-foot-long Lu Pu Bridge, which cost 2.25 billion yuan (over 300 million dollars) and took 38,600 tons of steel to build, is a masterpiece of Chinese engineering.

184-185 According to the precepts of feng shui, which are still a must, the people of Shanghai recognize Nanjing Xi Lu as the zhongxin, the pulsating heart of the city.

Teeming with people even at night and illuminated with dazzling and colorful neon signs, this street is the paradigm of a country that has discovered well-being and consumerism.

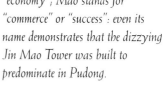

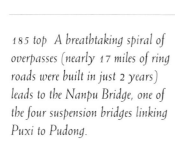

185 top *A breathtaking spiral of overpasses (nearly 17 miles of ring roads were built in just 2 years) leads to the Nanpu Bridge, one of the four suspension bridges linking Puxi to Pudong.*

185 bottom *Jin means "gold" or "economy"; Mao stands for "commerce" or "success": even its name demonstrates that the dizzying Jin Mao Tower was built to predominate in Pudong.*

31°14'N - 121°27'E

Shanghai

and the former headquarters of the Hong Kong & Shanghai Bank. Nanjing Xi Lu, the main commercial thoroughfare, starts from the Bund. With the astonishing sea of people crowding it day and night, and the dazzling neon signs of thousands of stores, this street offers further proof of the urban well-being of the new China.

For those of you who wonder if anything is left of the "old China," the answer is that everything, or nearly everything, has been lost. Surrounded by splendid pagodas, the Yu Yuan Gardens, which were the pride of the old Chinese village, have been spared from the encroaching concrete. At the same time, however, the work done to restore the gardens has done little to respect tradition, making them an undeniably kitschy tourist attraction. Instead, the lovely European quarter of the French Concession has fared much better. Despite the development of luxurious residential areas on the city outskirts, this quarter, with its white Parisian-style buildings, remains one of the most sought-after places for the affluent of Shanghai

to live. And it is also the location of a place that best seems to represent the somersaults of modern-day China: an entire block composed of small red-brick houses that delimit a mawkish pedestrian square. On July 23, 1923, one of those houses – No. 76 on Xinje Lu – was the site of the meeting that established the Chinese Communist Party, the offshoot of an ideology that, in the spirit of its founders, "would overturn heaven and earth."

All the buildings on that block were purchased recently by a Hong Kong magnate, who has restored them and opened boutiques, restaurants and nightspots. The central square has become the most fashionable rendezvous in Shanghai, and there is even a Communism Museum with an annexed shop selling gadgets with images of Mao Zedong. In what can only be called a marvelous taste for paradox, the area has been baptized Xintiandi: "new heaven and new earth." But not even in their wildest dreams would the founding fathers of the People's Republic of China have expected heaven and earth to be overturned in quite this way.

186-187 *The island of Hong Kong and the peninsula of Kowloon have developed vertically and are home to 7 million people, making Hong Kong the 15th largest city in Asia. Great Britain returned the territories to China on June 30, 1997.*

186 bottom *The Tsing Ma Gigantic Bridge, which cost more than $7 billion dollars and was inaugurated on April 27, 1997, crosses the crowded Ma Wan Channel. It is over 7200 feet long, making it the second longest bridge in the world. However, it is the longest one designed to carry both automotive and rail traffic.*

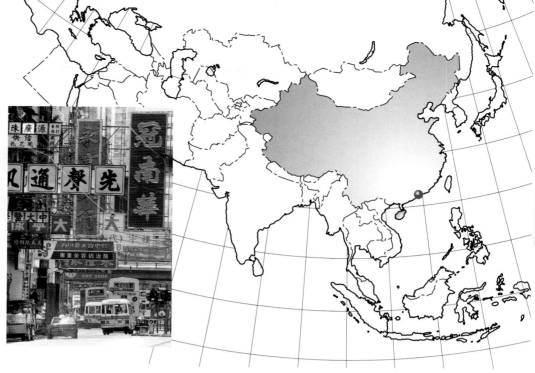

Hong Kong
PEOPLE'S
REPUBLIC OF CHINA

187 top left The typical sampans have disappeared and now the Hong Kong skyline has become one of the city's unmistakable attractions.

187 top right Crowded at all hours of the day, the former British colony is one of the most important trade cities in the world and is a leading exchange center.

187 bottom The futuristic Hong Kong Convention & Exhibition Centre, visible towards the bottom of the picture, was inaugurated in 1988 and was expanded to nearly double its original size in 1997 to host the Handover Ceremony, when the British colony was returned to China. Victoria's Peak, the city's only park area, rises in the background.

On June 30, 1997 in the lavish setting of the Hong Kong Convention & Exhibition Centre – a futuristic building, shaped like a bird poised in flight, which was specially constructed for the occasion at a colossal cost – the Handover Ceremony unfolded with parades, fanfare, fluttering flags and a plethora of prestigious spectators, and the British colony of Hong Kong was returned to the People's Republic of China. Awaited with ill-concealed terror by its 7 million inhabitants and with apprehension by Western investors, that fateful day was expected to mark the end of a bastion of the market economy. Defying all forecasts, what happened in Hong Kong proved to be one of the biggest "non-events" in history. Today we can say that nothing – or almost nothing – has changed here. It was not Hong Kong that had to adapt China, but just the opposite: China used Hong Kong as its model. It created the SAR here, a free-market zone that includes the nearby city of Shenzhen and Guangdong Province, with its capital Guangzhou (Canton), to become the most aggressive economic power in the world.

Hong Kong is composed of the island by the same name, which ends at Victoria's Peak, the hill that represents the only green space in the city center, and the peninsula of Kowloon, from which the island is separated by a mile-long stretch of sea. The financial district is concentrated in the former, which was the original British settlement (of which few traces remain), whereas the latter has always been involved in commerce. In addition to these key centers, Hong Kong encompasses a series of small islands as well as the New Territories, which stretch across the rural inland areas and are now in the midst of the fast-paced construction work that has characterized China's new course of action. In fact, on the island of Hong Kong and on

188 top Thousands of cars and public vehicles flow through the heart of the city day and night. Nevertheless, according to statistics this is "sustainable" traffic: 90% of all daily transits involve public transportation (11 million people).

188 bottom The 1230-foot-tall Bank of China Building, in the center of the picture, is the third tallest building in Hong Kong. Designed by I. M. Pei, it was completed in 1990 and is one of the city's most widely admired skyscrapers.

189 City lighting in the evening showcases some of the tallest towers in Hong Kong: from the Cheung Kong Centre, in the middle, to the Bank of China Building just behind it, and Central Plaza, the tallest building, visible in the background.

Kowloon, both of which were constructed vertically, there is not an inch of room left unless buildings are torn down to make room for new skyscrapers. For over thirty years now, Hong Kong has suffered from a chronic lack of housing and has repeatedly been forced to "steal" land from the sea. For example, the city's ultramodern international airport is located on an artificial extension of Lantau island. The new airport was built to replace the old one in Kowloon, where planes would take off and land on a runway bordered by skyscrapers: an experience that gave passengers heart palpitations.

Famous worldwide as a shoppers' paradise – though the locals prefer to face hours of traffic in order to shop in Shenzhen, which is much cheaper – Hong Kong looks like a Western city. Skyscrapers and shopping centers, subway lines and streets that cross the bay via tunnels built under the sea (although some people still use the Star Ferry, for a trip from Hong Kong to Kowloon with a view of the phenomenal skyline), texts in English set alongside Chinese ideograms and, above all, the use of the Hong Kong dollar rather than the yuan

are aspects that somehow make the city comforting. Beneath this façade, however, Hong Kong is ever Oriental in spirit.

The story about three of its most famous skyscrapers fully demonstrates this. The "oldest" one is the headquarters of the Hong Kong & Shanghai Bank, designed by architect Sir Norman Foster in 1985. To select the building site, the clients commissioning the building contacted a famed *feng shui* expert. Thus, in accordance with the dictates of geomancy, the building was constructed at the intersection of the five lines of the dragon, where *chi*, or positive energy, is concentrated. In 1989 another spectacular skyscraper, the Bank of China Building designed by Chinese-American architect I. M. Pei, was built nearby. However, its reflecting walls and diagonal lines ruined its rival's *feng shui*. In 1999 another skyscraper rose between the two giants: the Cheung Kong Centre, designed by Cesar Pelli in collaboration with a geomancer. And it seems that this building, decorated with miles of optic fiber programmed to change color every minute, has managed to reestablish harmony between the two banks!

190-191 *Nam Dae Mun, or the Great South Gate, is now the site of a shopping center. It is the only monumental gate to Seoul that is still standing. The gates were built in 1392 by General Yi Song-Gye, founder of the Chosun Dynasty.*

190 bottom left *Seoul Tower, which is 777 feet tall, rises above all the other skyscrapers in city center. The tower, which affords a stunning view, is on top of luxuriant Mount Namsan and can be reached by a cable railway.*

190 bottom right *Teheranro, Apgujong-dong and Chongro-gu, the hub of South Korea's flourishing publishing industry, constitute the economic and financial heart of the city.*

191 top *Built in the area of Sangam-dong for the 2002 World Soccer Cup, Seoul Stadium, which can seat 65,000 people, is composed of an underground level and six floors above the ground. The roofing evokes traditional Korean kites.*

191 bottom *A terrible spiral of invasion and destruction, the most recent of which in 1950 at the hands of North Korean and Chinese troops, destroyed many of Seoul's historic buildings, and the city is now "besieged" by fast-paced modernization. Approximately 3000 skyscrapers have been built in Seoul in the past ten years.*

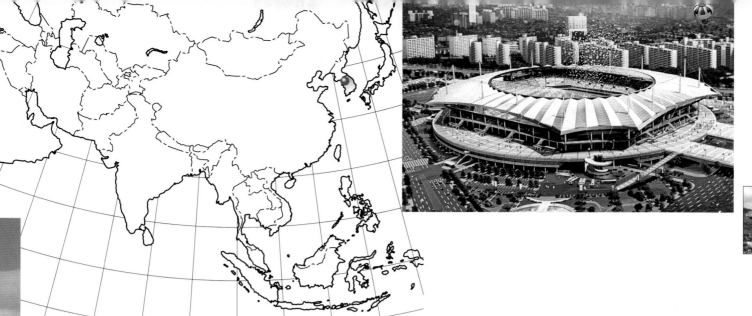

Seoul
REPUBLIC OF KOREA

ircled by hills, delimited to the south by the mighty granite mass of Mount Namsan and crossed by the Han River to the east, Seoul enjoys an enviable geographical position in the middle of the Korean peninsula. Unfortunately, the same thing cannot be said about its political position. Barely 25 miles away from the heart of the city, the ill-fated 38th parallel, which the UN considers the "hottest" and most militarized border on the planet, divides South Korea from North Korea. In fact, anyone strolling through the capital of South Korea who carefully observes its buildings will have no trouble noticing the loudspeakers installed by the government to warn citizens of the danger of an attack by their "cousins" from the north.

Today, however, foreigners are the only ones who notice them. The people of Seoul seem to have learned to live without worrying about this latent threat, just as they have stopped trying to reveal the mystery of what happens across the border. In all likelihood, extraordinary economic well-being and a still-young democracy seem sufficient to guarantee a future of prosperity and stability. In all honesty, the Koreans deserve it. Since 1392, the year it was established as the capital of Korea under the Chosun Dynasty – its name comes from the ancient word *Seobeol*, meaning capital – Seoul has been involved in a spiral of invasion and destruction, the most recent of which in 1950 at the hands of North Korean troops and Mao Zedong's Chinese army.

The city that was a mournful pile of rubble half a century ago now has a population of 10.5 million and an area of over 230 square miles. It has 522 *dong* (quarters) and 25 *gu* (districts), nine subway lines covering a total of 62 miles, and one million registered motor vehicles jamming urban roads that are up to 12 lanes wide. The exact opposite of the North Korean capital Pyongyang, Seoul is a metropolis open to the world; it hosted the Olympic Games in 1988 and the World Soccer Cup in 2002. Most importantly, however, its skyline full of skyscrapers clearly looks toward the future.

Today many areas in Seoul are developing vertically. One is Teheranro, the headquarters of the IT business and the new economy, and another is Apgujong-dong, the exclusive fashion district. And there is also Chongro-gu, the hub of Korea's flourishing publishing industry. For trivia lovers, this district claims the invention of printing. Nevertheless, the areas that are proudly considered the "Manhattans" of Seoul are Youido, the river island that encompasses its financial center, and Kangnam, a residential area in which Tower G has just been completed. This astonishing building, which is 866 feet tall and has 73 floors, is composed of three oval structures, is part of a futuristic complex of seven towers. However, the capital's tallest building is in the middle of Namsan Park, on the slopes of Mount Namsan. This is Seoul Tower (1,584 feet), a telecommunications tower with a terrace affording a magnificent view.

Even from this vantage point, amidst all of Seoul's modern buildings it is difficult to pick out the pagoda roofs of the few

192 top Built in 1395 by King Taejo, founder of the Chosun Dynasty, the Kyongbokkung – the "Palace of Shining Happiness" – is the oldest and most impressive of the five royal complexes in Seoul, and it encloses a ten-story pagoda.

192 center At Chongmyo, the temple built in 1385 as the burial site of the kings and queens of the Chosun Dynasty, the members of the royal family celebrated elaborate rituals five times a year to honor of the dead. Today, the ceremony is held only once a year, in May.

buildings that have survived the city's eventful history. Some of the most notable are the royal palaces of Changdeokgung, Changgyeonggung, Deoksugung and Kyongbokkung, all which were built by the Chosun Dynasty that, despite various vicissitudes, ruled Korea from the late 14th century until 1910. Each of these palaces is composed of numerous halls and pagodas, and is set in an elegant garden. However, it is Changgyeonggung, whose original structures date back to the 16th century, which conveys Korea's finest traditions. In the splendid garden where there is now a large pond, the royal family once allocated an area for cultivating rice, as a tribute to Korea's agricultural vocation and to recall that kingdoms progress only if they are in harmony with nature. This is a philosophical lesson that, if frenetic Seoul is any indication, its current rulers have yet to learn.

192 bottom The hexagonal pavilion of Hyang Wongjong was built by the Chosun Dynasty as a place to relax. It is located in the middle of a romantic lake and is connected to Kyonghokkung Palace via a picturesque wooden bridge.

192-193 Of all the royal palaces in Seoul, Changgyeonggung is the one that best represents the Korean tradition, thanks to the uniformity of its architecture and the variety of landscapes that can be admired in its immense gardens.

193 bottom The "Secret Garden" of Changdeokgung Palace boasts elegant pavilions, maple trees, orchids, chrysanthemums, ginkgo biloba, ponds dotted with lotus blossoms and rocks in symbol shapes, making it the finest example of a traditional Korean garden. Chosun architecture was influenced by Confucian principles of simplicity and harmony, and the capital city was built by respecting and exploiting the natural features of the territory and landscape to create a highly dramatic effect.

194-195 The skyscrapers of Makati, Manila's financial district that is crossed by Ayala Avenue, or the "Wall Street of the Philippines," rise over the broad verdant area of Greenbelt Square.

194 bottom left The ruins of the fortifications of Intramuros form the heart of old Manila. In the 16th and 17th centuries, this was the main Spanish port between Mexico and China.

194 bottom right The city is congested by chaotic but picturesque traffic.

195 top The cathedral of Manila is located on the site of a religious building constructed by the Spanish in 1583.

195 bottom Neglected and polluted for decades, the Pasig, the river flowing through Manila, was recently cleaned up through the enormous efforts of the city government.

Manila
PHILIPPINES

There is no doubt about the fact that the capital of the Philippines is a troubled metropolis. Its history – like that of the country itself – has been subjected to profound political instability over the past several decades. Nevertheless, a look back through the centuries reveals that Manila has always been a "fiery" city. Founded in about the 12th century at the mouth of the Pasig River, the city was long a trade center for the local population, the Chinese and the Arabs. In 1521, the Europeans' first attempt to colonize its territory culminated in violent warfare, during which the Portuguese explorer Ferdinand Magellan was killed. Its inhabitants also created plenty of trouble for the Spanish, who ruled there for 327 years, starting in 1565, as well as the Americans, who exercised virtually direct control over the vast archipelago of the Philippines during the early 20th century.

Manila, or Metro Manila as it is officially called, is an urban area covering 240 square miles, extending from Manila Bay to the inland area. It encompasses four cities and 13 municipalities, and has a population of 13 million. Because of the city's temperament as well as intense bombing during World War II, few of its historic buildings have been preserved, and those that remain are located within the two-mile perimeter of the walls the Spanish built at the end of the 16th century at the point were the Pasig River flows into the sea. In the 16th and 17th centuries, Intramuros – this was the ancient name of this city – was the main Spanish port between Mexico and China. The city had 15 churches, 6 monasteries, countless buildings symbolizing colonial power, and Asia's oldest university, founded in 1611, all of which surrounded by 20-foot-tall walls covering a perimeter of over 1.8 miles. In terms of historic events, the most invasive one dates back to the beginning of World War II, when U.S. General MacArthur razed the city's priceless Baroque architecture to build depots and housing for his troops. A cathedral, reconstructed in 1950, and the ruins of Fort Santiago and of Puerta Real, the main access to the citadel, are all that remain of Intramuros, which is now protected by UNESCO. Destroyed by the bombings of 1945, the Iglesia de San Agustín, the oldest church in the Philippines (built between 1587-1604) has now been restored in all its ancient glory. Likewise, Casa Manila, built in the mid-19th century, has been reconstructed and transformed into a museum, with furnishings and artwork from the colonial period.

Several buildings in the institutional center of Manila, which have been promoted to "antiquity" status, are separated from Intramuros by the river and by a park named in honor of José Rizal, the intellectual who was executed by the Spanish on December 30, 1896 and is considered the ideologue of Filipino independence. These are the Congress Building and the Finance Ministry, both of which now house the National Museum, the Metropolitan Theater, City Hall and the Post Office Building. All of these were built between 1920 and 1950, the period in which work was done under American auspices to give the city a modern and monumental layout.

Instead, the city of the new millennium has countered the animated chaos typical of major Asian cities with vertical architectural development. The new districts of Makati, Ermita and Ortigas are now jungles of skyscrapers conveying the illusion of "American" well-being. However, what captures one's attention even more than the five-star hotels, bank buildings, the stock exchange and multinational headquarters are the city's luxurious residential complexes. One of these is Global City – and its very name reflects the capital's expectations for the future – in which construction is being completed on Essensa, twin towers designed by one of the most famous contemporary architects, I. M. Pei.

196-197 The twin towers of the Municipality of Tokyo (right) stand out in this panoramic view, with Mount Fuji in the background. The building is nearly 800 feet tall.

196 bottom A dizzying ramp leads to the Rainbow Bridge, the suspension bridge built between 1987 and 1992 across the port of Tokyo. The structure is over

3000 feet long, and its two main piers are 1870 feet apart. Its pedestrian walkway affords a spectacular view of the bay and of the city.

197 top Artificially divided into 23 districts, 26 cities, 5 towns and 8 villages, the Tokyo Prefecture is actually a sprawling urban area crowded with 30 million residents, making it the largest metropolis in the world.

197 bottom The shinkansen, the remarkable trains connecting Tokyo, Kyoto, Nagoya and Osaka, were inaugurated in 1964 – the year the city hosted the Olympic Games – on a track that allowed for 125 miles per hour. Today's trains can reach speeds of about 200 mph.

Tokyo

JAPAN

According to a recent study on spoken Japanese, *kawaii* is the most commonly heard term among the Japanese – at least among the younger generation. It can be translated more or less as "cute," and it identifies everything that is small, soft, sweet and innocent. And in Japan, the market of *kawaii* items (childlike gadgets) has a sales turnover approaching that of electronic products. Tokyo has immense kawaii stores like Sanrio Ginza Gallery and Puroland, the haunts of kitsch and fairytale, but the iconography of "cute" is not merely for teens. In response to this fashion, the city government had police booths built around town – in the shape of gingerbread houses – and the new *mini kazu*, or runabouts, have intentionally been designed as children's car replicas.

Oddly enough, to the rest of the world Japanese style means rigor, minimalism and elegance. Indeed, as soon as visitors arrive in Tokyo – to paraphrase *Lost in Translation*, a recent film directed by Sofia Coppola – they cannot help but feel out of place, unsettled, overwhelmed. They can smile over the military-style march that resounds in the streets as soon as traffic lights turn green, to urge pedestrians to move quickly. They can admire the city's public transportation network, the most efficient on the planet, and its stations (Tokyo Central, Ueno, Ikebukuro, Shinjuku and Shibuya), which handle between 400,000 and 1.7 million transiting passengers a day. These stations are the hubs for the *shinkansen*, the "bullet trains" that are the pride of Japan. They can be enchanted by the thousands of neon lights and all the LCD screens, flashing on the façades of city buildings to keep passersby up to date on the latest news, the stock market and the weather forecast, or to entice them to buy. Unless you happen to be Japanese, however, you must immediately stop trying to understand.

Let's take Tokyo itself as an example. According to the Japanese, their capital is not a city but an extremely complex urban entity known as *Tokyo-to* (Tokyo Prefecture), which has a population of approximately 30 million. In turn, it is divided into 23 special districts called *ku* that, together, form the city "center" (about 12 million residents). Added to them are 26 cities (*shi*), each of which with a population of at least 300,000 people, five towns (*cho*) with at least 50,000

residents, and eight villages (*son*) of 5,000 people, most of which are on the islands of Tokyo Bay, which were incorporated into the urban area in 2003. In short, this is a mass of concrete and people (which nonetheless has 5,000 well-hidden public parks), in which construction went vertical due to lack of space. In fact, though Japan has been devastated by a constant string of violent earthquakes, Tokyo's residential buildings are normally 40 to 50 stories tall. Moreover, technologies continue to evolve to create earthquake-proof systems in the foundations (like the "cushions" tested recently to absorb seismic oscillations) that

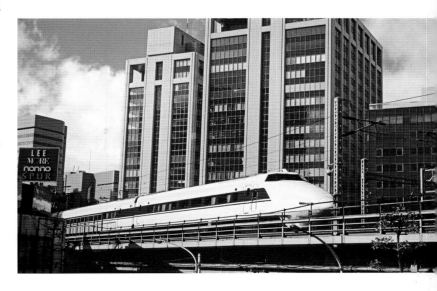

make it possible "to move onward and upward."

The Tokyo area, which is set on the east coast of Honshu, the largest island in the Japanese archipelago, has been inhabited for millennia, but until the end of the 16th century all that stood here was a fishing village by the name of Edo. Starting in 1600, under the rule of the powerful Tokugawa shogun (military administrators), Edo began to expand, swelling to a population of over one million just a century later. In 1853, the Europeans landed in Japan, breaking a thousand years of isolation and triggering profound social upheavals that weakened the Tokugawa in favor of the pro-Western emperor of the Meiji Dynasty. In 1863 the emperor moved his capital from Kyoto to Edo, which he renamed Tokyo, or "Eastern Capital."

Tokyo

198 bottom Designed to resemble a microchip – a tribute to the industry that made Japan a world economic power – the Municipality of Tokyo is flanked by two towers reminiscent of the spires of Notre-Dame in Paris.

Despite the fact that the city is four centuries old, its historic monuments can be counted on the fingers of one hand – even the Imperial Palace was reconstructed in the 1960s – in part because the old buildings were made of wood, and in part because Tokyo had experienced numerous earthquakes (the most catastrophic one was in 1923) and was then bombarded repeatedly during World War II. Nevertheless, it must be said that until the second half of the 19th century the Japanese did not have a single word in their language to express the concept of architecture – their aesthetics were based on the forms of nature – and their entry to modernity was inspired by an imitation of the West.

Ironically, though the latest trends in architecture and contemporary design in today's globalized world have been inspired by Japanese Zen concepts, the leading designers who helped give Tokyo its futuristic face are the children of modernism and Western functionalism. And they have even succeeded in elevating these concepts to excessive levels, as in the case of Kisho Kurokawa, who in 1971 built the Nakagin Capsule Tower in the overpopulated area of Ginza. This skyscraper holds prefabricated capsule dwellings measuring just 7.5 by 12.5 feet, with a height of 6.9 feet, and they are fitted with every comfort – so to speak – for a single occupant. Japan's most famous 20th-century architect, Kenzo Tange, who designed the remarkable Olympic Stadium in 1964, likewise looked to the West for his training, observing the works of Frank Lloyd Wright and Le Corbusier (the latter designed Tokyo's splendid National Museum of Western Art). A prolific architect, in 1991 Tange also designed the monumental skyscraper that houses Tokyo's City Hall Complex. Located in the technological district of Shinjuku, it is 797 feet tall; its shape is reminiscent of a microchip, but at the same time, with its two apical towers it is a tribute to the cathedral of Notre-Dame in Paris. The tallest structure in the city – and in all of Japan – is also "French." This is the Tokyo Tower (1,092 ft), built in 1958 and modeled after the Eiffel Tower.

Tokyo now has 2,300 skyscrapers – and they become more and more innovative – designed by notable Japanese architects such as Tadao Ando, Arata Isozaki, Kiyonori Kikutake, and Kisho Kurokawa. There are also works by Philippe Stark, who in the Sumida-ku area designed the Asahi Super Dry Hall, a singular structure topped by a flame that acts as a "showcase" for Japan's leading beer brewer. And the firm of Kohn Pedersen Fox designed Roppongi Hills, a

198-199 The Shibuya area, the location of the Olympic Village in 1964, has been transformed into one of Tokyo's main commercial districts.

200-201 Thousands of neon lights brighten the night sky in Tokyo, the prototype of the gigantic urban conglomerations that are destined to predominate in the 21st century.

surprising multipurpose skyscraper that cost $5.4 billion to build.

Nevertheless, what makes Tokyo such an alienating yet stimulating megalopolis is the city as a whole, rather than its individual buildings. Despite Tokyo's modernity and unfettered consumerism, which invents and absorbs fads in a matter of days, there are rituals that have not changed for centuries, and places – concealed amid the psychedelic colors and high-tech shopping malls of the Ginza, Roppongi, and Shinjuku districts – where it is still possible to attend a tea ceremony, watch an equally traditional sumo wrestling match or encounter the serene monks of a Shinto temple. But the things that probably astonish and intrigue visitors most are the follies of the "Japanese world," like the lively Tsukiji Fish Market, the biggest one in the world, as well as the city's "virtual" entertainment spots. One of these is Marine City, built on the sea, where young people from the Nintendo generation, raised on sushi and videogames, flock en masse to incredible theme parks to experience what the future will be like. As if the future did not already exist right here in Tokyo.

AUSTRALIA AND OCEANIA

I f the ancient rock paintings in Kakadu National Park, which testify to the long history of the Australian Aborigines, are any indication, our species colonized the planet's southernmost continent at least 40,000 years ago. At the time, Australia was probably connected to New Guinea by a low isthmus, and the islands in the Sonda archipelago were probably also joined to the continent, forming a vast peninsula. Taking advantage of particularly favorable climatic conditions, isolated groups of the first modern *Homo sapiens* crossed the narrow stretch of sea that separated continental Asia from Australia, and they settled in these new lands.

Since then, the Australian Aborigines have lived according to traditions handed down from generation to generation, creating their own myths and social structure while continuing to live like the hunter-gatherers of the Paleolithic, never developing a metal age. It was not until 7000-5000 BC that a new wave of migration from Southeast Asia introduced agriculture and brought in techniques for building canoes and making the continent's first ceramics.

In the Western world, where complex technological societies had developed in the meantime, in the early centuries of our era people already fantasized about the existence of an austral continent, which was thought to be south of the Indian Ocean. But it was not until the age of exploration, after the discovery of America, that more systematic searches for those faraway lands began. The first circumnavigation of the globe, which began in 1519 and was completed in 1522, followed a route that crossed the Pacific far north. According to the diary of Antonio Pigafetta, the Spanish fleet under the Portuguese

commander Ferdinand Magellan, who was killed on April 27, 1521 in a battle on one of the Philippine islands, sailed back and forth between the Sonda Islands, almost touching the western coast of Australia before turning west to head home.

It would take nearly a century before the first European – the Dutch navigator Willem Janszoon – set foot on the Australian continent; the year was 1606. However, Janszoon was convinced he had reached New Guinea. Ten years later, his compatriot Dirck Hartog realized that the Dutch schooners had reached the west coast of the *Terra Australis Incognita* posited by Claudius Ptolemy, the southern continent that, according to the ancients, had to exist to counterbalance the weight of Asia and Europe on this restless planet. Yet another Dutchman, Abel Tasman, discovered New Zealand and Tasmania between 1642 and 1644.

Nevertheless, the Dutch found the climate in this new world unbearable (in fact, they had landed on the least hospitable coast, characterized by long torrid summers), and from their very first contact they decided that the lands south of Sonda had no economic potential whatsoever. Thus, the arrival of the Europeans was deferred until 1770, when Captain James Cook rediscovered the continent on his way from the idyllic Polynesian islands. The *Endeavour* had left England on August 25, 1768 to sail to Tahiti, with 94 people aboard, namely the ship's crew and a group of scientists led by Sir Joseph Banks. The scientists had been appointed by the Royal Society of London to observe and document the transit of Venus across the solar disk on June 3, 1769. After leaving the Society Islands, so named in honor of the "sponsor" of this journey, the legendary English navigator continued

westward, finding shelter for the *Endeavour* in a splendid cove he named Botany Bay. He subsequently moved up the coast, and a little further north he discovered a vast jagged inlet that extended to the interior for miles.

Less than twenty years later – on January 18, 1788 – following Banks's indications Captain Arthur Phillip sailed up that inlet with a boatload of 800 prisoners from England and decided to establish the first English settlement in Australia, calling it Sydney Cove in honor of British minister Thomas Townshend, first Viscount Sydney. Life was difficult at first. Crops had to be planted as quickly as possible or the colony would starve. However, the prisoners had never worked the land before and many of them showed no intention of doing so, whereas the sailors were unconcerned with maintaining discipline. Just a few years later, the life of the approximately 2000 inhabitants of the colony of New South Wales slowly became more stable, and soon new colonists began to arrive.

More than two centuries after that first settlement of "immigrants," Sydney, with its population of four million, can be considered the only true metropolis on an endless semidesert continent. Australia alone has a population of less than 20 million inhabitants in a territory of nearly 2.9 million square miles. But to complete the geographical picture of Oceania, we must add New Zealand, Papua New Guinea, New Caledonia, and the myriad of islands that compose the remote archipelagos of Micronesia, Melanesia and Polynesia, many of which are exotic and virtually unexplored destinations even now – at least the ones that have not been transformed into exclusive tourist resorts.

Thus, it comes as no surprise that, even today, Oceania is still an incredibly wild continent where nature reigns supreme and man is concentrated in only a few areas. This is due also to the fact that much of Australia's territory is covered by an immense desert plateau – the largest deserts are the Great Sandy Desert, Gibson Desert and the Great Victoria Desert – accounting for 60 percent of the country's area. As a result, human settlements are inevitably concentrated in only a few areas. Though there are only a few cities with more than one million inhabitants (in addition to Sydney, Adelaide, Perth and Brisbane in Australia, and Auckland in New Zealand), a very large part of the population lives in urban areas. Given the harsh environmental conditions in the interior, however, all these urban areas are located along the coast. The interior of Australia is practically uninhabited.

From an architectural standpoint, due to the fact that they were founded fairly recently, the cities of Australia and New Zealand (the capitals of the other countries cannot be defined as cities, save for Papeete, Tahiti, the capital of French Polynesia) are modern. For the most part they have none of the charm of cities whose history goes back thousands of years, like many of the ones in Europe and Asia. In fact, many of them developed by annexing new residential areas to the original settlements, without a general plan to regulate their growth.

One of the few exceptions – indeed, probably the only one – is Sydney, which for years now has garnered international attention with impressive works like the legendary Opera House, as well as its residential areas and infrastructures, many of which designed for the 2000 Olympics. The result is one of the most modern and fascinating metropolises on the planet. This place, where the English established their first settlement in Australia, is where the new world has launched its challenge for the 21st century.

203 left Honolulu and Waikiki Beach stretch past the magnificent cone of Diamond Head.

203 center Aerial view of the center of Sydney. The ocean horizon is visible in the background.

203 right With its skyscrapers, downtown Melbourne dominates Port Phillip Bay.

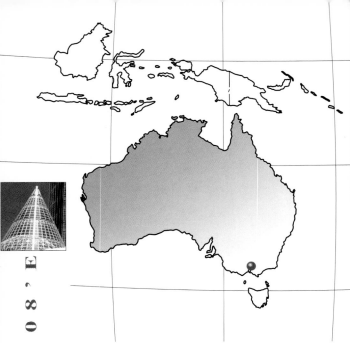

Melbourne
AUSTRALIA

Judging from the race to purchase one of the 556 apartments in the Eureka Tower, one can't help but wonder what has happened to the residents of Melbourne and the Australian dream: buying a single-family house surrounded by greenery, with enough room (at least 2.5 acres) for children to play and two cars parked in the driveway. In a country with plenty of space, it is odd that the most sought-after address in the capital of the State of Victoria is a high-rise set on a plot of land reclaimed from the bed of the Yarra River.

The Eureka Tower, whose blue glass walls rise to a height of nearly 1000 feet and stand out against the skyline, is one of the tallest residential buildings in the world. Slated for completion in 2005 and costing approximately $250 million, it was designed by Nonda Katsalidis, one of the continent's most brilliant

architects – and it is Melbourne's latest hot topic. Vying with Sydney, Melbourne is Australia's second-largest city in terms of population and economic importance, and it has long realized that it cannot compete with its rival when it comes to natural beauty. The scenario of the river and of Port Phillip Bay pales in comparison to Sydney Harbour, and Melbourne's climate, reminiscent of English weather, certainly doesn't help. As a result, the city's only option was to turn to unconventional architectural works and attempt to become a leading cultural capital.

Melbourne's competition with Sydney, which began about 15 years ago, spurred Australia's second city to move ahead by leaps and bounds, and today it can proudly affirm that it has won this challenge, at least in the area of art and culture. The city has an array of contemporary architecture, and multicolored

204 top left The Eureka Tower, which is over 1000 feet tall and has 556 apartments, making it one of the tallest residential buildings in the world.

204 top right Behind La Trobe Street, a cone-shaped structure covers the historic Shot Tower, a 20-story tower built in 1889 and now inside the Melbourne Central Shopping Center.

204 bottom and 204-205 The glass-clad Rialto Towers rise over the Yarra River. The buildings, on the left in these two panoramic views, are over 850 feet tall and have 63 floors; they were completed in 1986. Founded on Port Phillip Bay by John Batman in 1834, the city was named after British Prime Minister Lord Melbourne. With a population of 3.5 million, Melbourne is the second largest city in Australia, yet it is also one of its most "livable."

205 bottom left A façade decorated with panels covered with classical-style sculptures marks the Ian Potter Museum of Art, the deconstructionist building that houses the Australian art collection of the National Gallery of Victoria.

205 bottom right Quintessentially Victorian, Melbourne is famous for its 19th-century homes with porches and beautifully decorated balconies. This may be one of the reasons the residents of other Australian cities consider Melbourne a bit snobbish.

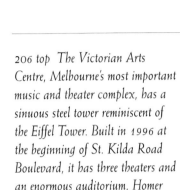

sculptures characterize its urban furniture. Its districts are dotted with avant-garde galleries (like the New Australian Centre for Contemporary Art, a building-sculpture designed by the architectural firm of Wood Marsh), extravagant university campuses, concert venues, restaurants and fashionable shops. The influx of immigrants, notably the Greeks – Melbourne has the third-largest population of Greeks in the world, after Athens and Thessalonica – but also Italians, Slavs, Chinese, Cambodians and Vietnamese, have mitigated its Anglo-Saxon severity, making Melbourne a laboratory for new models of coexistence. Constantly evolving, the city felt the need to create a new meeting place. Consequently, Federation Square, which can hold 25,000 people, was built. Overlooking the square are the headquarters of the major television network SBS, the Australian Centre for the Moving Image and, above all, the Ian Potter Centre, which houses the Australian art collection of the National Gallery of Victoria. This extraordinarily impressive deconstructionist building is one of the most talked-about works by the firm of Denton, Corker and Marshall, the architects who were responsible for the zoning plans of the entire square and are the main movers behind the renewal of Melbourne. The firm's architects also designed the bridges and tunnels leading into the city, as well as Melbourne's most important museum complex. Topped by an extraordinary metal spire that is nearly 132 feet tall, the Melbourne Museum is set in a sprawling park on the Yarra River, and it shares the area with the Royal Exhibition Hall, built in 1880 for the Universal Expo. The hall has recently been inscribed on UNESCO's World Heritage List as the most significant expression of Victorian architecture in Australia.

Melbourne has been ambitious ever since 1835, the year it was founded, and by the end of the 19th century it had earned the nickname of "The Paris of the Antipodes." Today, its historic memories – all in the purest British style – engage in a bizarre harmony with the futuristic buildings that have redesigned the city's skyline. Though Melbourne has earned a front-row spot as far as the future is concerned, to recount its history the city is forced to resort to stratagems. The most visited monument in the city is the birthplace of James Cook, the man who discovered Australia: The house was dismantled in Yorkshire, England, and reassembled here as the kind gift of Queen Elizabeth II to the former colony.

207 bottom left Federation Square is the city's most futuristic project. The outcome of 6 years of work, it was designed to become the artistic, cultural and geographical center of Melbourne.

207 bottom right The Southgate Walking Bridge over the Yarra River was specifically designed to give pedestrians the feeling that they are walking on a "living" structure.

Sydney

AUSTRALIA

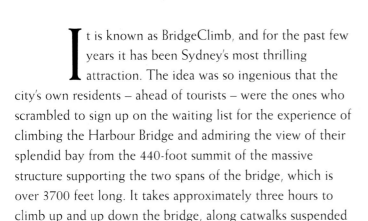

It is known as BridgeClimb, and for the past few years it has been Sydney's most thrilling attraction. The idea was so ingenious that the city's own residents – ahead of tourists – were the ones who scrambled to sign up on the waiting list for the experience of climbing the Harbour Bridge and admiring the view of their splendid bay from the 440-foot summit of the massive structure supporting the two spans of the bridge, which is over 3700 feet long. It takes approximately three hours to climb up and up down the bridge, along catwalks suspended midair and steep staircases and narrow metal pathways.

For those not afraid of heights, the climb is well worth the effort: Sydney Harbour – its official name is actually Port Jackson, but no one ever uses this name – is matched only by the bay of Rio de Janeiro for the title of the most spectacular urban scenario on earth. In this marvelous basin, dotted with small islands and set at the mouth of the Parramatta River, dazzling city architecture alternates with steep cliffs and

golden beaches, with the Blue Mountains outlined starkly in the background. The Harbour Bridge itself is the pride of Sydney. Completed in 1932, it is the widest suspension bridge in the world, extending 160 feet, the width required to accommodate two carriageways, two railroad lines, a bike path and a pedestrian walkway. It took 1500 workmen ten years to build, and the structure required 52,800 tons of steel, over 3.3 million cubic feet of cement, and 18,000 granite blocks. In short, it was a magnificent feat of engineering, and its inauguration marked Sydney's triumphant addition to the list of the world's most modern metropolises.

Thirty years later – in 1973, to be precise – the bridge would lose it 'triumph of modernity' cachet to the formidable Sydney Opera House, now considered an icon of 20th-century architecture. Designed by Danish architect Jørn Utzon, the building rises on a promontory and seems to float on the blue waters of the bay, with roofing created like a set of sails swollen by the wind. The extraordinary complex boasts approximately a thousand rooms, including concert auditoriums, theaters and rooms that are interconnected to create flexible and functional areas with a powerful visual impact. On average, 3000 events are performed here every year for a total audience of about two million.

In 2004, the entire city proudly hailed the nomination of the Opera House for inclusion in UNESCO's World Heritage List – just as Sydney felt "directly involved" when Utzon was awarded the prestigious Pritzker Architecture Prize in 2003 – but at the time it was constructed, the Opera House it was the target of harsh criticism. Its development phase took 15 years because of numerous clashes between the architect and the city governments, budget cuts, and changing ideas. In fact, Utzon indignantly abandoned his position as director of works before the structure was completed.

These disputes are now just a hazy memory, and the Opera House has become the model of inspiration for all of Sydney's architecture. In the designer's mind, the building was meant to create a dialog – an interplay of geometry and symmetry – with the Harbour Bridge (in fact, the height of the middle "sail" is exactly half that of the bridge). In time, however, that dialog was transformed into a stimulating conversation of different voices. The latest addition to the

208-209 The Opera House, whose roofing is reminiscent of a set of sails swollen by the wind, has been the symbol of Sydney ever since it was opened in 1973.

209 bottom right An aerial view of some of the outlying areas of Sydney, overlooking coves that are perfect natural shelters for countless yachts.

208 top left St. Mary's Cathedral, the most important Catholic church in Australia, was reconstructed between 1866 and 1928 over the site of the first cathedral, burned in 1865.

208 top right The 1014-foot-tall AMP Tower (formerly Centrepoint Tower and Sydney Tower) is the tallest building in Sydney: 1504 steps lead to the top.

208 center St. Andrew's Cathedral, founded in 1819, is the oldest Anglican cathedral in the country.

208 bottom e 209 bottom left Record-breaking bridges: Pyrmont Bridge (left), inaugurated in 1902, is the oldest swingspan bridge in the world, whereas the Harbour Bridge (right), inaugurated in 1932, is the world's widest suspension bridge.

210 top Originally created for sports competitions and recreational events, Hyde Park is an immense public green area in the center of Sydney; it was inspired by the London park after which it was named. The sole legacy of its 19th-century layout is the giant chessboard at its western end, which still attracts numerous chess enthusiasts.

210 center The Archibald Fountain, which was built in 1932 through sponsorship of J.F. Archibald, publisher and editor in chief of The Bulletin, is at the northern edge of Hyde Park. Archibald wanted to commemorate the alliance between France and Australia in World War I, and as a result Frenchman François Sicard was commissioned to design the fountain.

city skyline, in the heart of the Central Business District and less than half a mile from the Opera House, is the masterly complex known as Aurora Place, designed by Renzo Piano. Piano, likewise unfurled a soaring stylized sail, composed of evanescent glass panels, that stands out in a urban space in which skyscrapers – like the luxurious Chifley Tower by the firm of Kohn Pedersen Fox and Harry Seidler's Grosvenor Place – are conceived and intensified in a collective dimension.

Indeed, with its exceptional location Sydney can best be defined as a joint venture between man and nature. In fact, to the rest of the world the harbor-city is the very symbol of Australia and its spirit – even more than the red expanse of the outback, the primordial interior of the country. Despite this, however, the city is merely the capital of New South Wales, whereas the otherwise unremarkable city of Canberra is the Australian capital. Though the country's institutions are located in the latter city, Sydney is where Australians have focused their investments and ambitions. In 2000 the city hosted the Olympics, and for the occasion the city's efforts made entire areas literally blossom, among them Darling Harbour, the former industrial port that was transformed into an entertainment venue, and it completed infrastructures that placed it on a par with the most important cities in the world.

In fact, any attempts to compare the city to New York or London seem to offend Sydneysiders. They weigh aspects like the climate (the sun shines here 300 days a year), safety, and the area's stunning landscape: first of all, the bay, followed by the vineyard-covered hills, the mountains and an array of national parks just a few miles from the center of town. One is the Royal National Park, which was established in 1879 and is one of the oldest protected areas on the planet. And they rightly state that the atmosphere here is priceless. The nearly four million people who live here feel as if they are on a perennial vacation. Few people have the privilege of enjoying the services, job opportunities and culture of a cosmopolitan city while also having the chance to go sailing or surfing near a beach as beautiful as the famous Bondi Beach.

210 bottom left French fashion designer Pierre Cardin has described the Queen Victoria Building as "the most beautiful shopping center in the world." An extraordinary example of Neo-Byzantine architecture, it was built in 1898 to replace Sydney's general market.

210 bottom right The Grand Organ, which was once the largest pipe organ in the world, is the pride of Sydney Town Hall, which was completed in 1889. The building, designed by J.H. Willson, has a 187-foot-tall clock tower.

210-211 The Rocks, on the west coast of Sydney Cove, is the oldest district in Sydney. This is where the founders of the British colony in Australia landed on January 26, 1788. The area was recently transformed into an entertainment district with restaurants, pubs and discotheques.

211 bottom The trim houses dear to British tradition – but with more exotic frontons and façades – line Argyle Square, located in the city's historic district between Sydney Cove and Darling Harbour.

Sydney

212-213 The tower of the MLC Centre, completed in 1977 and the tallest building in the country until 1985, soars to a height of nearly 750 feet in the heart of Australia's most important financial center, Sydney's Central Business District. The area has attracted the most famous architects in the world. Renzo Piano designed Aurora Place, which was completed in 2000, and the firm of Kohn Pedersen Fox recently designed Chifley Tower, one of the most prestigious office complexes on the continent.

212 bottom With its little tables set outside overlooking the bay, the Opera Bar in Sydney, next to the Opera House, enjoys a truly enviable location. Live concerts and performances by famous Australian DJs make it a lively spot all night long.

213 top With approximately 4 million inhabitants, Sydney is the most populous city on the Australian continent. Its skyline makes it one of the most admired metropolises in the world, thanks also to the splendid bay that provides the city with an impressive natural harbor.

213 bottom Today the extraordinary appeal of the Opera House is universally acknowledged (tellingly, the building is on UNESCO's World Heritage List), but initially this work was harshly criticized. In fact, it took 15 years to build and its designer abandoned his position as director of works before the structure was completed.

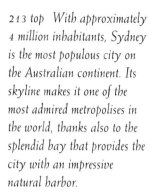

Looking at Circular Quay, the coast road that represents the postcard-pretty portion of the bay lined with fabulous residential complexes, no one would guess that Sydney, the first European colony in Australia, was established in 1778 as a terrifying penal colony. However, the city's main historic monuments, most of which are along Macquarie Street, close to Circular Quay, are the work of Francis Greenway, an architect who arrived here as a prisoner. Some of the most noteworthy are the elegant Parliament House, the State Library, Sydney Hospital, St. James Church and the Mint Building, all of which were built between 1809 and 1821 under Lachlan Macquarie, the enterprising governor of New South Wales. And the splendid Royal Botanic Gardens, at the edge of Hyde Park (a "London" park in both name and appearance), are located where the early colonists once grew

vegetables. With its cobblestone alleys, the district known as The Rocks, once the unsavory haunt of ex-convicts, is a charming place for a stroll.

Quarters with wide avenues, lined with fragrant citrus and eucalyptus trees, radiate out from the center of town. In addition to the original British population, these areas are home to large communities of European descent (first and foremost Italians and Greeks) as well as Middle Easterners and Asians. The only ones missing are the original inhabitants of Australia, the Aborigines. However, their spirit remains in the city's place names. Though Wooloomooloo and Kirribilli may now be all-white residential areas, their names evoke the hypnotic sounds of the didgeridoo, the ancient wind-instrument formed out of hollowed eucalyptus wood, whose sound helped create the world and everything in it.

Auckland
NEW ZEALAND

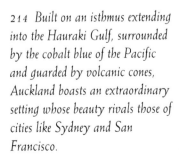

In the Maori language, Auckland is called *Tamaki Makau Rau*, the City of 100 Lovers, because all the Polynesian tribes that arrived there were bewitched by the beauty of this place. According to legend, its first inhabitants were the Turehu, light-skinned people with magical powers who are cited as the forebears of all the *iwi*, or the Maori tribes of the region. Regardless, the first material testimony of human settlements in the Auckland area dates back to 1350, and in the centuries that followed numerous *iwi* built their fortified villages (known as *pa*) on the tops of the 48 volcanic cones that surround it. These tribes coexisted quite peacefully until the mid-18th century, when the Ngati Whatua *iwi* subdued them all and the tribe proclaimed itself *tangata whenua*, the "people of the earth." A little less than a century later, however, what the Ngati Whatua had achieved with force they lost to the English, commanded by Captain William Hobson.

214 Built on an isthmus extending into the Hauraki Gulf, surrounded by the cobalt blue of the Pacific and guarded by volcanic cones, Auckland boasts an extraordinary setting whose beauty rivals those of cities like Sydney and San Francisco.

214-215 The main attractions along the capital's modern and lively waterfront are the Princess Wharf and the America's Cup Village, which has an extraordinary number of yachts moored in front of it. Sailing is the

national sport, and the most eagerly awaited event is the Auckland Anniversary Day Regatta, held in January to commemorate the date Captain William Hobson reached New Zealand.

215 bottom left Built in 1912, the majestic Central Post Office is the most representative building in lively Queen Elizabeth II Square, the heart of the city's social and cultural life. The entrance to Britomart Terminal, the futuristic hub for sea and rail transport, is also located here.

215 bottom right Since 1929 the War Memorial Building, an impressive Neoclassical building located in the Auckland Domain, has houses the Te Papa Whakahiku, New Zealand's most prestigious museum, which has an extraordinary collection of Maori and Polynesian artifacts.

216-217 Visitors should not be misled by the skyscrapers of the Central Business District: in reality, the city is powerfully pervaded by nature and traditional values of the Maori.

216 bottom The Auckland Harbour Bridge, which is about half a mile long and extends over Waitemata Harbour, was inaugurated in 1959 and triggered the urban development of the wilds north of the capital. This area is now covered with densely populated suburbs, and 160,000 vehicles cross the bridge daily.

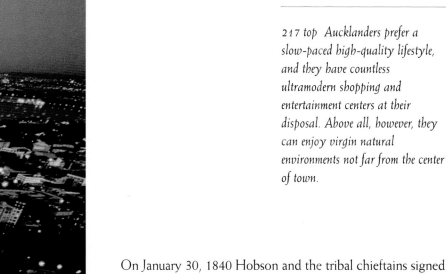

217 top *Aucklanders prefer a slow-paced high-quality lifestyle, and they have countless ultramodern shopping and entertainment centers at their disposal. Above all, however, they can enjoy virgin natural environments not far from the center of town.*

217 bottom *The 1076-foot-tall Sky Tower is the tallest structure of this kind in the Southern Hemisphere. It was inaugurated in 1997 and took just 2 years and 9 months to build. At the top there is a panoramic lounge area with stunning views extending for 50 miles on clear days.*

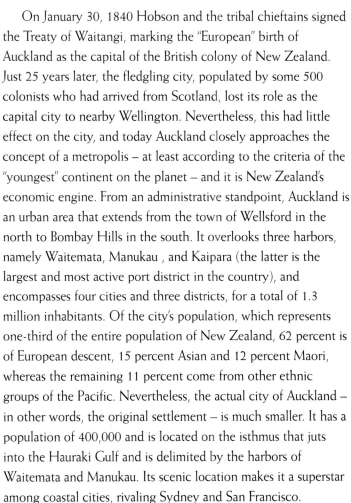

On January 30, 1840 Hobson and the tribal chieftains signed the Treaty of Waitangi, marking the "European" birth of Auckland as the capital of the British colony of New Zealand. Just 25 years later, the fledgling city, populated by some 500 colonists who had arrived from Scotland, lost its role as the capital city to nearby Wellington. Nevertheless, this had little effect on the city, and today Auckland closely approaches the concept of a metropolis – at least according to the criteria of the "youngest" continent on the planet – and it is New Zealand's economic engine. From an administrative standpoint, Auckland is an urban area that extends from the town of Wellsford in the north to Bombay Hills in the south. It overlooks three harbors, namely Waitemata, Manukau , and Kaipara (the latter is the largest and most active port district in the country), and encompasses four cities and three districts, for a total of 1.3 million inhabitants. Of the city's population, which represents one-third of the entire population of New Zealand, 62 percent is of European descent, 15 percent Asian and 12 percent Maori, whereas the remaining 11 percent come from other ethnic groups of the Pacific. Nevertheless, the actual city of Auckland – in other words, the original settlement – is much smaller. It has a population of 400,000 and is located on the isthmus that juts into the Hauraki Gulf and is delimited by the harbors of Waitemata and Manukau. Its scenic location makes it a superstar among coastal cities, rivaling Sydney and San Francisco.

Auckland's splendid natural surroundings, with a sea full of dolphins and whales, numerous city parks and botanical gardens, streets lined with oaks and *kauri* (rubber trees), and its ring of volcanoes make it a relaxing place to live, and its residents devote time to sports and outdoor activities in a way inconceivable elsewhere. In fact, Auckland has the largest number of pleasure boats per capita in the world, earning it the title of "City of Sails."

Auckland's residential districts are characterized by low houses and gardens, whereas the Central Business District has an impressive array of vertical structures. The center is dominated by the 1,076-foot-tall Sky Tower, built in 1997 for the sole

purpose of giving citizens and tourists a spectacular belvedere with a 360-degree view. Today, dozens of skyscrapers are reflected in the waters of the gulf, creating a charming architectural dialog with the city's late-19th-century Victorian buildings. The Britomart Terminal has also been completed recently. This futuristic building, a hub for sea and rail transport, has become the heart of an area designed to offer cultural events and entertainment. Work is also underway to expand the city's most prestigious museum, which houses a noteworthy collection of Polynesian art. Its prized possession is the *waka Te Toki a Tapiri*, an ancient 82-foot Maori war canoe. And perhaps this is the very vessel that carried the first of the "hundred lovers" to the city.

218-219 The Diamond Head Crater owes its name to the fact that the first white colonists of Hawaii were convinced that the formations of calcite crystals at its summit were diamonds.

218 bottom left The Honoluluans' favorite building is Iolani Palace, residence of the last rulers of the archipelago until the monarchy was overthrown.

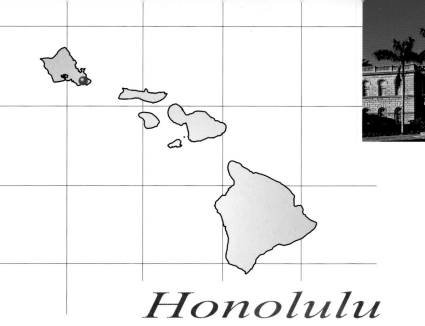

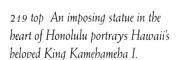

Honolulu

USA

218 bottom right Despite the fact that it is full of skyscrapers and office buildings, downtown Honolulu has a relaxed atmosphere.

219 top An imposing statue in the heart of Honolulu portrays Hawaii's beloved King Kamehameha I.

219 bottom A tourist port dotted with boats is visible next to the green promontory of Magic Island.

Honolulu's urban district embraces the southern coast of the island of Oahu and extends for over a thousand nautical miles to encompass the little islands dotting the immense Pacific Ocean. Because of this administrative oddity, the capital of Hawaii, America's 50th state, is listed in the *Guinness Book of World Records* as the longest city in the world. Nevertheless, this is merely the most apparent peculiarity of Honolulu: With a population of about 400,000, plus about 70,000 tourists arriving daily, it is the only major city of the archipelago. Despite the fact that – at least compared to its "cousins" from the continental United States – it is anything but a metropolis, Honolulu is home to an unparalleled blend of races and cultures, the outcome of the waves of immigration from every world continent that have succeeded each other over the past two centuries of its history, or ever since 1778, when Hawaii was discovered by the great English navigator and explorer, Captain James Cook.

Though critics consider it the "least Hawaiian spot" in Hawaii, only the most inattentive observer will fail to notice the luxuriant scenery surrounding the city's explosive and ultra-American modernity. It doesn't take much to see that the population of Honolulu lives under the beneficial influence of land, sea and wind rather than the effects of stress and concrete. The State Capitol Building, constructed in 1969, is emblematic of the Hawaiians' visceral bond with nature. Its columns look like coconut palms, the halls that house the two legislative houses are shaped like volcanoes, and the entire complex is surrounded by pools, confirming the state's insularity – both geographical and philosophical. Not far from here is Iolani Palace, shaded by the city skyscrapers: The building can be touted as the only royal residence in the United States, and it was built by King David Kalakaua in 1879 for the birthday of his consort, Queen Kapiolani. Its style combines Renaissance and Neo-Classical elements with motifs typical of the native tradition, and the sumptuous

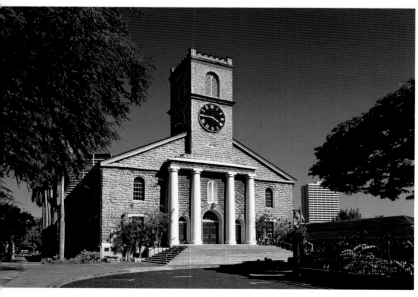

furnishings of the monarchy can still be seen inside it. The nearby monument built to commemorate Kamehameha I, the sovereign who united the archipelago into a single kingdom in 1810, bears witness to Hawaii's monarchic past. The gilded bronze statue is venerated by the local population and is always adorned with leis, the flower garlands typical of Hawaii.

Downtown Honolulu and the adjacent and lively Chinatown have numerous religious buildings. Among the most noteworthy are Kawaihao Church, the first Christian church built in Hawaii (1842); the Buddhist temple of Kuan Kin; and the Shinto shrine of Izumo Taisha. The harbor is another of Honolulu's focal points. It is dominated by the 184-foot-tall Aloha Tower, built in 1926 in the Art Deco style; the traditional Hawaiian greeting "Aloha," engraved in enormous letters across its façade, welcomes the numerous cruise ships that crowd the harbor.

Honolulu boasts museums and prestigious cultural institutions, including the University of Hawaii, located in the lush suburbs of the Moana Valley. This is also the location of the Kennedy Theater, one of the first works designed by Chinese-American architect I. M. Pei. For tourists, however, cultural venues are not nearly as attractive as Waikiki Beach, which is connected to the downtown area by Ala Moana Boulevard. Waikiki is not merely a beach: it is a legend that has been consecrated by hundreds of Hollywood movies and the dreams of thousands of vacationers. Protected by the spectacular volcanic crater of Diamond Head, it is now an enormous stretch of hotels that are as dazzling as they are gargantuan. At the same time, however, in the collective imagination this resort has become the paradigm of a "vacation paradise." Like downtown Honolulu and its statue of King Kamehameha I, Waikiki also has its own tutelary deity. This is the monument dedicated to Duke Kahanamoku, worshipped as the "father" of the sport that has played a leading role in creating the legend of Hawaii: surfing.

220 top The Falls of Clyde, docked at the pier of the Hawaii Maritime Center, was built in Scotland in 1898 and is the last full-rigged four-masted ship in the world.

220 center top The celebrated sandy strip known as Waikiki Beach is famed as a vacation paradise and boasts one of the largest concentrations of hotels on the planet.

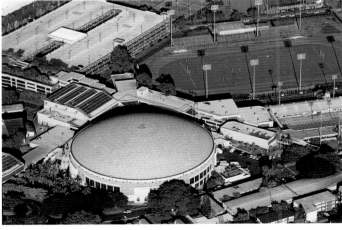

220-221 The tourist port of Honolulu is always crowded with cruise yachts.

221 bottom left The University of Hawaii has magnificent sports facilities.

221 bottom right The Ala Wai Golf Course, behind Waikiki, is one of the many golf courses near the city. Major tournaments are held here. Along with surfing, golf is one of most popular sports among Honolulu residents.

220 center bottom Another popular statue at Waikiki Beach is a tribute to Duke Kahanamoku, who was the Olympic swimming champion in 1912 and invented modern surfing.

220 bottom Consecrated in 1842 by American missionary Hiram Bingham, the Kawaihao Church was Hawaii's first Christian church.

NORTH AMERICA

great cities of the World

When we think of the word "city," the first thing that usually comes to mind is Manhattan, with its breathtaking skyscrapers, the Brooklyn and Verrazano Bridges, the lights of Times Square, Broadway musicals, the artists in Greenwich Village, and Wall Street, the mecca of capitalism. And, of course, the Museum of Modern Art, the Metropolitan Museum, and Yankee Stadium. Above all, however, we associate this Atlantic port city with the Statue of Liberty that has greeted the waves of European immigrants who have crossed the Atlantic over the centuries to pursue their American dream. There is no doubt about it: New York is the stereotype of the great metropolis of the 20th century and of the new millennium, despite the horrifying terrorist attack of September 11, 2001 that destroyed the World Trade Center, wiping out one of the symbols of the city and of world power, and killing several thousand people.

And yet the quintessential city was established here almost by chance. Founded in 1624 by a group of Dutch colonists who wanted to buy furs from the native population, it was originally named New Amsterdam. However, it quickly became a bone of contention between Britain and the Netherlands, the two powers that dominated the seas – and markets – in the early 17th century, after the fall of the Spanish Empire. Thus, despite the opposition of the settlement's last governor, Peter Stuyvesant, after the three Anglo-Dutch Wars of 1664-1674 the Dutch ceded that insignificant outpost on the estuary of the Hudson River in exchange for an island with valuable nutmeg plantations in the Sonda archipelago – or so the story goes.

Anecdotes aside, the history of New York is entwined with the events of the 20th century. By this time, its fame extended well beyond the New World and the city had become a point of reference and a paradigm of beauty and modernity. Like Chicago, it grew enormously between the 1870s and the 1880s, and by the year 1900 it had a population of over four million, second only to London.

During the 1880s the most important word in the history of American metropolises was coined: skyscraper. The invention of the enormous vertical structures that were destined to give virtually every American city a distinctive skyline can be attributed to architect George A. Fuller, who in about 1880 solved some of the problems related to the load-carrying capacity of large buildings. In 1889, using steel produced on an industrial scale via a process patented by the Briton Henry Bessemer, he built his first skyscraper: the Tacoma Building in Chicago, which, with 13 stories and a height of 165 feet, was hailed as a triumph of engineering. However, New York wanted its own place in the history of skyscrapers, and its wish was fulfilled in 1902 when Fuller completed the Flatiron Building, a 285-foot giant with 21 floors.

Then in the 1920s John J. FitzGerald, a reporter for *The Morning Telegraph*, gave the city its moniker "The Big Apple" in his articles, borrowing the name that African-American jazz musicians from New Orleans used in referring to New York. A short time later, the extraordinary buildings that have made the city immortal began to challenge the heavens. The Chrysler Building was completed in 1930 and rose to a height of over 1,000 feet – only to be surpassed just a year later by the 102-floor Empire State Building (1,250 feet), which remained the tallest skyscraper in the world for nearly half a century.

Nevertheless, even now that dozens of countries have risen to the challenge with dizzying constructions like the Petronas Towers in Kuala Lumpur or Taipei 101 in Taiwan, the allure of the Big Apple is unique: New York remains one of the biggest cities in the world, with a population of 8 million and a metropolitan area with an estimated population of about 20 million. And it continues to be a beacon on a continent characterized by its enormous cities. According to the figures supplied by the Population Division of the United Nations Department of Economic and Social Affairs, in the United States alone there are thirteen other metropolitan areas with populations in excess of three million people: Los Angeles, Chicago, Washington, San Francisco, Philadelphia, Boston, Detroit, Dallas,

Houston, Atlanta, Miami, Seattle and Phoenix, with Minneapolis, Cleveland and San Diego not far behind. In Canada, only Toronto and Montreal can compete with these numbers, whereas Vancouver and, to an even greater extent, Ottawa are smaller cities on a more human scale.

If we consider only Canada and the United States, due to the historic and cultural uniformity of these countries (though according to official cartography and international economic agreements the continent includes Mexico) North America covers an area of a little more than 7.7 million square miles, with a total population of about 320 million people, only 31 million of whom live in Canada. Considering the fact that 77% of the population lives in metropolitan areas, this probably makes it the world's most urbanized continent. Nearly 130 million people, or 40% of the total, are concentrated in the twenty largest cities of North America, and with the exception of Los Angeles and Vancouver on the West Coast, most of the continent's metropolises are clustered along the East Coast and around the Great Lakes.

And yet the continent that was discovered just 500 years ago by the Europeans and was colonized in the centuries that followed was unquestionably rural until at least the mid-19th century. In 1830, with most of the population engaged in farming, trade and mining activities, the level of urbanization in the United States was just 9%. New York, Philadelphia, Boston, New Orleans, Baltimore, Cincinnati and Montreal were North America's biggest cities, but they were still decidedly pre-industrial centers, as portrayed by Martin Scorsese's film *Gangs of New York*. Just forty years later, the first industrial revolution came to the New World, and by 1870 city residents represented 23% of the total population. The definitive transition from an agricultural and trade society to an industrial economy came at the turn of the 20th century. Hundreds of thousands of new immigrants – the lifeblood of the continent – arrived, domestic transportation systems improved, and technological innovations like the elevator, the radio and the automobile became widespread. With the California Gold Rush of 1849 the first major

settlements were also established in the West: Los Angeles grew to 100,000 inhabitants.

After World War II, the rapid ascent of America as a superpower and the baby boom of the Fifties and Sixties took care of the rest, transforming North America into what can be called an enormous semidesert continent with a handful of massive urban concentrations. Despite the undeniable appeal of many American cities, the hypertrophy characteristic of these enormous metropolises seems to have engendered inevitable problems that are not found in the smaller-scale cities of Canada. This may also be due to administrative decisions that have not always been adequate.

In their astonishing growth of the past few decades, many cities have expanded to encompass the urban area of other cities; in some cases these smaller cities have been incorporated in the administrative structure, but in others they have remained independent. Los Angeles is a prime example. Its metropolitan area is vast, and it includes dozens of other cities like Hollywood, Bel Air, Santa Monica and Beverly Hills. However, the first two are part of the city of Los Angeles, whereas the latter are independent. In some of these cities, this confusion on an institutional level has led to internal competition and difficult territorial management. Recently, the string of new quarters around the initial cities has created problems for the more central areas, which find themselves without any alternatives for economic development, since the pressure of the outlying areas has essentially atrophied them.

Nonetheless, the North American metropolis – or at least its idealization – has marked the technological dream of the 20th century, becoming the emblem of progress and human civilization, and a symbol encompassing new forms of architecture, new urban spaces and new social contexts. The image of these metropolitan worlds has circled the globe with Hollywood movies, which have celebrated their grandeur and harshly criticized their flaws. But they have always given other countries a taste of the legend of American cities. A telling example is Woody Allen's genteel and romantic portrait of Manhattan, to the tune of George Gershwin's *Rhapsody in Blue*: "New York was his city, and it always would be."

223 left The Manhattan and Brooklyn Bridges extend eastward over the East River.

223 center The white tower of First Canadian Place, which is 978 feet tall, rises above downtown Toronto.

223 right The waters of Puget Sound reflect the clear blue sky of Toronto.

Vancouver
CANADA

Over the past decade, all the studies conducted to identify the most "livable" city in the world have ranked Vancouver as one of the very best. Numerous factors contribute to the flattering status of the capital of British Columbia. The most evident is its spectacular location, ringed by the Grouse, Cypress, and Seymour Mountains (just 20 minutes away by car) to the north, and with the Pacific Ocean to the west, its waves tempered by splendid Vancouver Island and gently lapping on the shores of the city. Together with the False and Fraser Rivers, the ocean forms a "waterway" that makes the Vancouver suburbs look like a charming archipelago. One of these suburbs is Stanley Park, with 1000 acres of birch trees, maples and conifers, and it is the largest city park in Canada. As far as climate is concerned, the temperature rarely drops below freezing in winter, and the summer resembles a long, balmy spring. The only drawback is that the area gets plenty of rainfall. But one can't have everything – and, after all, Vancouver is located in gelid Canada.

It is no accident that Vancouver has Canada's highest per capita spending for outdoor activities and sports equipment. Tellingly, it also happens to be the urban area with the highest population growth in North America. If one adds its many entertainment opportunities, its vibrant economy (Vancouver is the main port of trade with Asia and the Pacific) and its cosmopolitan atmosphere (its nickname "Hongcouver" reflects that it is second only to San Francisco in the size of its Chinese community), it is natural that many have chosen to call this city home.

The metropolitan area has 18 municipalities with a population of about 2,150,000 people, 568,000 of whom live in

224 top left Vancouver began to develop vertically in the 1930s, and its now-historic skyscrapers, made of stone and embellished with small towers, are reflected by the glass façades of the modern giants that have been built next to them.

224 top right The majestic elliptical Vancouver Public Library was inaugurated in 1995. Architect Moshe Safdie wanted to create a structure that would offset the city's soaring skyscrapers because, as he noted, "Vancouver needs to anchor itself to the ground."

224 bottom Protected by the Grouse, Cypress and Seymour Mountains to the north, and set along the Ocean, Vancouver enjoys a spectacular position. In fact, together with the False and Fraser Rivers, the ocean forms a "waterway" that gives its suburbs the appearance of a charming archipelago.

224-225 The capital of British Columbia holds the record as the North American city with the most skyscrapers per capita. It has been constructed vertically because its residents want to enjoy the fabulous panorama of the sea and mountains from the own homes. At the same time, however, there is also a lack of space. Vancouver trails New York and San Francisco as the cities with the highest population density on the continent.

225 bottom Robson Square, the heart of the city's business district and social life, also boasts a prestigious museum. This is the Vancouver Art Gallery, where paintings by local artist Emily Carr are also exhibited. Born in 1871, she was the most intense and expressive interpreter of the colors of her land.

the core city, which covers the western end of Burrard Peninsula. Of the latter residents, 25 percent are in the 25-45 year range. In short, Vancouver is a young city, founded just over 100 years ago. To celebrate its first century, in 1986 Vancouver hosted the World's Fair. This event gave the city buildings like Canada Place and the geodetic dome of Science World, which are part of a dazzling skyline that has over 700 high-rise residential complexes – far more than New York City. After all, an apartment with a view of the ocean or the mountains makes city living even more desirable.

In spite of their size, however, the buildings in Vancouver do not offend the landscape, but miraculously add to its charm. As early as 1957, starting with the inauguration of the BC Electric Building – decorated with tiles colored blue like the ocean, green like the forest and black like winter clouds – scores of architects have strived to forge a dialog between modernism and nature. Some of the most interesting examples of this "school" include the Central Library, the Museum of Anthropology at the University of British Columbia, and the Law Courts, all of which were designed by the famed Canadian Arthur Erickson (b. 1924), a pioneer of the rebirth of Modernism in Canada, and known for his unique ability to handle large-scale contemporary architecture which is sensitive to its location by exploiting the effects of various materials and structural systems. He is the chief architect of Simon Fraser University

Likewise, a naturalistic philosophy is evident in One Wall Centre, the 492-foot-tall elliptical building designed by the prize-winning Peter Busby, which was selected as the skyscraper of the year in 2001, and the Newton Public Library, which covers 16,000 square feet in the verdant suburban area of that name. A team from Patkau Architects designed it as a "primitive" structure inspired by biological cycles.

In keeping with its role as a model city, Vancouver has been chosen as the venue for the World Urban Forum in 2006. This meeting unites public agencies, private concerns and international experts under one roof to discuss forms of sustainable development for urbanization. For the city government, the Forum will also effectively serve as a dress rehearsal for 2010, when Vancouver will host the first "green" Winter Olympics in history. Eco-compatible buildings and sports complexes powered by clean and renewable energy are currently being built for the Olympic Games.

226 top The dome of the Science World, also known as the "golf ball," has a roof composed of 766 glass triangles. Built for the 1986 Expo, today it houses the OMNIMAX Theatre, with a circular screen covering a diameter of 27 meters.

226 center Built in 1937 to connect the center to the suburbs of North Shore, the Lions Gate Bridge is one of the symbols of the city. The bridge is often congested with traffic, but the people of Vancouver have criticized plans to widen it, as this would ruin its appearance.

226 bottom Making the Vancouver Public Library a lively and joyous place was imperative for its designer, who created the Promenade, which winds its way along the entire length of the building. A glass roof allows natural light to "color" the space.

226-227 At sunset, the glass façades of the skyscrapers in the City are tinged with gold. The tall buildings do not mar the seascape, and instead they miraculously augment its appeal by creating an expressive dialogue with the natural surroundings.

227 bottom This general view clearly shows that the structure of the Vancouver Public Library is a contemporary allusion to the Colosseum in Rome. Architect Moshe Safdie designed all of Library Square, which covers an entire city block and is also the site of the Federal Office Tower and numerous shops.

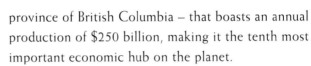

Seattle

USA

With the cry "the world is not for sale," on November 30, 1999 tens of thousands of people from many countries – ordinary citizens, union members and representatives of over a thousand organized civic movements – took over the streets of Seattle, preventing the inaugural session of the Third Ministerial Conference of the World Trade Organization. These events have now gone down in history, and the term "people of Seattle" is used to refer to anyone who fights globalization and the power of multinationals.

Why did this episode, which made world headlines, take place in Seattle? Because the city is a symbol: not only for the advocates of global trade, but also for those who view the WTO as an enemy to be vanquished. The capital of Washington State, Seattle ranks first in the United States in terms of economic growth, and it is tangible proof of the benefits of world trade. Every year, about $34 billion in exports go through its ultramodern port on the Pacific. In turn, it is part of a macro-region – Cascadia, which extends from Eugene, Oregon, to Vancouver, in the Canadian

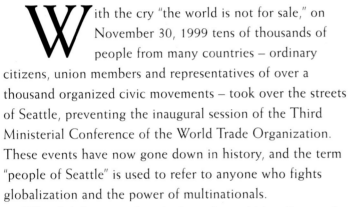

province of British Columbia – that boasts an annual production of $250 billion, making it the tenth most important economic hub on the planet.

Seattle is also home to Boeing, America's top exporter, and Microsoft, the most important company on the worldwide software market; Microsoft founder Bill Gates (the world's richest man) was born here. What's more, Seattle is also the location of the headquarters of AT&T's cellular telephone division, the home of Amazon, the world leader in online book sales, and Starbucks Coffee, the multinational coffee company that has been blacklisted by anti-global activists.

At the same time, Seattle has traditionally been a "left-wing" city. This tradition dates back to 1919, when the city's longshoremen, together with the Industrial Workers of the World, coordinated the first general strike in American history, right here in Seattle. At the same time, this informal and unconventional city – Seattle feels closer to the more Nordic-style Canadian culture than to the glitz of Southern California – has long been the place that spawned many of America's "alternative" fads and cultures.

In spite of its extraordinary concentration of financial resources, Seattle is a small city with a population of just over 500,000 (this figure rises to about 3 million if its lush green suburbs are included). Even today, the city has managed to live in close contact with its enchanting natural surroundings, as it sits on Elliott Bay and is protected by Lake Washington and Mt. Rainier. Though it was a modest frontier town at the end of the 19th century, it prospered during the Gold Rush. Today, its focal points are the historic district around the Victorian-style Pioneer Square, austere-looking Capitol Hill with homes surrounded by parks and gardens, and the lively student area of University District. Just beyond this area, but accessible by monorail, is Seattle Center, the skyscraper district that arose in 1962, when the city hosted the World's Fair. This is the location of the Space Needle, the soaring tower that has become the

228 top Some of the most prestigious companies in the United States are concentrated in Seattle's financial district.

228 bottom Pier 59 is located along the Waterfront, which offers a splendid view of Elliott Bay. The long wharf, built in the late 19th century, now serves as an access to the underwater dome at the Seattle Aquarium.

228-229 Every year, $34 million in export goods transit through the ultramodern port of Seattle.

229 bottom left The sinuous Lake Washington Ship Canal divides the city into two sectors.

229 bottom right Seattle, with its financial district crowded with dazzling skyscrapers, is surrounded by stunning natural scenery.

230-231 The Space Needle is the hallmark of the Seattle skyline. Over 600 feet tall, this tower was built in just 400 days and was inaugurated in April 1962 for the "Century XXI" World Expo.

230 bottom Financed by Paul Allen, cofounder of Microsoft, and inaugurated in 2000, the Experience Music Project is an interactive venue designed to stir enthusiasm about music. Mementos of the great stars of American rock are also displayed here.

symbol of Seattle, and the area also boasts theaters, exhibition centers and an amusement park.

It is here that Frank O. Gehry, a genius of contemporary architecture, fully vented his creativity – in the utterly unconventional and "jumbled" way that distinguishes him – to design the Experience Music Project, a museum devoted to the creative evolution of American music. The complex, which was funded by Microsoft cofounder Paul Allen, who thus fulfilled his dream of displaying his Jimi Hendrix mementos, is a cluster of different buildings in undulating shapes and psychedelic colors. The buildings represent the energy of music and are inspired by the legendary Fender Stratocaster guitar that Hendrix would destroy after every concert. In addition to the gallery devoted to the great rock star, Gehry's masterpiece also features extraordinary spaces devoted to two illustrious citizens of Seattle: Quincy Jones and Ray Charles.

231 top From above, the Experience Music Project looks like a conglomeration of different buildings in dazzling colors, connected by a monorail. The fragmented, undulating forms of the complex, designed by Frank O. Gehry, were inspired by Jimi Hendrix's famous Fender Stratocaster guitar.

231 center The observation platform of the Space Needle (which also boasts a stylish restaurant) is shaped like a missile. The elevators rising to the platform also have a "space-age" appearance, and the ride to the top takes just 41 seconds.

231 bottom In the middle of historic Pioneer Square, the replica of an Indian totem pole is a tribute to the earliest residents of the area where the city was founded during the Gold Rush. The square is lined with late-19th-century buildings, all of which have carefully been restored.

Seattle

San Francisco

USA

San Francisco is a thorn in the side of America's neo-cons. For the 800,000 denizens of San Francisco (and the 7 million in the outlying county), however, it is "the last stronghold of civilization." Indubitably, both sides are exaggerating, but one thing is certain: San Francisco is the most liberal city in the United States. The gay marriages that were celebrated here are merely the latest proof of the atmosphere that reigns in this "happy peninsula" of Northern California, where all forms of prejudice are banished and no one – with the exception of neo-conservatives – feels out of place. Talking about the atmosphere, the air in San Francisco is also special from a strictly climatic standpoint. The city is a notable exception in the West Coast state that is the epitome of sunshine and beaches, especially if we are to believe Mark Twain, who said, "The coldest winter I ever spent was summer in San Francisco." The famous writer may have exaggerated somewhat, but the breeze blowing in from the Pacific in August makes wearing a jacket a must, and a blanket of fog often covers the bay. In reality, however, San Francisco enjoys an eternal springtime: sometimes capricious but always stimulating; it makes flowers bloom like new and revolutionary ideas.

In 1953, the City Lights Bookstore, the first bookshop in the United States dedicated to paperbacks, opened in North Beach, in district founded by Italian immigrants. Lawrence Ferlinghetti, the bookshop's owner was also a poet and novelist and he soon became friends with other "dissolute" colleagues, namely Allen Ginsberg and Jack Kerouac. Together, in 1957 they spawned an extraordinary albeit controversial literary movement – and attitude – better known as the Beat Generation. Ten years later, San Francisco had its "Summer of Love," and this time it was a very hot summer indeed. The Grateful Dead, the Jefferson Airplane and Janis Joplin played in the parks. To the cries of peace and freedom, the hippie movement was born, while the seeds for the legendary student revolts of 1968 were sown at the nearby university campus in Berkeley.

With all due respect to its critics, San Francisco is widely considered one of the prettiest cities in America. The bay, dominated by the great orange span of the soaring Golden Gate Bridge, is one of the key elements in the beauty of this city. The bridge, which opened in 1937, is one of the world's engineering icons; it was named for the fact that, during the great California Gold Rush of 1849, the bay it spans was an entry point for hopeful miners flooding in in search of fortunes and a departure point for them when leaving for the Klondike Gold Rush in Canada in the late 1890s. Today, however, nature itself represents the true wealth of the bay: Golden Gate National Park is one of the largest protected urban areas in the world. In addition to 40 miles of coastline, it includes Alcatraz (the island that, until just a few decades ago, was a fearsome penitentiary) and Angel Island, and it encompasses 19 ecosystems with

232 center With a population of just 800,000, San Francisco does not resemble the typical sprawling American metropolis.

232 bottom The unmistakable white outline of Coit Tower stands out in this view of the Bay Area.

233 bottom right San Francisco City Hall, built between 1913 and 1915 to house city government offices, was inspired by the Italian Renaissance. The interior is finished in California marble, Indiana limestone and oak, and the dome on the building has a diameter of over 115 feet. It has been the site of a number of historic events, like the wedding of Joe DiMaggio and Marilyn Monroe in 1954.

232-233 Opened to traffic at exactly noon on May 28, 1937, the bright red-orange Golden Gate Bridge is indubitably the symbol of San Francisco.

233 bottom left This aerial view shows the pavilion of the Palace of Fine Arts, built for the 1915 World's Fair.

234-235 *The splendid Victorian houses of Alamo Square, referred to as "The Painted Ladies," stand out against the skyline dominated by the slim profile of the Transamerica Pyramid and the monumental Bank of America Center.*

234 bottom left *The Piedmont Boutique on Haight Street owes its fame to the legs of a gigantic blowup doll that stick out from the first-floor window over the shop.*

234 bottom right *Introduced in the late 19th-century as horse-drawn carriages, San Francisco's famous cable cars are now operated electrically, and they are one of the city's leading tourist attractions.*

235 top *Lombard Street, an exhausting climb of curves and sharp bends, is one of San Francisco's most fashionable spots. Splendid flowerbeds decorated this street, which is paved with original brickwork and is lined with magnificent Victorian homes.*

235 bottom *San Francisco's Chinatown is the largest and oldest one in the United States, covering an area of eight neighborhoods. The Chinese began to move to the California city in the mid-1800s, after China was defeated by Great Britain in the Opium War.*

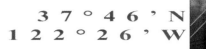

numerous rare animal species. From a "morphological" standpoint, the unique aspect of San Francisco's urban fabric comes from the hilly landscape on which the city was built. Many of its streets are so steep that, to help pedestrians get around, horse-drawn tramlines were inaugurated at the end of the 19th century. Today, some of those nostalgic cable cars, which are operated electrically, have been declared historical assets and represent one of the city's main attractions. Though most visitors flock to Fisherman's Wharf, the old fishing port that has now been transformed into a tourist attraction, complete with ferries that leave for the traditional tour of Alcatraz, San Francisco has plenty of other sights to see. The skyline is dominated by the skyscrapers of the Financial District, including the impressive Bank of America Building and the Transamerica Pyramid. The former, which is the largest

building in the city, boasts a thousand windows with a view of the bay. Designed by Skidmore, Owings & Merrill in collaboration with Wurster, Bernardi & Emmons, it was constructed in 1969 and became famous as the set for the movie *The Towering Inferno* starring Paul Newman. The Transamerica tower, designed in 1972 by the leading Californian architect William L. Pereira, boasts a daring pyramidal shape that rises to a height of over 850 feet. Its foundations rest on a site that is part of the city's literary history: the hotel where famous figures stayed – from Rudyard Kipling to Robert Louis Stevenson and Mark Twain. This was also where Sun Yat-Sen drew up the first Chinese constitution and organized the overthrow of Pu Yi, who has gone down in history as China's last emperor, scarcely a despot, with most of his life dominated by the Japanese. Also in downtown San Francisco, located next to the Financial District,

San Francisco

is the oldest and liveliest Chinatown in America.

San Francisco was founded by the Spanish in 1776, but only a handful of historic buildings survived the catastrophic fire of April 18, 1906. It broke out following the most violent earthquake in the history of Northern California, which occurred along the Pacific Plate. (According to modern estimates, the earthquake was an 8.3 on the Richter scale.) Thus, the city's oldest building is the Mission Dolores, which was built by the Jesuits in the late 18th century. This is also the name of one of the city's most bohemian neighborhoods, which is famous not only for the more than 200 murals decorating its walls (the most colorful and spectacular one is a tribute to Carlos Santana, who began his musical career here) but also for the factory of one of most beloved "inventions" of America: Levi-Strauss jeans, which were originally work pants worn by

gold miners. However, every neighborhood in San Francisco has its own distinctive personality. Two examples are Castro, the colorful gay enclave, and Nob Hill, the historic upper-class district with splendid homes (many of which made of wood) surrounded by gardens dotted with hydrangeas.

The city has recently become a leading venue for fans of contemporary architecture, since many of the buildings that have been completed or are currently under construction have been designed by prestigious figures. Among them is San Francisco Museum of Modern Art, the work of Swiss architect Mario Botta in 1993. The museum is the most important of the extraordinary exhibition spaces of the recently restored Yerba Buena, the site of the first Spanish settlement in the area. Another museum has just been completed nearby, incorporating an old power plant built in 1907; its collections are dedicated to the Jewish community and its history. The museum is the work of Daniel Libeskind, who also designed the Jewish Museum in Berlin, and here as well the architect has managed to create forms with a dramatic symbolic impact. Yerba Buena is also the location of a museum complex devoted to Hispanic culture. The architect, Mexican Ricardo Legorreta, has conceived a powerful red structure freely inspired by the traditional buildings of his homeland. The restoration work required to repair the damages caused by the earthquake that struck San Francisco in 1989 has also led to the innovative interpretation of historic buildings. Italian architect Gae Aulenti renovated the Neo-Classical Old Library, which since 2003 has housed the splendid Museum of Asian Art, and the new Academy of Science, located in Golden Gate Park, is scheduled for completion in 2008. Architect Renzo Piano designed an impressive structure that, to use his own words, "belongs to nature," as it will be covered with a rippling roof that encloses a "living space." In short, it is architecture that reflects the landscape and perfectly expresses the ideals of the sophisticated and unconventional San Franciscans.

236 top Built by Baron Makoto Hagiwara for the California Midwinter International Exposition in 1894, the Japanese Tea Garden is one of the most picturesque spots in Golden Gate Park.

236 center Fisherman's Wharf, the traditional dock for San Francisco's fishing boats, is one of the city's most popular attractions. It is famous for its historic promenade, spectacular view and excellent restaurants.

237 bottom left Golden Gate Park covers an area of about 990 acres, and there are several prestigious museums on its grounds. The Botanical Gardens have over 7000 plant varieties.

237 bottom right Mission Dolores, founded in 1791 by Franciscan father Francisco Palóu, is one of the few buildings that withstood the terrible earthquake of 1906.

236 bottom Ghirardelli Square is a popular tourist destination. It was named after Domenico Ghirardelli, an Italian immigrant who founded the Ghirardelli Chocolate Company in 1852.

236-237 The San Francisco Museum of Modern Art at Yerba Buena was Swiss architect Mario Botta's first work in the United States. The monumental building is composed of squared elements.

238 top right A view of the Hollywood Walk of Fame on Hollywood Boulevard: for 18 blocks, the sidewalk is studded with countless stars bearing the names of the movie personalities of yesterday and today.

238 top left No. 6925 Hollywood Boulevard is the address of the famous Grauman's Chinese Theater, inaugurated on May 18, 1927 with the premiere of Cecil B. DeMille's movie King of Kings.

Los Angeles
USA

238 bottom Sunset Boulevard, which is nearly 20 miles long and is lined with palm trees, has been immortalized by dozens of films. It "starts" at Olivera Street, in downtown Los Angeles, and ends in Malibu, on the Pacific Ocean.

238-239 There are about 480 skyscrapers concentrated in the financial district. These giants tower over the Hispanic-style buildings of El Pueblo de Los Angeles, the earliest settlement of what is now the most sprawling metropolis in the United States.

To get an idea of what Los Angeles is, one needs to look down on it from the window of an aircraft. For a good half hour before touchdown at Los Angeles International Airport – and 30 minutes in the air covers plenty of ground – identical images move before the viewer's eyes: a sea of roofs of low houses, yards of different sizes, swimming pools in a surreal shade of turquoise, palm trees here and there, and ten-lane highways with interchanges tied up into knots that seem impossible to exit.

According to city demographic data, Los Angeles has a population of 4 million. However, this is only the population of the city proper. In reality, with its many individually named suburbs, the urban area stretches seamlessly for hundreds of square miles and encompasses nearly 18 million residents. What is even more worrying is the fact that Los Angeles County has more registered cars than all of Russia.

Based on these preliminary figures, a typical visitor might just want to get off the plane on landing – and catch the next one out. And yet LA deserves to be given a chance. After all, the "City of the Angels" is the place where dreams are made. In turn, it is a hill with the word "Hollywood" written across it in enormous letters; it is Beverly Hills, dotted with the lavish homes of the rich and famous. Los Angeles is the glowing temple of kitsch – Grauman's Chinese Theater – at 6925 Hollywood Boulevard, with the footprints of movie stars set in concrete. It is also the trendy shops of Melrose and convertibles zipping down Sunset Boulevard. It is the beaches of Santa Monica and Venice, with all the "local color" of beach volleyball, skateboard fanatics, surfers and body builders. It is the fantasy world of Disneyland, in the suburbs of Anaheim, which attracts 6 million children of all ages every year. Indeed, the list could go on forever, because as monstrous, heavily trafficked and crowded as it might seem, Los Angeles is familiar . . . we have all already "experienced" it through countless movies.

239 bottom left A classic postcard view of Hollywood Hills, with the San Fernando Valley in the background. This famous sign was installed in 1929 and originally said "Hollywoodland." The suffix "land" fell off in 1949.

239 bottom right An aerial view of one of LA's wealthiest intersections: Rodeo Drive – famous for luxury shopping – and Wiltshire Boulevard, with the impressive Regent Beverly Wiltshire Hotel.

240-241 *The Los Angeles Philharmonic commissioned architect Frank O. Gehry to design the Walt Disney Concert Hall, an awesome building/sculpture clad with titanium panels. The complex was funded by a $50-million donation made by Lillian Disney in 1987 to commemorate her husband. Together with the nearby Museum of Contemporary Art, the auditorium has ushered in a new and exciting chapter in the cultural life of downtown LA.*

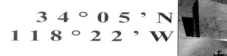

Even its residents define Los Angeles as a set of "villages" in search of a city. At the end of the 19th century, the immense valley of Southern California, where the city was eventually built, was dotted with widely spaced ranches owned by Spanish farmers and cattle breeders. They were built in rapid sequence starting in 1781, when the Spanish missionaries founded El Pueblo de Nuestra Señora la Reina de los Angeles del Río Porciúncula. Though it has radically been transformed, the "center" of Los Angeles, about 12 miles from the ocean, remains the territory of that ancient pueblo, and it is home to an enormous Hispanic population. Likewise, it boasts buildings reflecting "Mediterranean" architecture. One example is Union Station, built in 1939 in an Art Deco style mixed with Moorish elements. Today, the new heart of the Hispanic community is the splendid Catholic Cathedral of Our Lady of the Angels, designed by Rafael Moneo and built in 2002.

So-called Downtown Los Angeles is a grid of anonymous high-rise office buildings, but on its outskirts, the city manages to shed its stereotype as a "lightweight" spot – a place to follow movie stars and laze about on beaches and in nightspots – and it transforms itself into a cultural destination. In fact, this is the location of the Museum of Contemporary Art, an extraordinary space devoted to the latest art trends; it was designed by Japanese architect Arata Isozaki as a "village in the valley of skyscrapers." This is also the location of the Disney Concert Hall, the remarkable structure that is the brainchild of the modernist architect Frank O. Gehry.

In reality, all of Los Angeles County, from Malibu to Long Beach, is a curious collection of architecture. It has everything from trim little suburban houses to faux-mediaeval castles, Palladian villas and astonishing high-tech homes, like the eco-sustainable villa that Robert Redford recently completed in Santa Monica and the numerous houses designed by Richard O. Gehry. And speaking of Gehry, the architect's studio is housed in a bizarre construction overlooking the hippy beach of Venice, one of Los Angeles' most distinctive areas.

240 bottom The Universal Studios are a leading tourist attraction in Los Angeles. Shows by stuntmen, concerts and reconstructions of the sets of famous major motion pictures – like Jaws, King Kong *and* Back to the Future – *give visitors the chance to experience the magic of Hollywood for a day.*

241 top The broad courtyard at Two California Plaza features inventive "dancing fountains." The 750-foot-tall building is one of the giants of downtown LA. Designed by Arthur Erickson, the skyscraper was completed in 1992.

241 center The Hollywood and Highland subway station of the Red Line is famous because it is located under the Kodak Theatre, where the Academy Awards ceremony is held every year.

241 bottom The immense glass-and-steel structure of the West Hall of the Los Angeles Convention Center, near the financial district and the Civic Center, attracts 3 million visitors annually.

Los Angeles

242-243 Santa Monica is the oldest and largest of LA's resort suburbs, and it has long been home to a varied community of writers, artists, actors and rock stars, from mystery writer Raymond Chandler to Elton John.

243 top left A spectacular aerial view of the coastline stretching from Malibu to downtown Los Angeles. These beaches are popular with Pacific Coast surfers.

243 top right Inventive murals color the houses in Venice, the city's most liberal suburb. It was founded in 1905 by businessman Abbott Kinney, who transformed a marshy coastal area into a resort town.

242 Built in 1922, the Santa Monica Pier features a Ferris wheel and small roller coaster. The exclusive Sun and Sea Beach Club is located on the beach north of the pier. The complex once housed the servants' quarters of the villa (now demolished) of billionaire William Randolph Hearst.

243 center A picturesque view of the Washington Boulevard Pier, which marks the southern boundary of the long sandy strip of Venice Beach.

243 bottom Located between Venice and Redondo Beach, Marina del Rey is the world's largest manmade harbor. It opened in 1965.

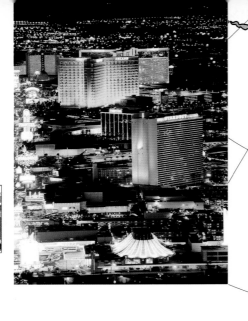

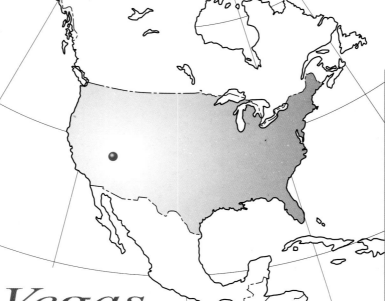

Las Vegas

USA

244 top Naturally, the night offers the best views of the spectacular panorama of the "city of sin," a nonstop extravaganza of neon lights, psychedelic colors and ostentatious architecture in the middle of the wild desert of Nevada.

244 bottom The Tropicana: which was established in the Fifties, earned its place in history because this is where the celebrated Parisian Folies Bergères staged their first show abroad.

I n the space of just a few hours, visitors can have dinner at the top of the Eiffel Tower, enjoy a show in the Colosseum, visit the Egyptian temple of Karnak and take a picture of the Statue of Liberty. And in between they can get married and even win a little money. All this – and a lot more – can only happen in dreams. Or in Las Vegas.

"Only in Las Vegas" is the slogan of the world's acknowledged capital of entertainment. Here, however, this is more than just a clever advertising concept. The "city of sin" – this is its best-known sobriquet – is truly one of a kind, not only because of the millions of visitors who come in here each year (spending an average of 3.9 hours a day at gaming tables or in front of slot machines) and the 100,000 couples who come here to get married, but due also to the 4,000 people who move here every month, attracted by the city's endless employment opportunities and the State of Nevada's low-demand tax policies. In fact, Las Vegas holds the record as the fastest-growing city in the United States: Between 1950 and today, its population has increased fifty-seven-fold.

Notably, Las Vegas is also a young city. The valley in which it is located was not even discovered until the mid-19th century, and in 1905 – when the railroad arrived – there was only an encampment there. Immediately after that, a saloon was opened and people began to gamble as a pastime. Curiously, in 1910 Las Vegas became the first place in the United States to ban gambling (after all, a Mormon community was also established here). It was not until the Thirties that this restriction was lifted, in order to use gambling proceeds to fund the establishment of schools. As a result, Las Vegas was untouched by the Great Depression and began to prosper. Today, 43 percent of Nevada's tax revenues come from gambling, and 34 percent of state's annual income from taxes is used for education.

Two other dates – among the many that have also revolved around less-than-upstanding figures – are fundamental in the history of Las Vegas. One is 1941, when the first hotel-casino

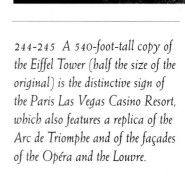

244-245 A 540-foot-tall copy of the Eiffel Tower (half the size of the original) is the distinctive sign of the Paris Las Vegas Casino Resort, which also features a replica of the Arc de Triomphe and of the façades of the Opéra and the Louvre.

245 bottom left Marked by a Disney-like entrance, the MGM Grand Hotel & Casino, with 5034 rooms distributed in four buildings, is the biggest hotel in the world. One of its attractions is a park that recreates a natural habitat for a family of lions.

245 bottom right The Flamingo was inaugurated on New Year's Day of 1946, making it the oldest hotel-casino on the Strip. Its first owner was Benjamin Siegel, the gangster who "created" the legend of Las Vegas. Hollywood dedicated the movie Bugsy to Siegel.

246 top left A copy of the Winged Victory of Samothrace decorates one of the pools at Caesar's Palace. The theme of this resort casino, inaugurated in 1966, is classical antiquity. For example, the waitresses wear a peplum.

246 top right Copies of the Empire State Building and the Chrysler Building, both of which are part of the mega-resort New York, New York, dominated the Vegas skyline.

246 bottom The Montecarlo Resort & Casino is one of the most dazzling stars in the empire of Steve Wynn, the king of Vegas casinos. One of his creations is Le Rêve, a mega-resort named after a Picasso painting. In fact, Wynn is also one of the most envied art collectors in the world.

246-247 Casinos housed in wooden buildings have survived next to the skyscrapers along the Strip, and their atmosphere evokes the early days in the history of Las Vegas. Oddly enough, Las Vegas was the first town in America to ban gambling in 1910. The first permit granted to a casino dates back to the 1930s.

247 bottom left The only way to see the immense Aquapark of Las Vegas in its entirety is from the air. For years now, the "city of sin" has been promoted as a peaceful vacation spot for the entire family.

247 bottom right Rising to a height of 1,150 feet, Stratosphere Tower is the tallest building in the Western United States. On top there is a lounge bar, a restaurant, an observation deck, a wedding chapel and the Big Shot, an attraction that allows adventurous souls to experience the thrill of freefalling at a speed of 50 mph.

was opened. Named El Rancho Vegas, it was located on Highway 91, which was later renamed the Las Vegas Strip and is also the most brightly lit street in the world. The other is 1976, the year Atlantic City, New Jersey, was granted a license to open casinos. Las Vegas lost its national monopoly on gambling and had to come up with a new idea to remain unique and inimitable. Thus, mega-resorts were annexed to the casinos.

Today, the Strip has the world's highest concentration of mega-resorts, which have up to 6,000 rooms each and feature halls for shows of all kinds and entertainment for all ages. To name a few, the New York-New York Hotel has replicas of the Big Apple's most important buildings, the Venetian boasts a Grand Canal, and the Luxor, where guests stay in a pyramid, is topped by a beam of light that is visible even to planes flying over Los Angeles, 300 miles away. And there are places like the Stratosphere, which has the tallest tower in the western United States, the Paris, which has reproductions of the Eiffel Tower and the Arc de Triomphe, and the Mirage, with a volcano that erupts every 15 minutes.

In short, Las Vegas is the planetary temple of kitsch, which borders on the sublime here. But in this Disneyland for adults, there are also people who think about culture. One of them is billionaire Steve Wynn, the king of casinos, who recently inaugurated Le Rêve, a colossal resort named after Picasso's famous painting (which is owned by Wynn, one of the world's biggest art collectors). Among the attractions, there is also room for his extraordinary collection of artwork. As of 2001, the Strip is also the location of two extraordinary exhibition spaces, designed by Rem Koolhaas: the Guggenheim Las Vegas, which hosts prestigious temporary exhibits, and the Guggenheim Hermitage, created through the joint efforts of the American foundation and the famous museum in St. Petersburg.

248-249 The phenomenal skyline of the capital of Illinois overlooks Lake Michigan. It is no accident that its complex of buildings is considered a veritable textbook of modern architecture. Even at the turn of the 20th century, Chicago was nicknamed "Paris of the Prairies."

248 bottom In 2003, Sears Tower – rising majestically on the left side of the picture – celebrated its thirtieth birthday, but it still maintains its record as the tallest building in the United States. Its gleaming black walls have an astonishing number of windows: 16,100.

249 top left The top of Two Prudential Plaza has a distinctive pyramidal shape. The 995-foot-tall skyscraper was completed in 1990.

Chicago
USA

249 top right Four ornamental lantern-shaped towers crown the skyscraper at 900 Michigan Avenue. The building, designed by Kohn, Pedersen and Fox, is a tribute to the architecture of Otto Wagner and the Viennese Sezession movement.

249 bottom By the bend in the Chicago River just before it flows into Lake Michigan, the futuristic curved shape of the 475-foot-tall building at 333 Wacker Drive perfectly exploits the space of this site.

In Chicago, the Sears Tower is one building that certainly does not go unnoticed: Rising to a height of 1,450 feet, it dominates the city skyline and is the tallest skyscraper in the United States. Its base, which covers two city blocks, extends over an area of more than 4300 square feet. Ever since it was completed in 1973, this building, designed by Bruce Graham of Skidmore, Owings & Merrill, has continued to draw attention. On March 12, 2004, the *Chicago Tribune's* page-one headlines announced that two New York real-estate tycoons, Jeffrey Feil and Joseph Chetrit, had purchased the Sears Tower for the astonishing price of $835 million. For Chicago's nearly three million residents, this New York "assault" must have come as an unpleasant surprise. The two metropolises are historic rivals, each claiming to be Number One in both the financial and architectural arenas. Though New York is home to the world's most important stock market, Chicago counters this with its commodities exchange, which handles one-third of the global trade volume of grain and meat. And while New York's skyscrapers are more famous, Chicago is the city that can pride itself on having spawned the very idea of modern architecture.

But let's take things one at a time. The area around the capital of the state of Illinois was explored as far back as the late 17th century. However, it was not until 1779 that Jean Baptiste Point du Sable founded the first permanent settlement at the point where Lake Michigan meets the Chicago River. Interestingly, the river and the city itself were named after the wild garlic that grew on its banks, which the native population called *checagou*. Because Point du Sable was dark-skinned – his father was French-Canadian and his mother Haitian – he managed to win the natives' trust and established a fur-trading post. In 1833 Chicago was recognized as

250 top *Magnificent Mile is the wealthiest and most dazzling stretch of Michigan Avenue, the boulevard that extends from the lakeshore to Lincoln Park, northwest of Downtown Chicago and its skyscrapers.*

250 bottom *Opened in 1916 as a recreational area, Navy Pier extends for about half a mile on Lake Michigan. After a long period of decline, in 1989 – thanks to heavy investments – the pier was restored to its original splendor and it now attracts about 8 million visitors a year.*

250-251 *Buckingham Fountain is one of the largest in the world. Surrounded by bronze seahorses, it set in the middle of Grant Park. It represents Lake Michigan and the four states along its shores.*

251 top left *More modest in size compared to its neighbors (is it "only" 670 feet tall), the R.R. Donnelley Building stands out because of its elegant postmodern lines. The building was designed by Catalan architect Ricardo Bofill.*

Chicago

the city's official name, and four years later construction work began on the Illinois & Michigan Canal, a navigable route connecting the Great Lakes region to the Mississippi and thus to the port of New Orleans. With the canal, Chicago became a trade hub between the Caribbean area and New York, and the construction of the railroad in 1850 made the city the crossroads between the civilized East Coast and the Wild West.

From then on, Chicago's flourishing trade and job opportunities attracted enormous numbers of Irish and Eastern European immigrants (today, the city has the largest Polish population after Warsaw), as well as African Americans from the South. Chicago was also the birthplace of America's most important labor unions. Likewise, it played a key role in the movement for racial equality; in 1981, it elected the first African American mayor in the United States, Harold Washington. Two of its most famous citizens – albeit with a negative connotation – are old history: the "founding fathers" of American organized crime, John Dillinger and Al Capone. Jazz and blues also started out in Chicago to move on to worldwide acclaim. And, again in the

music field, Chicago's main street became part of the legend of rock with the Rolling Stones' record 2120 S. Michigan Avenue. When it comes to literature, Chicago is the birthplace of no less than Ernest Hemingway, and home to Carl Sandburg, Nelson Algren, Studs Terkel, and Ben Hecht, among other modern giants.

In architecture, Chicago's preeminence is linked to two exceptional names: Frank Lloyd Wright and Ludwig Mies van der Rohe, the fathers of functionalism and minimalism. Nevertheless, these masters would not have had the chance to express themselves and experiment with modernity if the city itself had not been revolutionary in its own right.

It all started with a tragedy: the Great Chicago Fire of 1871 – Chicago had grown to a population of 300,000 by this time – that reduced much of the city to cinders. The city fathers embarked on highly ambitious reconstruction work and astonished the world in 1893 by hosting the World Columbian Exposition, commemorating the discovery of America. The idea of constructing vertically came in response to the astronomical rise in the price of land allocated for construction, coupled with the need

251 top right The Wrigley Building was built in 1922 over the site of the home of Jean Baptiste Point du Sable, the founder of Chicago. Its clock tower is a copy of the Giralda bell tower of the Seville cathedral.

41°51'N 87°41'W

to provide office space for businesses, insurance companies, the stock exchange and the banks that were opening branches in the city. The first skyscraper, designed by William Le Baron Jenney in 1885, was owned by Home Insurance; it was 180 feet tall and its weight was supported by a cast-iron structure that was used as a model for the skyscrapers built immediately after that. Its demolition in 1931 was a loss to architectural history. In 1909, Daniel Burnham was commissioned to come up with a sweeping plan for the city: The outcome was a project that earned Chicago its sobriquet "Paris of the Prairies." Louis Sullivan, Martin Roche, and William Holabird were among the architects who designed the city's distinctive buildings.

Though it has expanded substantially since then – the city limits encompass 25 miles of the Lake Michigan shoreline – the city has remained faithful to that project, and Downtown Chicago is considered a veritable "textbook" of modern architecture. It is circled by the Loop, the elevated railway that effectively acts as an enclosure, and there are countless fascinating buildings here. In addition to the Sears Tower and Chicago's more recent giants,

there are noteworthy historic monuments such as the Old Colony Building (1894), the first skyscraper that made extensive use of glass, and The Rookery, a magnificent office building constructed in 1888 by John Root in a style that combines Gothic and Moorish elements. In 1905 the Rookery gained a splendid lobby with its famed winding staircase designed by Frank Lloyd Wright.

The city's main thoroughfare, Michigan Avenue, is northeast of the Loop and the street has been dubbed "The Magnificent Mile" because of its majestic buildings. These include the Tribune Tower, the headquarters of the daily newspaper *The Chicago Tribune*, built in 1925 in a daring Neo-Gothic style, and the Wrigley Building, constructed by the chewing-gum magnate who also had Wrigley Field, the baseball stadium where the Chicago Cubs play, built in the Twenties. One of the most prestigious museums in the United States is located at the other end of Michigan Avenue. This is the Art Institute of Chicago, for which architect Renzo Piano has designed a new extension.

One of Chicago's most notable suburban areas is Oak Park, and this is where Hemingway was born. However, the area also

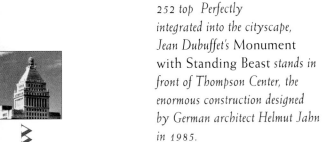

252 top Perfectly integrated into the cityscape, Jean Dubuffet's Monument with Standing Beast stands in front of Thompson Center, the enormous construction designed by German architect Helmut Jahn in 1985.

252 bottom Chicago is an outdoor art gallery, in which the forms and colors of sculptures by the leading contemporary artists dialogue with starkly impressive buildings like the Tribune Tower, the headquarters of the prestigious Chicago daily.

boasts 25 houses designed by Frank Lloyd Wright in his Prairie Style, including the home where the architect lived with his wife and five children, and the one that housed his studio. In addition, the marvelous Robie House, designed by Wright in 1909, and the campus of the University of Chicago are in the Hyde Park area. About twenty of the university campus buildings were designed by the influential Mies van der Rohe and, in keeping with the well-established tradition of commissioning famous architects, the Illinois Institute of Technology retained the Dutch architect Rem Koolhaas to design its new campus center, currently under construction.

For the events celebrating the year 2000, the city decided to create Millennium Park, a green "lung" set amidst the skyscrapers and

complete with a visionary concert space designed by the contemporary American architect Frank O. Gehry. Visitors to the park must now divide their attention between this structure and the equally extraordinary sculpture by Anglo-Indian artist Anish Kapoor, completed in June 2004. The work is entitled *Cloud Gate*, because 80 percent of its bean-shaped metal surface reflects the sky. Initially perplexed by the work, Chicagoans now love it. As the wind pushes the clouds across the sky, the sculpture seems to be in constant motion and is never, ever the same. Indeed, it is a paradigm for Chicago's vivacity and for its nickname, the Windy City, given to it about fifty years ago when an envious New York journalist was overwhelmed by the crisp breeze blowing in from the Great Lakes.

252-253 The sculpture by Alexander Calder is entitled Flamingo. *It stands in Federal Center Plaza, the complex of three buildings that is considered the perfect union of technology, function and artistic expression.*

253 bottom A sinuous stylized human figure counters the linearity of the Aon Center, which is 1,136 feet tall and was built in 1973.

254-255 New Orleans was built on a crescent-shaped bight of the Mississippi – hence the name Crescent City – and, with Lake Pontchartrain behind it, the city seems to rise magically from the water. The entire urban center is 3 to 10 feet below sea level.

254 bottom A white building houses the station of Downtown New Orleans. Though tourists are concentrated in the historic French Quarter, this area offers numerous points of interest, including an Art District, with contemporary artists' galleries located in the old port warehouses.

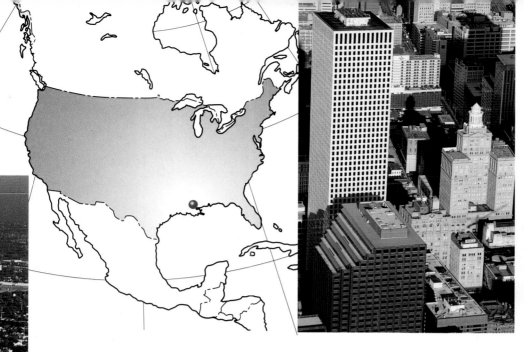

New Orleans

USA

Anne Rice, the queen of horror, lives and wrote most of her novels in New Orleans' Garden District, in a Neo-Classical house that has a haunted air. Other great names in American literature lived in the city and in its French Quarter: when living at 632 St. Peter Street Tennessee Williams wrote *A Streetcar Named Desire*, inspired by the metallic clatter of the now-historic St. Charles streetcar. William Faulkner wrote *Soldier's Pay* at 624 Pirate's Alley, which now houses a bookshop named after him. And Truman Capote, who was born in New Orleans in 1924, wrote his first book, *Other Voices, Other Rooms*, at 27 Royal Street.

In short, New Orleans is "different" from other American cities. Whereas New York is "The Big Apple," just waiting to be grabbed with gusto, New Orleans is "The Big Easy," where time moves more slowly and everything is a little simpler. It is

255 top left One Shell Square, nearly 700 feet tall, is the "giant" of New Orleans. Built in 1972, the building is starkly clad in white Italian travertine, which gives it a sophisticated look.

255 top right The World Trade Center, built in 1967, is located between Canal and Poydras Streets, and it is the hub of the New Orleans financial district.

It is just over 400 feet tall, and its unusual cross layout makes it one of the city's most distinctive skyscrapers.

255 bottom Located on the outskirts of the Central Business District, the Louisiana Superdome is an immense structure. It is 680 feet across and covers nearly 52 acres. This is the home stadium of the city's beloved football team, the New Orleans Saints.

LOUISIANA STATE MUSEUM CABILDO

256 top *The Cabildo was once the seat of the Spanish government, and after Louisiana was sold to the French (the deed was stipulated in this very building) it became City Hall, then the Supreme Court Building and, finally, a part of the State Museum.*

256 center *Loyola University, located at the edge of Audubon Park, is distinguished by buildings in the Gothic Tudor style, like stately Marquette Hall.*

256 bottom *Many buildings around Jackson Square, as well as numerous residences in the Garden District, were built between the late 18th century and the first half of the 19th century in an elegant Neo-Classical style.*

257 *St. Louis Cathedral, built in 1794, stands next to the Cabildo in Jackson Square. The park across from it was known as Place d'Armes during the French period and the gallows were located here.*

decadent, seamy and sublime, all in one. In a word, it is literary. As to its nicknames, it has been called the Crescent City because of its unique geography. It is located on a muddy crescent-shaped bight of the Mississippi – hence the name – and, with Lake Pontchartrain behind it, the city seems to rise magically by the water.

New Orleans has never abandoned its French heritage. Its home state is Louisiana (named after the French monarch Louis XIV), the only state in the United States that is divided into "parishes" rather than counties. The city was founded in 1718 by a French-Canadian officer, Jean Baptiste le Moyne, Sieur de Bienville, as a military outpost to protect France's territorial interests. In 1762, Louis XV ceded it to his Spanish cousin, Charles III. In 1801, New Orleans (or Nouvelle Orléans, as it was called then) reverted to the French, only to be sold by Napoleon to the United States in 1803.

History confirms that the Americans got a real bargain, though back then they may not have thought so: New Orleans, already flourishing port town, was too "merry" for their Puritan tastes. During the years of European rule, the French-Canadian colonists (called "Cajuns," from the mispronunciation of Acadia, their homeland) were joined by Spanish notables, wheeler-dealers, women of dubious morals, about 10,000 refugees from the French Revolution, and former Haitian slaves who had fled their homeland's bloody rebellions. They quickly intermarried, creating a unique breed and culture: the Creoles. While the French Quarter was their domain, Americans of British descent built the Garden District as theirs. In remembrance of this separation, even today the median strip along the streets of New Orleans is referred to as "neutral ground."

New Orleans boasts 35,000 buildings that are listed as historical treasures, ranging from wooden cottages to stone residences complete with stuccowork and lacy-looking cast-iron columns and balconies. Some of them are in a Neo-Classical style, whereas others flaunt "tropical" colors and a hybrid style that is the architectural transposition of the city's culture. Notable examples include the Cabildo, the splendid building where the Louisiana Purchase was signed, the St. Louis Cathedral (built in 1724 and reconstructed following a fire in 1794), and the Ursuline Convent (1745); these last two are, respectively, the first Catholic cathedral in America and the oldest building in the Mississippi Valley. Then there are the houses along Royal Street and Charles Street, and the nightspots of Bourbon Street, which are open around the clock and have become the main attraction of the French Quarter. Here jazz was born, and immortals like Louis Armstrong brought it and themselves fame. And this is also the site of the wild and colorful Mardi Gras parade.

In short – and with all due respect to the Puritans – in New Orleans the fun never ends. Today, the city's newest attraction and most important modern building is the Louisiana Superdome, a high-tech arena covered by the largest steel roofing structure in the world. Here, however, it is great sports events, rather than music, that steal the show.

New
Orleans

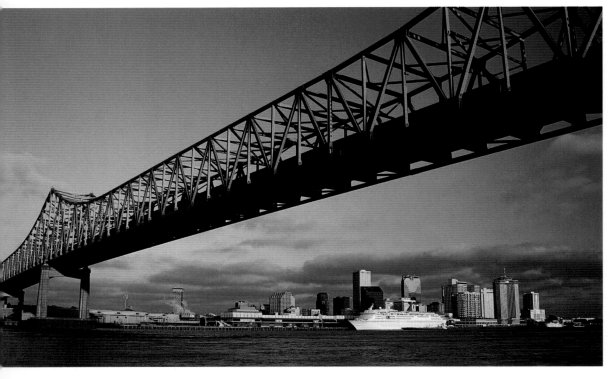

258 left Jazz clubs, restaurants offering Cajun specialties, and shops filled with antiques and souvenirs stretch seamlessly along Bourbon Street, which is always packed with tourists. This is also the site of the wildly colorful Mardi Gras parade.

258-259 The historic Royal Café, on Royal Street, is one of the main attractions of the French Quarter; the street is also referred to in French as the Vieux Carré. Its lacy cast-iron balcony resembles a luxuriant forest of tropical plants and flowers.

258 bottom The completion in 1988 of the Greater New Orleans Bridge No. 2, nearly 1,600 feet long and built at a cost of $78 million, bolstered the road network across the Mississippi. The first bridge over the river was built in the 1950s.

259 right The notes of a jazz orchestra create the perfect soundtrack for the French Quarter. The music genre that blends African and Caribbean rhythms was created right here at the beginning of the last century, quickly spreading across the United States (and around the world) thanks to two extraordinary musicians: Louis Armstrong and Joe "King" Oliver.

259 bottom In New Orleans, no one passes up a chance for entertainment — not even in the modern financial district, where the dazzling Harrah's Casino stands between austere skyscrapers. The city has rightfully earned its sobriquet "The Big Easy."

261 center The 1024-foot-tall NationsBank Plaza is the tallest skyscraper in the South.

261 bottom One Atlantic Center, built in 1987, is one of the many skyscrapers "designing" the Atlanta skyline.

Atlanta

USA

260 The Georgia State Capitol Building was completed in 1889, and is the expression and symbol of Atlanta, which became the "capital of the New South" after the defeat of the Confederate Army. Built in the Neo-Classical style, this immense dome on this majestic edifice is covered in gold leaf and culminates with a lantern topped by an allegorical statue of freedom.

261 left The Westin Peachtree Plaza, which is 722 feet high and has 73 floors, is one of the tallest hotels in the world.

261 top Stone Mountain, about 15 miles east of downtown Atlanta, is part of a protected area that is one of Georgia's main tourist attractions. A colossal relief sculpted on its granite surface depicts Confederate generals Jefferson Davis, Robert E. Lee and Stonewall Jackson.

In the summer of 1886, people passing in front of Jacob's Drug Store in Atlanta were drawn to the sign praising the taste and tonic properties of a beverage called Coca-Cola, which was sold for a nickel. Many evidently read the ad and walked past it. According to the drug store's ledgers, that year Jacob's sold only nine glasses of Coca-Cola a day. This meant meager earnings for its inventor, John Pemberton, who in 1890 decided to sell the drink's secret formula to another pharmacist, Asa Griggs Candler. Candler, who had a good head for business, eventually became the first leader of the Coca-Cola Company. Everyone knows how the story ends: Coca-Cola is now the world's most popular soft drink, each day selling 1.3 billion cans and bottles to consumers in 120 countries.

It is no accident that Coca-Cola hails from Atlanta. Georgia's state capital has a unique penchant for producing universal icons. When Coca-Cola was "baptized" Atlanta was still a fairly small town. Though it had been founded just 40 years earlier near the southern slopes of the Appalachian Mountains, it had already earned its place in American history. In 1864, as the tide turned in the Civil War, the Union Army, led by General Sherman, burned it to the ground. That dramatic event would have been relegated to the pages of schoolbooks if Margaret Mitchell had not recounted it in her novel *Gone With the Wind*, and, above all, if millions of people had not been moved to tears by the scenes of Tara being burned and by the last kiss between Scarlett O'Hara and Rhett Butler, in the timeless classic starring Vivien Leigh and Clark Gable.

Moving ahead in history, on January 15, 1929 Martin Luther King, Jr. was born in a middle-class house on Auburn Avenue, in the Afro-American district of Atlanta. King is another figure who needs no introduction. With his words "I have a dream," millions of African Americans understood that their time had come; they demanded rightful recognition and equal standing in America's workplaces, schools, neighborhoods, courts, and social and cultural forums – and continue to find their rightful place. Atlanta is also the home of CNN, Ted Turner's television

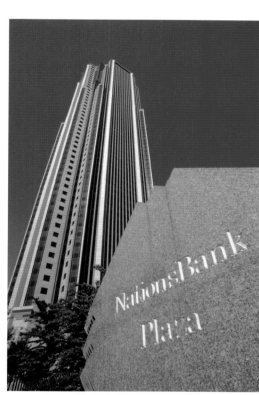

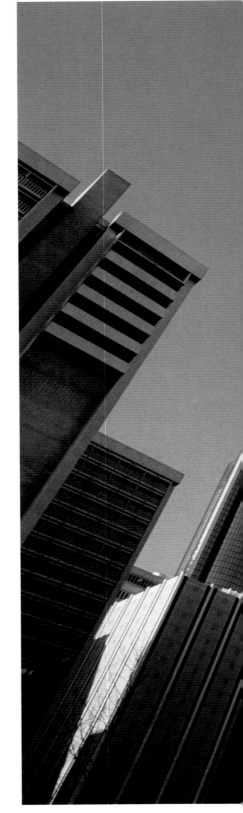

262 top left The picture shows one of the entrances to Underground Atlanta, the starting point of the Heritage Trails.

262 top right Peachtree Street crosses the downtown area from north to south. Unlike most American cities, Atlanta does not have an orderly grid layout.

empire that revolutionized the dissemination of information on a planetary level. And in 1996 the city had the honor and onus of hosting the Olympic Games. As of 1999 its airport has also earned the title of the busiest one in the world, handling 78 million passengers and 900,000 arriving and departing flights every year.

Atlanta is a typical American city. Its downtown area bristles with skyscrapers – including the Gulf Oil Building (1952), one of I. M. Pei's first major projects, and the Bank of America Plaza (1992), which, with a height of over 1,000 feet, is the tallest building in the Southern United States. Not to be missed is the "traditional" shopping area, known as the Underground, which was built over the site of the Atlanta fire, the parting gift of the Union Army. The center devoted to Coca-Cola memorabilia is also located here. Visitors can also enjoy the historic district of middle-class African-American homes, marked by a Heritage Trail that leads to the birthplace of Martin Luther King, Jr., the legendary Royal Peacock Club where Louis Armstrong and Aretha Franklin played, and the Atlanta Life Insurance Building, which from 1920 to 1980 was the headquarters of the most successful private Afro-American business in the country. Then, in contrast, the Midtown area houses the High Museum of Art, which has an extraordinary collection of artwork and recently inaugurated a new wing designed by Renzo Piano, which is annexed to the sleek 1983 building designed by Richard Meier. The city also prides itself on the Centennial Olympic Park, which hosted the Olympic Games and has now been converted into an entertainment complex.

The city is also ringed by residential suburbs with spotless albeit anonymous-looking homes. However, one of these areas is quite surprising. This is Sandy Springs, which is the location of the Concourse Corporate Center, America's tallest suburban building. Despite this record, however, Atlanta's nearly four million residents still consider the enormous granite mass of Stone Mountain, which dominates the eastern part of the city, their favorite "skyscraper."

262 bottom The Dorothy Chapman Fuqua Conservatory was added to the Atlanta Botanical Garden in 1989. Its greenhouses – dedicated to the rainforest environment, desert flora, fruit trees and carnivorous plants – have numerous rare and endangered plants. The building was constructed thanks to the $5.5-million donation made by entrepreneur J.B. Fuqua in memory of his wife.

262-263 This lovely view showcases an original sculpture, "Ballet Olympia."

263 bottom left This fountain is in the World of Coca-Cola exhibition pavilion devoted to the world's most famous beverage, which was invented in Atlanta in 1886 by pharmacist John Pemberton.

263 bottom right Water spurts from the five Olympic rings of the fountain in the middle of Centennial Park, the area constructed in 1996 to host athletes and now transformed into a sports center.

264 bottom right Now transformed into a museum, Casa Loma is indubitably the city's most extravagant spot. Sir Henry Pellatt, founder of the Toronto Electric Light Company, built this pseudo-mediaeval castle, with its complex architecture, between 1911 and 1914. The tycoon decorated it with furnishings and artwork from all over the world.

264-265 The CN Tower (over 1,800 feet tall) is the continent's tallest telecommunications tower. Its observation platform, the Sky Pod, affords a marvelous view of the city and of Lake Ontario.

264 bottom left The two sinuous and asymmetrical skyscrapers of the New City Hall – almost sculptural in appearance – mark off the circular Nathan Phillips Square.

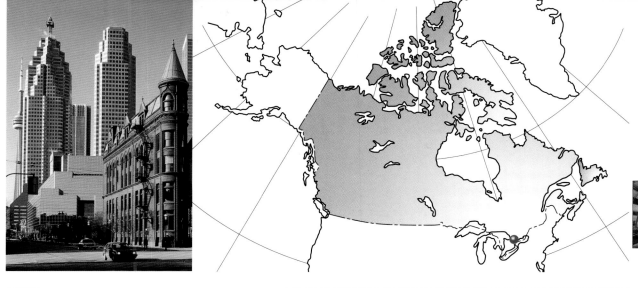

Toronto
CANADA

265 top The architecture of the turreted Gooderham Building contrasts with the postmodern structure of the Canada Trust Tower and Bay Wellington Tower.

265 bottom King Street West, the hotbed of the financial district, is dominated by First Canadian Place, 980 feet tall, and by the 900-foot-tall Scotia Plaza.

To find out the weather for the day, all the people of Toronto have to do is gaze up at the Canada Life Assurance Building, at the corner of University Avenue and Queen Street West. There is a cube-shaped beacon at the top: Green means a sunny day, red tells them they'll need their umbrellas, and white (a common occurrence in winter) indicates snow. In addition to its utility, the device can also be credited with bringing a touch of color to the city's austere financial district, whose skyscrapers recall the fact that, first and foremost, Toronto is a working city – sun, rain or snow.

On the other hand, by following the adage "Early to bed, early to rise" typical of Anglo-Saxon Puritanism, the capital of Ontario has become the engine of the Canadian economy. Indeed, it no longer measures itself against its "cousin" Montreal but vies with New York. However, Toronto's critics consider this business city to be too serious, commenting that it is "a Swiss-run New York." Nevertheless, the fact that a metropolis of

approximately 4.5 million people is also clean, orderly and open, has a very low crime rate and has park areas covering 18 percent of its urban territory verges on the miraculous. Virtually the whole world is represented here: its population includes 535,000 Scots, 480,000 Irish, 415,000 Italians, 435,000 Chinese, 225,000 Germans, 160,000 Poles and 130,000 Greeks. Of the nearly 100 languages spoken in Canada, 80 are spoken in Toronto, and the administration has promoted the Heritage Language Program to encourage immigrants to preserve their culture of origin.

Before establishing a settlement on the muddy plains where Lake Ontario meets Georgian Bay, the Huron Indians had already perceived the area's multiethnic vocation: Toronto means "meeting place" in their language. The first European to meet the native population was French explorer Étienne Brûlé in 1615, and for 150 years the only ones to follow him were intrepid fur traders. It was not until the second half of the 18th century that the French built Fort Rouillé, a defensive structure that was unable to defend Ontario from the claims staked by the

British, who took over Toronto in 1793 and transformed it into a city.

Today, in the heart of Toronto the spires and towers of the red-brick buildings of the 19th and early 20th centuries – such as Old City Hall, Union Railway Station and St. Andrew's Presbyterian Church – are offset by the futuristic CN Tower (at over 1,800 feet, it is the tallest telecommunications tower on the continent) and reflected in the surfaces of impressive skyscrapers. The headquarters of banks and multinationals are concentrated between Queen Street and Yonge Street – this latter, according to the *Guinness Book of World Records*, is the longest street in the world, as it extends to the Rainy River at James Bay (1,178 miles). When it comes to roads, the PATH – the underground city – is equally remarkable. This network of

266 top Union Station has a hi-tech futuristic look, but it is "old" inside: Inaugurated in 1927, it is listed as a national monument.

266 bottom PATH's underground galleries extend from Union Station. This 7-mile pedestrian network spreads out under the city, connecting 50 office buildings, 1200 shops and dozens of bars and restaurants.

266-267 Topped by a glass-and-steel shell, Roy Thomson Hall is one of the most original-looking buildings in downtown Toronto. This extraordinary 2812-seat concert hall is the home of the Toronto Symphony Orchestra and the Toronto Mendelssohn Choir.

nearly 7 miles of subterranean walkways connects 50 office buildings, and 1,200 shops and restaurants in the center, and it is especially appreciated by the people of Toronto in the winter, when the temperature is often below freezing. Above ground, one of the hubs of this "parallel world" is BCE Place, a brightly lit square covered with metal and glass vaults, designed by Santiago Calatrava. Toronto boasts museums with internationally renowned art collections, as well as the Sky Dome. This stadium, which has a retractable roof, can seat 60,000 people. Since its inauguration in 1989 it has hosted over 2,000 events, from encounters with Pope John Paul II, Nelson Mandela and the Dalai Lama to concerts, the Blue Jays' baseball games and the Argonauts' football games. Together with the Maple Leafs, the ice hockey team that plays at the futuristic Air Canada Centre, the teams are the city's sports heroes.

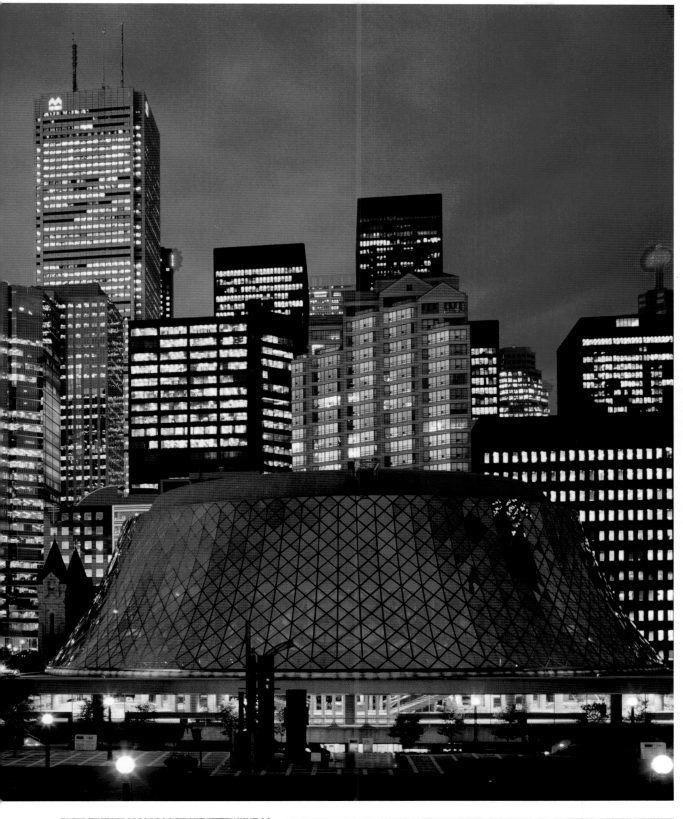

267 right The Sky Dome is the pride of Toronto. Since its inauguration in 1989, the stadium, which is equipped with a retractable roof, has hosted over 2000 major events of all kinds, before a total audience of 50 million people.

267 bottom left Located at the intersection of Bay and Yonge, at what is historically the sociocultural heart of Toronto, BCE Place is a gallery covered by slender white arches that Spanish architect Santiago Calatrava designed as a contemporary reinterpretation of Gothic cathedrals.

267 bottom right The Toronto Eaton Centre is one of the biggest and most luxurious shopping centers in Canada. Its daring architectural solutions and the unconventional artwork decorating it are extraordinary. The complex has 285 shops, as well as restaurants, cinemas and theaters.

268-269 This splendid picture conveys the profoundly European character of Montreal, which is the world's second largest Francophone city after Paris, despite the fact that today only one-third of its population is of French descent. These conditions help create a thrilling multiethnic and multicultural atmosphere.

268 bottom left The copper roof of the building at 1000 Rue de la Gauchetière (670 feet), the tallest in the city, blends in with the dome of the Cathédrale Marie-Reine-du-Monde next to it.

268 bottom right The Chapelle de Notre-Dame-de-Bonsecours is also known as "the sailors' church" because the statue of Our Lady at the top made it possible to distinguish the port even miles away. To pray for protection on their journey, crews would bring boat-shaped votive lamps to the altar.

269 top Opened in 1930 and named in honor of the first European to reach the site where the city was built, the Jacques Cartier Bridge – over 2 miles long – connects Montreal to Longueil, on the south bank of the St. Lawrence.

269 bottom The magnificently decorated Basilique Notre-Dame was inaugurated in 1829. The main altar is the work of Frenchman Henri Bouriché, whereas the stained-glass windows with scenes depicting the foundation of Ville Marie (the city's ancient name) were made in Limoges.

Montreal

CANADA

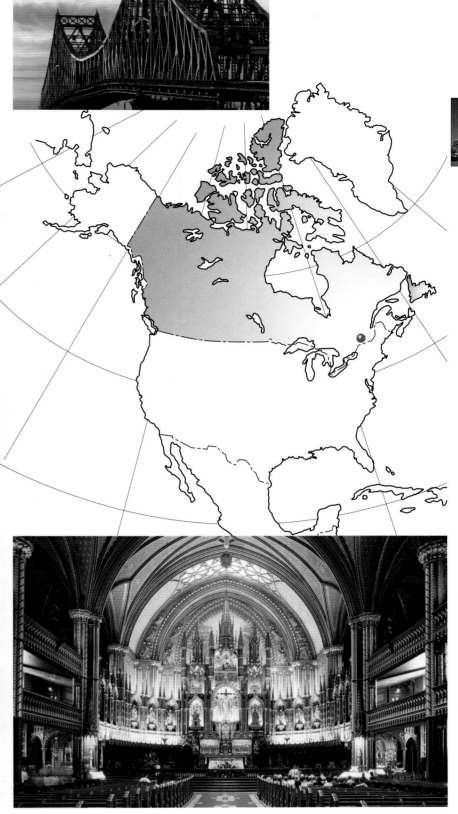

The Atlantic coasts of Europe are closer to Montreal than the Pacific coast at Vancouver, even though the latter city is also in Canada. Many hundreds of miles of ocean separate Montreal from Europe, but reaching Vancouver would entail crossing immense expanses of often inhospitable wilderness. Regardless, Montreal has made its choice, opting to remain a profoundly European city. In fact, it is the world's second largest Francophone city after Paris, despite the fact that today only one-third of its population of 1.8 million is of French extraction.

During the 1960s, the capital of the province of Quebec was also center stage for the violent separatist actions promoted by the French-speaking majority. This ultimately slowed down the city's economy and led to a loss of prestige in favor of Toronto, which has now become the country's driving force. Now that these tensions have been settled, however, Montreal has come to the fore as a cultural hub, with countless museums, theaters, art centers and cultural venues like McGill University, one of the most distinguished universities in North America.

Every corner of Montreal reveals noteworthy testimony to the city's European history, which began in 1535 when explorer Jacques Cartier arrived at the island at the confluence of the St. Lawrence and Ottawa rivers. A little more than a century later, Louis XIV appointed Paul de Chomedey de Maisonneuve to establish Ville Marie "to celebrate the glory of God and bring salvation to the Indians." In honor of the king, the French aristocrat named the city's only hill Mont Royal. Though it is just 738 feet tall, the locals respectfully refer to it as "la Montagne" and it is the origin of the name Montreal. In 1875 the city appointed architect Frederick Law Olmsted –

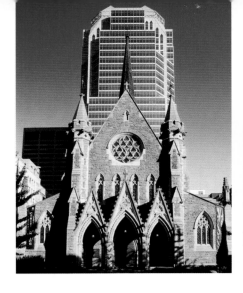

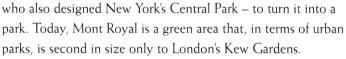

*270 top left Built in 1859 and
now dwarfed by skyscrapers, the
Anglican Christ Church Cathedral
is on Rue Sainte-Catherine, the
main shopping street in Montreal.
The Maison des Coopérants rises
majestically behind it.*

who also designed New York's Central Park – to turn it into a park. Today, Mont Royal is a green area that, in terms of urban parks, is second in size only to London's Kew Gardens.

This bucolic setting acts as a counterpoint for noteworthy historical buildings, most of which are located in the charming quarter of Vieux Montréal – Old Montreal – on the banks of the St. Lawrence. Lining the quarter's cobblestone streets and squares are gems like the Neo-Gothic Basilique Notre-Dame; Château Ramezay, which was the residence of the French governors and one of the oldest buildings in North America (1756); the Hôtel de Ville (1870); and the Marché Bonsecours, formerly the headquarters of the municipal administrative offices and now converted into a space for boutiques and art exhibitions. Behind Vieux Montréal are the Quartier Latin, which has the bohemian atmosphere of its Parisian namesake, and the Vieux Port, a warehouse area that is currently part of an architectural renovation project. Even the modern area, now the location of numerous skyscrapers, has a refined aura, with constructions like the Cathédrale Marie-Reine-du-Monde,

a late-19th-century replica of St. Peter's Basilica in Rome.

Though the 19th century was characterized by the frenzied construction of religious architecture – Mark Twain even described Montreal as "a city where you couldn't throw a brick without breaking a church window" – the 20th century has seen the advent of public architecture with a powerful impact. These works include "the underground city," a network of pedestrian walkways extending for nearly 20 miles under the city and lined with shops, restaurants, cinemas and theaters, as well as the sensational exhibition venue of the Centre Canadien d'Architecture and, above all, the stadiums built in 1976 for the Olympic Games. As a way of justifying their enormous construction costs, these stadiums are widely used not only for sports events but also as tourist attractions. One example is the Biodôme, the former cycle-racing track that now houses the Environmental Museum. If history represents the wealth of Montreal, its hinterlands – Canada's vast and still generally unspoiled wild regions – represent a second valuable treasure.

270-271 and 271 bottom left
In recent years, Vieux Port (top)
and Vieux Montréal (bottom) have
been redeveloped and turned into a
recreation area and sought-after
residential district.

271 bottom right The Montreal
Casino is located in what were the
French and Quebec pavilions for
the Expo '67. The complex is in
Parc Jean Drapeau, near Vieux
Port.

270 top right A view of Place
des Arts, dominated by the
enormous twin skyscrapers of the
Complexe Desjardins. The Musée
d'Art Contemporain de Montréal
is located in this lively central
plaza.

270 bottom Built for the Olympics
as bicycle racetrack, the futuristic
Biodôme has been converted into the
Environmental Museum. The Tour
de Montréal or Montreal Tower
Observatory (575 feet tall) stands
out in the background.

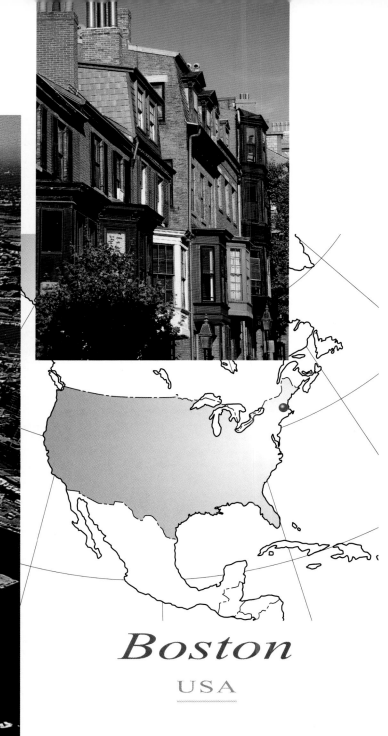

272-273 The spectacular Boston Waterfront extends along the mouth of the Charles River.

272 bottom left Despite its rather small size, Boston's financial district is one of the most important in the country, as it is the home to major hi-tech companies.

272 bottom right Rising to a height of 790 feet, the John Hancock Tower dominates the city skyline.

273 top The red-brick façades, stuccowork and bow windows of the elegant homes of Beacon Hill, the city's refined upper-class neighborhood, reflect Boston's Victorian soul.

273 center top Harvard University, founded in 1636, is one of the most prestigious universities in the world, and it is the oldest one in the United States.

273 center bottom Cambridge, separated from the center of town by the Charles River, is home not only to Harvard University but also to the highly prestigious Massachusetts Institute of Technology.

273 bottom The view takes in the entire Back Bay, a sprawling district of quaint brick houses that was planned in 1856 and is now one of the most sought-after neighborhoods in Boston.

Boston

USA

Bostonians call it "the Big Dig." Big as it might be, however, the term is actually a euphemism for the largest and most complex engineering project in American history. With ten years of work costing $14.6 billion, the project has catapulted New England's oldest city into the 21st century. Traffic in the Massachusetts' state capital now moves through re-engineered or new highways, tunnels, and bridges. The new system, offering some 10-lane roadways, has dramatically improved speed and convenience and has sharply decreased hydrocarbon pollution. Last but not least, the project has made Boston a much handsomer city, since the old elevated roads have been torn down to "clean up" the view of the bay and make room for park areas. The highlight of the Big Dig is the Leonard P. Zakim Bunker Hill Bridge, designed by Swiss architect Christian Menn. With its single 1433-foot span supported by steel cables, it has earned the title of America's most beautiful bridge.

But Boston has long been accustomed to being at the head of the class. Founded in 1630 by a group of English Puritans led by John Winthrop, who named it after his hometown in the England's county of Lincolnshire, it is considered the "cradle of modern America" and it has more historical sites

274-275 For over 250 years, Faneuil Hall Marketplace has played a key role as a rendezvous, trade and entertainment center. It is the starting point for the Freedom Trail, which leads to the city's most important historic monuments.

274 bottom left The John F. Kennedy Library and Museum is a national memorial to the 35th president of the United States. The complex was built with donations offered by 36 million Americans.

274 bottom right Designed by Frank O. Gehry, the Ray and Maria Stata Center at the Massachusetts Institute of Technology is one of the most futuristic works yet designed by the famous American architect. It houses the Computer Science and Artificial Intelligence Laboratory, together with the Department of Linguistics and Philosophy.

275 top *Now surrounded by skyscrapers, the Old State House played a central role in the political life of colonial Boston. It was built in 1713, and in 1776 the Declaration of Independence from British Crown was first read publicly from its balcony. Today it houses the Boston History Museum.*

275 bottom *The impressive Church of Christ, Scientist is the most important religious building for Christians of this denomination, which was founded in Boston in 1879 by Mary Baker Eddy. This is where the religious movement publishes* The Christian Science Monitor, *considered one of the most authoritative dailies in the United States.*

than any other city in the United States. Among these sites, which are now marked as part of the Freedom Trail, special mention goes to Boston Common, the "green lung" that also happens to be the oldest public park in the country, as well as the upscale area of Beacon Hill and the Old State House. The square in front of the State House was the site of the Boston Massacre, and the Declaration of Independence was read from the balcony of this building in 1776.

Today these historic districts – including the North End, which has the biggest Italian community in America – are mirrored in the new high-rises such as I. M. Pei's superlative Hancock Tower that characterize the city skyline and bear witness to Boston's extraordinary affluence. Though in terms of size, Boston cannot be compared to "giants" like New York, Chicago and Los Angeles, it is nonetheless one of the United States' leading urban areas. But Boston is also "old money." Being a true Bostonian means having at least one forebear who was described in the novels of Edith Wharton, the writer who, in the second half of the 19th century exposed the virtues and vices of the city's upper crust. And it also means being sophisticated, elegant and "European" in nature. Tellingly, the Kennedy family is Bostonian, and the city has dedicated a library and museum – in another building designed by I. M. Pei – to JFK, an American icon. Boston also

boasts prestigious venues like the Museum of Fine Arts, founded in 1909 and recently expanded to become one of the largest exhibitions spaces in the world, displaying masterpieces of American art.

Boston is also one of America's leading technological hubs. The greater Boston area is home to 57 colleges, above all, the "Free Republic of Cambridge" with Harvard University and the Massachusetts Institute of Technology, separated from the center of town by the Charles River. Even at these brain factories, however, both the "burden" of history and the city's explosive vitality are extraordinarily tangible. This is also true from an architectural standpoint. The austere 17th and 18th century red-brick buildings that line Harvard Square are juxtaposed against the buildings of MIT, the hi-tech village that also happens to be a compendium of contemporary architecture. At the MIT campus, architecture runs the gamut from Alvar Aalto's Baker House to the Kresge Auditorium by Eero Saarinen and the Ray and Maria Stata Center, designed by Frank O. Gehry. Inaugurated in 2003 on the site that once held Building 20 (where scientists experimented with new radar technologies during World War II), Gehry's remarkable work also houses the Computer Science and Artificial Intelligence Laboratory. In other words, this is the place where the world of tomorrow is being planned.

New York

USA

With the Freedom Tower, a steel-and-glass skyscraper with an asymmetrical spiral slated to rise of 1776 feet, designed by Daniel Libeskind and by David Childs of Skidmore, Owings & Merrill, the site of the 9/11 tragedy will be reborn. Every day, thousands of office workers will flock here along with New Yorkers and tourists who will go shopping and visit an array of museums and cultural centers as children play in the park. As night falls, people will flock to cinemas and theaters, one of which by Frank O. Gehry, who has taken the classic English courtyard theater of the Shakespearean age and given it a contemporary interpretation. At the site where the Twin Towers once stood, the families of the victims can visit a memorial commemorating their loved ones. Designed by Michael Arad and Peter Walker, the memorial, entitled "Reflecting Absence," will bear the engraved names of those who perished in the attack on the walls marking the perimeter of the two towers that were destroyed. To reach the reborn World Trade Center, the heart of a new and densely populated district offering the best of urban living, an ultra-efficient interchange for the subway and railroad lines will be in operation. In short, everything will be greater, and better, than before; a reflection of New York City's determination to commemorate yet transcend its tragedy and to give New Yorkers' courage and optimism free rein.

Though the memory of 9/11 and the fear of future terrorist attacks have changed the way America operates, New York has chosen to move beyond the tragedy and to focus on building a vibrant future. In the wake of the fear it experienced, the city was overcome by a desire for renewal, planning the renovation of entire neighborhoods (like Manhattan's West Side, where luxurious residential complexes are being constructed), building high-tech skyscrapers designed by leading architects (for example, the *New York Times'* futuristic headquarters, designed by Renzo Piano and located in Times Square, the vibrant, brilliantly lit heart of Manhattan) and creating new museums or expanding existing ones. The new MOMA, opened at the end of 2004, was designed by

277 bottom left The Brooklyn
Bridge stands out in this view of
Manhattan, which is the heart of
New York City. This masterpiece,
designed by John Roebling, was
built between 1867 and 1883.

277 bottom right The South Street
Seaport is located in the central area
of the old port. Excursion boats leave
from this pier, and there is also a
museum dedicated to the history of
New York Harbor and of navigation.

276 top The Statue of Liberty,
dedicated on October 28, 1886, is
the symbol of New York.

276 bottom The New York skyline
is matchless.

276-277 Founded in 1624 by
Dutch colonists, who named it
New Amsterdam and then sold it
to the English 40 years later, the
city was not named New York
until 1664.

278-279 Located at the southern tip of Manhattan, the Financial District is the economic hub of New York – and of the United States.

278 bottom and 279 top The 34-story Municipal Building, which is 580 feet tall, was built in 1914 by McKim, Mead & White. On the right is the United States Courthouse. Designed by Cass Gilbert, it was built in 1936.

Yoshio Taniguchi and cost the astronomical sum of $858 million. Covering an area of over 645,000 square feet (only 20 percent of which devoted to exhibition space), it ushers in what can be considered a new era in the "philosophy" of museum space from both an architectural and conceptual standpoint.

Nevertheless, as far as restoration is concerned, the most symbolic work involved the Statue of Liberty. In addition to enjoying a 360-degree view of New York Harbor, visitors can now see the interior of the intricate iron framework that supports it. The statue (the work of French sculptor Frédéric-Auguste Bartholdi) was completed in 1886, and was intended to represent the values and dreams of the world's most celebrated democracy. Located on Liberty Island, at the entrance to the splendid New York Bay, it served as a "beacon" for the millions of immigrants for whom arrival at New York marked the beginning of a new life on the other side of the Atlantic.

Despite the fact that it is one of the oldest cities in the country, countless people – in the United States and abroad – insist that New York is not America, and this concept applies not only to its positive traits but also its negative ones. Indeed, like an apple – and "The Big Apple" is its most famous nickname, given to the city in the Twenties by John J. FitzGerald, a reporter with *The Morning Telegraph* – New York is a "finite universe" destined to be special and, at times, even paradoxical. The city that in the 20th century would become the world capital was founded in 1624 by Dutch colonists, who named it New Amsterdam. Forty years later, Peter Stuyvesant, Director-General (governor) of the Dutch possessions in North America reluctantly surrendered the city of New Amsterdam to superior British forces. In the subsequent settlement, the Dutch received what today is a little island in the middle of the Indian Ocean, valued for the fact that it had nutmeg plantations, as the spice was worth its weight in gold at the time. In any event, in 1664, the city was renamed New York.

The city, which is centered on the island of Manhattan, covers an area of over 300 square miles with the boroughs of Brooklyn, The Bronx, Queens, and Staten Island. Its population totals about 8 million, plus another 12 million in the sprawling greater metropolitan area. Demographics aside, all its figures are astonishing, and they demonstrate New York's amazing vitality. It has a road network of about 6,375 miles, and its subway system, one of the word's earliest and largest, operates 24 hours per day carries 4.8 million passengers daily, is the busiest and most hectic on the planet. Nearly 11 million spectators a year attend performances at New York theaters, and the number of patrons eating at its 17,000 restaurants is incalculable. Central Park, the splendid natural area in the heart of Manhattan, is the habitat of 215 bird species, not to mention thousands of squirrels. As if that

279 center Built between 1930 and 1931 as the world's tallest office tower, at the time the Empire State Building was considered the largest financial investment in history. The building, designed by the firm of Shreve, Lamb and Harmon, is 1250 feet tall and has 102 floors. It held the record as the world's tallest building until 1972. Nonetheless, it is a record-breaking building in many other aspects: it weighs 365,000 tons, is clad with over 2 million cubic feet of limestone and granite, has 6400 windows and uses 1172 miles of cables for its elevators.

279 bottom The Chrysler Building was the world's tallest building for just one year, only to lose this title to the Empire State Building. Walter P. Chrysler commissioned William van Alen to design this 77-floor building, which is 1043 feet tall.

280 top left In 1902 the Flatiron Building, designed by Daniel Burnham, became the city's first skyscraper. This unusual triangular construction sits at the intersection of Broadway and Fifth Avenue.

New York

were not enough, New York is one of the most filmed cities in the world. At least 250 films are made here every year, from romances to disaster movies . . . because, after all, in the United States (and thus in the world), everything begins and ends right here.

The very symbol of capitalism, New York is home to the most important stock exchange in the world, and $5.5 trillion ($5,500,000,000,000) or more in securities are traded here annually. The New York Stock Exchange itself is located on Wall Street, one of the streets in Lower Manhattan that was named after the wall marking the southern boundary of the ancient Dutch colony. Even in its dazzling modernity, New York has maintained profound ties to its history. Broadway, the historic avenue that cuts diagonally through Manhattan's strict grid layout, faithfully follows the Wiechquaekeck Trail, the old trade route of the Algonquin Indians who lived here long before the Europeans arrived. Yet at the same time, one could say that the very concept of modernity

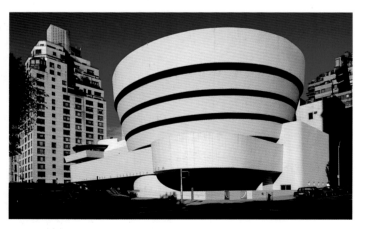

arose in New York. To handle the demand for space created by the massive influx of immigrants into Manhattan's limited area, in the 1890s the Chicago-born concept of vertical residential and office structures was widely adopted. Among the early exemplars of this "new architectural species" was the Flatiron Building (1902), which was followed by dozens of others from the Gothic-trim Woolworth Building (1913), the Chrysler Building (1930), whose Art Deco lines made it one of the most elegant buildings of its kind, to the majestic Empire State Building and Rockefeller Center (both of which built in 1931), and the countless steel-and-glass giants that have made the New York skyline the most famous one in the world.

But the city's uniqueness also comes from its museums – led by the Metropolitan Museum of Art and the Guggenheim, located in the striking helical building designed by Frank Lloyd Wright – and its capacity to be a driving force for ideas, combined with the astounding mélange of people who, over the years, have given New York its unmistakable character. To these of course must be added the Museum of Modern Art (MOMA), with its elegant, austere addition designed by Yoshio Taniguchi.

Though Manhattan has been the focus of this brief overview of New York City, it must be noted that it is inseparable from its four outer boroughs, home to various ethnic, cultural, social centers and even sports hubs. Among the boroughs Brooklyn deserves special mention. This proud and once independent city is connected to Manhattan by the magnificent Brooklyn Bridge, the world's most famous suspension bridge. Opened in 1883 after 14 years of construction, often involving pioneering techniques, and considered the spiritual forerunner of New York's first skyscrapers, it links Manhattan to the area that boasts what is probably the "highest creative density" of modern New York. The old working-class neighborhoods of Brooklyn are where the most unconventional artists now live and where new fashions are born and where exhibition spaces devoted to avant-garde movements are being built. Here too are found vibrant if anachronistic communities of Orthodox Jews. It is no accident that Brooklyn is the hometown of Woody Allen, the figure who, probably in spite of himself, has become the very icon of "New Yorkness," that unique penchant for wit and, above all, self-deprecation that is rarely found anywhere else in the United States.

280 top right The Federal Hall National Monument was built in the first half of the 19th century to house the city's customs offices, and it is now a museum. A bronze statue of George Washington stands at the museum entrance.

280 center and bottom The Solomon R. Guggenheim Museum, built in 1959, is one of Frank Lloyd Wright's undisputed masterpieces. Its design moves away from the precepts of modernism to establish a direct rapport between form and function.

280-281 The focal point of Rockefeller Plaza is the fountain with the gilded statue of Prometheus.

281 bottom left The façades of the turn-of-the-century buildings, with their fire escapes, are the distinctive features of New York City.

281 bottom right Little Italy was settled by Italian immigrants in the mid-19th century. However, in the second half of the 20th century the district shrank considerably as neighboring Chinatown expanded.

282 top The unrelieved bulk of the MetLife Building dwarfs its distinguished neighbors, the New York General Building (shown) and Grand Central Terminal.

282 center The skyscrapers facing the East River enjoy a view of the city's most important bridges.

282 bottom The construction of a new wharf on the East River began in 1982 at the site of the old fish market. The Pier 17 Pavilion, which opened in 1985, features 3 floors of boutiques, cafés and restaurants. It is surrounded by docks and promenades that offer an incomparable view of Brooklyn.

New York

282-283 This view shows Midtown, the area of Manhattan between 14th and 59th Streets. This where the Garment District and the Theater District are located, not to mention the most dazzling stretch of Fifth Avenue.

283 bottom left Times Square – the very heart of New York – was originally called Longacre Square, but was renamed in 1904 when The New York Times moved its headquarters here.

283 bottom right Rockefeller Center is an enormous complex built by oil magnate John D. Rockefeller in the early Thirties. By 1940 it already had 14 skyscrapers of various heights. The first one, now the GE Building (in the photograph), seen from the Avenue of the Americas, was completed in 1933 and is 850 feet tall.

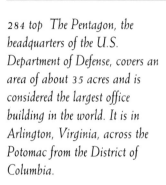

Washington

USA

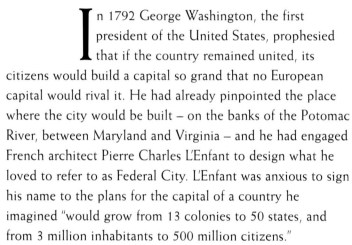

284 top The Pentagon, the headquarters of the U.S. Department of Defense, covers an area of about 35 acres and is considered the largest office building in the world. It is in Arlington, Virginia, across the Potomac from the District of Columbia.

284 center A south view of the White House, the home of all American presidents starting with John Adams. Each of them has made changes of some kind to this 132-room residence. For example, Franklin D. Roosevelt had a pool installed, and Harry Truman built a terrace.

In 1792 George Washington, the first president of the United States, prophesied that if the country remained united, its citizens would build a capital so grand that no European capital would rival it. He had already pinpointed the place where the city would be built – on the banks of the Potomac River, between Maryland and Virginia – and he had engaged French architect Pierre Charles L'Enfant to design what he loved to refer to as Federal City. L'Enfant was anxious to sign his name to the plans for the capital of a country he imagined "would grow from 13 colonies to 50 states, and from 3 million inhabitants to 500 million citizens."

In October of that year, work began on building the presidential residence, designed by the Irish architect James Hoban. Washington himself supervised its construction after budget and timeframe problems arose. However, Washington would never live in what everyone now refers to as the White House. The first president to live there was his successor John Adams, in 1800. Since then, for the entire duration of his term of office every U.S. president has moved into the 132 rooms of the sumptuous Neo-Classical residence at 1600 Pennsylvania Avenue, the most famous address in America – and perhaps in the world.

Unfortunately, Washington did not live long enough to see much of his namesake city completed, one whose historic buildings – because of L'Enfant's visionary plans – make it the most European metropolis in the United States. An area of 100 square miles was envisaged for the capital, but part of the land, where Arlington Cemetery and the Pentagon are now located, was returned to the State of Virginia. Thus, the District of Columbia – the area where the city was built was named in honor of Christopher Columbus – covers 69 square miles. At the very heart of this area are the Capitol Building, which houses the U.S. Congress, and the National Mall, the enormous park-like expanse dominated by the Washington Monument. This white obelisk, which is 555 feet tall, was built in 1885 to commemorate the first president, and even today it is the tallest stone building in the world.

As the country's governmental center, Washington has

284 bottom The Smithsonian Quadrangle is the site of one of the most prestigious cultural institutions in the world, and it includes museums, galleries and a zoo.

284-285 The imposing National Mall, lined with 2000 elm trees, is 2.5 miles long, with the Capitol Building on one end and the Washington Monument on the other.

285 bottom Construction of the Capitol Building – the "heart of America – began in 1793 and took 24 years, spanning the terms of six presidents and six architects.

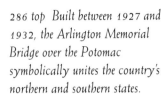

286 top Built between 1927 and 1932, the Arlington Memorial Bridge over the Potomac symbolically unites the country's northern and southern states.

286 center top The building that houses the National Archives is a superb example of Neo-Classical architecture. It was designed at the turn of the 20th century by John Russell Pope.

286 center bottom The Thomas Jefferson Memorial is reflected in the waters of the Tidal Basin at sunset. This splendid Neo-Classical building, a copy of the Pantheon in Rome, is a tribute to the third U.S. president.

286 bottom Lincoln Memorial, modeled after a Greek temple and completed in 1922, is a tribute to the 16th president of the United States, but it has also come to represent a monument to the American ideals of freedom and tolerance.

286-287 Splendid frescoed ceilings decorate the Great Hall of the Thomas Jefferson Building, built in 1897. The building is the central section of the complex housing the Library of Congress, which has one of the richest book collections in the world.

287 bottom left The Vietnam Veterans Memorial, by Chinese-American designer Maya Lin, was inaugurated in 1982. Its face is engraved with the names of the 58,209 soldiers who were killed in America's most controversial war.

287 bottom right The U.S. Marine Corps War Memorial honors the Marines killed in action since 1775. The group represents the capture of Mount Suribachi, on the island of Iwo Jima, on February 3, 1945.

many other buildings of great historical interest and political significance. The most important are the Library of Congress, which developed around the Jefferson Building and holds 100 million documents, including 26 million books and 36 million manuscripts, maps and photographs, as well as the immense National Gallery of Art and the Smithsonian Institution. Considered one of the world's leading research centers, the Smithsonian in its entirety comprises 14 museums, several galleries and a zoo. Its collections are endless, and only 1 percent of them can be displayed on a continuous basis.

Three other structures are fundamental in the democratic development of the United States and the country's recent history. Completed in 1922, the Lincoln Memorial has become a symbol of America's efforts in civil rights: standing on the steps of this monument, Martin Luther King, Jr. gave his most famous speech in 1963. Modeled after a Greek temple, the monument is composed of 36 columns, representing the 36 states that formed the country when Lincoln was president. The Holocaust Museum, dedicated to the victims of Nazism, is just a short distance from the Washington Monument, and the Vietnam Veterans Memorial is near the Lincoln Memorial. The Vietnam Memorial, built in 1982, was designed by Maya Lin, a twenty-year-old student at Yale. Today, it is the most visited monument in Washington.

Critics say that Washington is anonymous. And what is worse – given the American penchant for the colossal – it does not have a skyline, because planning regulations banned buildings taller than 13 floors. For its admirers, who are perhaps more hopeful, the city's domes and colonnades make it the continuation of Europe's Renaissance tradition. In reality, however, perhaps the capital of the world's most powerful nation is merely one president's vision come true.

Miami

USA

I f a revived Miami Beach has come to be considered America's Riviera, it owes its success to an unlikely cop who was always surrounded by beautiful women, drove a Ferrari and sported an Armani wardrobe. And in between, he trounced drug traffickers. We're talking about Don Johnson, star of *Miami Vice*, the television series that, during the Eighties, introduced Americans to fabulous scenes of that strip of sand extending into Biscayne Bay, as well as the tropical heat and *soupçon* of transgression that are the ingredients of any fabulous vacation.

Perhaps without this clever "advertising trick" Miami Beach – above all South Beach, set along the splendid beachfront of Ocean Drive – would have fallen into oblivion, and its marvelous Art Deco hotels, villas and businesses would have continued to deteriorate in the tropical breezes. Instead, South Beach now tops the list of American tourist destinations, and it is considered part of the country's historical heritage. Its perfectly restored buildings couldn't be more glamorous. They were built during the Great Depression by virtually unknown architects – L. Murray Dixon, Henry Hohauser, Albert Anis, Roy France, Robert Swartburg and Anton Skislewicz – who were commissioned to design homes for people who, after the stock market collapsed in 1929, had "champagne taste but a beer budget." They used European Modernism as their model, but then they let their imaginations run wild, turning to forms and colors inspired by Florida's flora and fauna, and the aerodynamic lines of cars, ocean liners and airplanes.

Today – as in the past – Miami Beach is a dream within everyone's reach. In contrast, Coral Gables and Key Biscayne have a different history. The former was built in the 1920s as a town of princely villas; today it is a cultural and artistic enclave. The latter, an island with lush vegetation and breathtaking beaches, was "colonized" by President Nixon, who had his winter *buen retiro* here and was then followed by the jet set. Interestingly, the first time the name "Miami" appeared on a map was the year 1896, when magnate Henry Flagler, the founder of Standard Oil, built a resort on what was merely a stunning deserted coastline and

288-289 Miami Beach is a separate township from Miami and gained the title of "city" in 1917. However, its most famous area – South Beach – began to be exploited in 1870, when Henry and Charles Lum set up a coconut plantation there.

289 top right Since the 1920s, the Berkeley Shores Hotel in South Beach, one of the island's most exclusive hotels located on Ocean Drive and Collins Avenue, has been a must for the rich and famous. It is also popular with many Hollywood movie stars.

288 top Founded at the turn of the 20th century by magnate Henry Flagler, who built the first resort on a stunning deserted coast, Miami now has a population of about 5 million and – in the true American style – has become a city of skyscrapers.

289 bottom left Work to dig the Miami Beach canal began in 1912 through the efforts of John Collins (a landowner who had purchased extensive property on the island) in order to transport commodities.

289 bottom right An architectural "relic" from the period prior to World War II, the Art Deco National Historic District, in the southernmost part of the island of Miami Beach, has been subject to strict conservation plans.

290-291 All around South Florida, and particularly along the coast in front of Miami, the sea is dotted with keys, luxuriant and charming little islands. The most famous is Key Biscayne, which has become a resort area for VIPs from all over the United States.

290 bottom Nicknamed "the Hearst castle of the East" by Miami residents, Villa Vizcaya is a splendid residence inspired by the Italian Renaissance. It was built in 1916 for industrialist James Deering.

291 top left Thanks also to the popular "Miami Vice" TV serial of the Eighties, Miami Beach has become one of the top tourist destinations in the country. It has become so famous and widely appreciated that it has been considered part of the historic heritage of the United States.

291 top right Rows of houses have been built along the Collins Canal, which connects the southern end of Indian Creek, a small waterway, to Biscayne Bay.

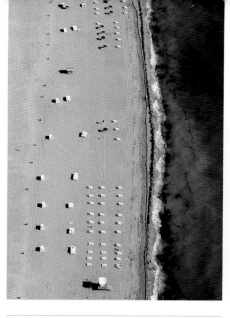

291 bottom *Extensive reclamation work, completed in 2005, has restored the original depth of Collins Canal and made it navigable again.*

brought in railroads. Since then, the progress of this area has always been linked with the concept of "escapism." Though this corner of Florida is widely referred to as the "portal to paradise" because of the millions of retirees from the northern United States who have decided to spend the last years of their lives here, it is the other fugitives coming in from the south that make Miami unique. Half of the metropolitan area's nearly five million residents are of Hispanic descent (many do not even speak English), and most of them are Cubans whom Fidel Castro "allowed" to leave. In the meantime, immigrants have turned Miami into the "capital of the Americas," the link between the Anglo-Saxon and Latino worlds.

Downtown Miami (which, curiously, is a separate township from Miami Beach) owes its appeal to Little Havana: ten blocks crossed by quaint Calle Ocho, the Latino name for the otherwise commonplace 8th Street, that form the main tourist attraction for Hispanic visitors. In fact, "all" the city has to offer – with the exception of the Miami Performing Arts Center, an elegant and sunny complex designed by Cesar Pelli – are dazzling shopping centers, high-rise office buildings and sports facilities, as well as the world's busiest cruise ship port. But this is also where Florida's extraordinary economy thrives, and where a new group of trendsetters is burgeoning: the YUCAs. The acronym stands for Young Urban Cuban-Americans, and this group seems destined to take up the legacy of New York's yuppies.

CENTRAL AND SOUTH AMERICA

great cities of the World

In the early centuries of the Christian era, well before the Europeans discovered Central and South America, these lands were inhabited by populations that developed rich and thriving civilizations. From Mexico to the territory of modern-day Peru and Bolivia, there developed cultures about which we still know very little, but that probably rivaled that of the ancient Romans in architectural marvels, social structure, crafts and trade.

Empires gradually dominated the lands between the two tropics, and the Mayas, Aztecs, Olmecs, Toltecs and Incas built lavish and prosperous cities, as demonstrated by the countless ruins dotting the entire region. For example, we can cite the marvels of Teotihuacán, the "city of the gods" that was founded in about the third century BC and literally vanished between 700 and 900 AD. The remains of at least 2,000 buildings have been classified in this city, which covered an area of nearly 60 square miles and is estimated to have had a population of 200,000 during its golden age. There are places like Copán, Tikal, Chichén Itzá, Palenque and the other major cities of what was the vast Mayan Empire, as well as magnificent Cuzco, the legendary capital of the Incan Empire, which developed in the shadow of the Andes.

According to legend, Cuzco was founded in approximately AD 1200 by two deities who emerged from the waters of Lake Titicaca. In reality, archaeological excavations have uncovered evidence that there was a village in this area as far back as the 8th century. The small town grew slowly at the beginning of the Incan civilization, and was transformed into a powerful imperial city in the early 15th century. In 1438 Pachacuti, a member of the dynasty of Manco Capac, the city's legendary founder, began to transform it into a grand, monumental capital. According to the original city plans, it was laid out in the shape of a puma, an animal sacred to the Incas. Its streets radiated from the puma's heart to reach the borders of an empire that continued to expand. The sides of the mountains were terraced to accommodate the agricultural activities of the city's more than 50,000 people; temples, ceremonial centers, houses and markets were built, and the

most important buildings were constructed using enormous stone blocks fitted together with extraordinary precision. Within just half a century, the Incan Empire dominated the western part of South America, extending nearly 2,500 miles down the Pacific coast, from Colombia to Chile.

During the 15th century, Cuzco mushroomed in both size and wealth. Indeed, when Francisco Pizarro and his troops reached the city on November 8, 1535, the conquistador was enchanted by it. The walls of the courtyard of Coricancha, the Temple of the Sun, were covered with solid gold, and in the middle there was a garden with a corn plant made of silver and gold, and studded with gemstones. For the last great capital of Central-South America, the arrival of the Spanish sadly marked the beginning of the end. As an insult to the vanquished population, the Iglesia de Santo Domingo was built over Coricancha, and the same fate befell the other symbols of the greatest civilization of the Andes.

This destiny was also in store for what is now the biggest metropolis of Latin America, Mexico City, which with its population of nearly 30 million vies with Tokyo and New York for the title of the most highly populated urban area in the world. Founded in 1325 by the Mexica, a population of Aztec descent, it was originally named Tenochtitlán. On August 13, 1521 it fell to the army led by Cortés, who left the magnificent capital of the legendary Montezuma in ruins.

The entire history of the cities of Latin America – and here we have included Mexico due to its cultural affinities with the continent – is thus linked with European colonization. Even in places that had important indigenous settlements, the conquistadors did nothing to safeguard the precious memory of those extraordinary civilizations. In fact, in many cases they committed horrendous crimes against these populations and against the products of those remarkable cultures.

For the most part, today's cities are the result of this colonization. They have a European soul, and were established after the Spanish and Portuguese conquered the continent. Thus, from Mexico City to Buenos Aires, the great metropolises of Latin America share a certain sense of

disorientation, a lack of cultural identity that has been manifested in exuberant and sometimes heedless growth due to the rapid urbanization of rural populations. Founded and developed by Europeans, they are home to millions of descendents of those ancient native populations and of the conquistadors, forming a multiethnic fabric that has nevertheless lost at least half of its social, religious and cultural roots.

Central and South America cover an area of nearly 8.9 million square miles, and with a little more than 500 million inhabitants, the continent is not densely populated. To be more precise, due to the enormous environmental and climatic variations that characterize it – from the equatorial areas of Ecuador and the forests of the Amazon to the more temperate areas of central and northern Chile, Uruguay and central Argentina, and down to the desolate plains of Patagonia and Tierra del Fuego – it presents striking demographic differences in relation to latitude. One-third of the total population lives in Brazil, which also covers one-third of the continent's surface area. However, because of the vastness of the Amazon rain forest, most of its inhabitants are concentrated in the easternmost regions of the country, above all along the Atlantic coast. And this is where – with only a few exceptions – the continent's leading metropolises are located. Of the 20 largest cities in Central and South America, 12 are in Brazil. Apart from Mexico City and Buenos Aires, São Paulo and Rio de Janeiro are by far the most populous urban areas, respectively with 16 and 11 million inhabitants.

Established for the most part as the offshoots of colonial settlements in the first half of the 16th century, when explorers crossed the Atlantic to reach the New World, the cities of Latin America experienced an initial phase of great development toward the late 19th century. This was followed by further growth in the first half of the 20th century, when waves of immigrants arrived from Europe, due also to the two world wars. Argentina, Brazil, Venezuela and Colombia mainly attracted Spaniards, Portuguese and Italians, who quickly gave South American cities a European appearance, also from an architectural standpoint, as was the case in Buenos Aires throughout the 19th century. An incredible melting pot of cultures, the city that was declared the capital of Argentina in 1880 gradually took in Basques, Italians, Czechs, Poles, Croatians and Ukrainians, to the point that by the end of the century seven residents out of ten were foreigners.

More recent urbanization is instead the result of internal migration, and this process has generated metropolises that are astonishing in size, like the ones we have already discussed, as well as the Peruvian capital Lima, which has a population of nearly seven million, Bogotá, Belo Horizonte, Porto Alegre, Recife and Medellín. This migration is due mainly to economic reasons, because the rural populations flock to the capitals in search of better-paying jobs, but it is also politically motivated. For example, Lima has recently experienced another rapid phase of immigration because many rural residents, particularly in the northern part of the country, have abandoned the areas where the terrorist group Sendero Luminoso has been active.

Thus, the great metropolises of Central and South America reflect stratified situations in which boundless wealth, held by the heirs of the ancient colonizers and large landowners, clashes with the poverty of slums crowded with new immigrants, most of whom are unable to find jobs and, driven by desperation, end up turning to crime. The continent of contradictions is one where a world that is still profoundly tied to agricultural tradition, which plays a leading role in the economy, is at odds with a rich and well-educated middle class that is pushing Latin America toward impressive modern industrial development, relying also on the availability of cheap labor.

Lastly, there are now divergences – though seemingly less evident – between the timid demands of a tradition wiped out by the colonizers, with its *curanderos* and animist religions, and a civilization that crushed the native populations for centuries, only to appreciate, too late, the immense cultural heritage that has been lost. And yet, contradictions have often been the source of the most dynamic momentum for the progress of humanity.

293 left An elegant early 20th-century building houses the Civic Museum of São Paulo in Brazil.

293 center "El Angel de la Independencia" stands proudly over Paseo de la Reforma in Mexico City.

293 right The Capitolio in Havana replicates the architecture of the Capitol Building in Washington.

294-295 *The Zócalo, the immense rectangular square in the heart of town, overlays the Aztec ceremonial center of México-Tenochtitlan. The Catedral Metropolitana, the Palacio Nacional and the remains of the Templo Mayor line the square.*

294 bottom *The Catedral Metropolitana, facing the Zócalo Square, was built in various stages between 1567 and 1788. It combines the Spanish Baroque, Mestizo-Churrigueresque and Neo-Classical styles. The two towers were built with stones from Aztec temples.*

Mexico City

MEXICO

W ith a metropolitan area of almost 580 square miles and a population of 28 million, a figure that grows by nearly 700,000 people a year, Mexico City is the largest urban agglomeration on the American continent – and perhaps on the planet. It is actually a city-state whose official name is México Distrito Federal, which in turn is divided into 16 *delegaciones* or subdistricts and 400 *colonias* or quarters. Its denizens call it *México* (proudly referring instead to their country as *La República*) or, more simply, *D.F.* Or they affectionately but ironically call it *El Monstruo Querido*.

Aside from its sheer enormity, the "Dear Monster" generates 25 percent of the Mexican economy (estimated to be worth approximately \$815 billion per year) and, in fact, the Distrito Federal alone is considered the thirtieth largest economy in the world. Its intellectual vitality is astounding. Playwright Harold Pinter says he comes here whenever he feels he needs to know what's new in the world, and in terms of the number of theaters Mexico City is rivaled only by New York and Paris. So far, we have talked about "dear" Mexico City. Instead, the "monster" part has one of the highest crime rates in the world, and is distinguished by the acrid smell of smog (there is one car for every five inhabitants), which is the cause of the respiratory problems most of its citizens experience. The city's enviable position at an altitude of 7,500 feet does virtually nothing to counter this. The number of days in a year that one can stand in the Zócalo, the main square, and admire the view of Popocatépetl and Iztaccíhuatl, the two volcanoes that dominate the city, can be counted on one hand. The two volcanoes, which are still active, often spew smoke, making the gray mantle over the city even denser.

It is a high-energy city of glaring contrasts – going from magnificent streets as wide as highways, like Paseo de la Reforma and Avenida Insurgentes, to intimate little alleys – but it is also a city of intriguing layers of history. The surfaces of its ultramodern skyscrapers, from the World Trade Center to the Torre Mayor (2003), which at 738 feet is the tallest American building south of the United States, the Torre Altos and the

295 top The façade of the Sagrario, next to the Catedral Metropolitana, is magnificent. Following the extensive work done on it and completed in 2000, the capital's most important religious complex has now been taken off the list of endangered world heritage sites.

295 center The nave, 4 aisles and 14 chapels in the Catedral Metropolitana house extraordinary artwork, such as the phantasmagoric Altar de los Reyes, sculpted by Jerónimo de Balbas in 1723.

295 bottom The Iglesia de Santiago dominates Plaza de las Tres Culturas, so called because its buildings evoke the country's mestizo present, Spanish past and Aztec origins. The ruins of Tlatelolco are located here: this was the site of the last battle for the conquest of Mexico, waged on August 13, 1521.

Torre Latinoamericana, reflect the elaborate Baroque architecture of the city's colonial buildings and even the monumental remains of the Aztec civilization. The immense Zócalo square is emblematic. Overlooking this square are the oldest cathedral in America and the Palacio Nacional, the seat of government. The foundations of the Palacio Nacional were laid by the conquistador Hernán Cortés, and its treasures include a series of splendid murals by the famous artist Diego Rivera. Just beyond it are the ruins of the Templo Mayor, a magnificent Aztec sanctuary discovered in 1978 during excavation work for the subway.

Each place and each building in Mexico City is a fabulous discovery. Despite the fact that they have been worn away by pollution, the brilliant colors of the Spanish *azulejos* and of the more recent buildings, like the Polyforum Cultural Siqueiros (1968), are dazzling. The Polyforum houses the *Marcha de la Humanidad*, the mural by David Siqueiros: Covering an area of 48,400 square feet, it is the largest work of its kind ever executed. Amidst this chaos, the clean and simple Bauhaus lines of the Bacardi Office Building, built by Mies van der Rohe in 1961, stand out starkly, and the care lavished on the city's countless museums is astonishing. One of these is the Museo Nacional de Antropología, which houses the most extraordinary collection of pre-Columbian artifacts in the world. Even its location is marvelous. It is in the middle of the Bosque de Chapualtepec, the park crisscrossed by navigable lakes that represent the last remains of the legendary "city of water" that was México before the arrival of Cortés. Back then, the Aztec capital was an array of pyramids, hanging gardens and white palaces, separated by bridges and canals and built on an immense lake. One can only wonder how famous Venice would have been if the Spanish had not destroyed the city of México to turn it into the capital of their colonial empire.

296 top With its daring asymmetrical architecture, the Centro Bursátil stands out among the skyscrapers of Paseo de la Reforma, the avenue in the center of Mexico City. The building houses the Mexican stock exchange, and the trading hall is located in the spherical building next to it.

296 center The Torre Latinoamericana, which is nearly 600 feet tall, towers over the business district of Cuauhtémoc. This impressive building was completed in 1956 and ushered in Mexico City's metamorphosis into a modern megalopolis.

297 bottom left The Museo de Antropología e Historia, was built in 1964 to house the largest and most valuable collection of pre-Columbian artifacts in the world.

297 bottom right The Nueva Basílica de Santa María de Guadalupe, opened in 1976, is a majestic building with a diameter of 328 feet. The church can hold 10,000 people.

296 bottom At the beginning of Paseo de la Reforma, a 118-foot-tall Corinthian column, topped by a statue of the Angel of Victory, was erected in 1910 to celebrate the centennial of Mexico's independence.

296-297 The Stadio Azul and Plaza de Toros represent a dream come true for magnate Neguib Simon, who financed their construction in the mid-20th century. They can respectively accommodate 80,000 and 50,000 people.

298-299 The most picturesque portion of Malecón, the seafront of Centro Habana (the street's official name is Avenida Antonio Maceo), is lined with splendid turn-of-the-century buildings. They are painted in bright colors that have been worn away by the elements, giving this thoroughfare an unmistakably decadent charm.

298 bottom Inaugurated as a hotel in 1930 and converted into a casino in 1955, the Hotel Nacional, which has 457 rooms and 16 suites, is one of the most impressive structures along the Havana seafront.

299 top left Castillo de San Salvador de la Punta was built on Havana's northern coast between 1589 and 1630 to "support" Castillo del Morro, the larger fortress across from it.

299 top right Designed by Italian military architect Battista Antonelli in 1610, Castillo del Morro — together with Castillo de la Punta — marks the entrance to the canal leading into the bay. In 1762 the British laid siege to the fortress, which finally surrendered after valiantly resisting for 44 days.

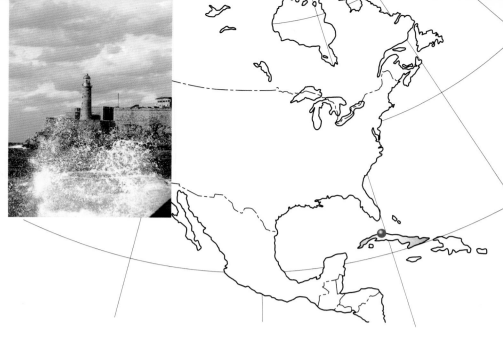

Havana

CUBA

First and foremost, Havana is a city of the sea. It was in 1519 that, as they gazed at the ocean, the Spanish founded it near a natural harbor guarded by a promontory of dark rock. It was here that, between 1589 and 1630, they built the Castillo del Morro and, across from it, the Castillo de la Punta, closing the access channel with a chain to bar entry to any enemies.

In the course of its history, galleons have landed in Havana, bringing treasures and slaves. The fleets of both Drake and Morgan crossed in front of the coast – both decided against attacking – and the British conquered it in 1762, holding the city for 11 months before returning it to the Spanish in exchange for Florida. In 1898, the American battleship *U.S.S. Maine* exploded in front of Havana Harbor, an incident the United States used as an excuse to claim credit for the Cubans' anti-colonialist struggle and take Spain's place in dominating the island. In more recent times, ferries arrived packed with Americans, who discovered paradise in Havana during Prohibition at home.

The only time the city has looked inland was in 1959, when it enthusiastically embraced the revolution led by Fidel Castro and Che Guevara. Then, once again, it turned its gaze back to the sea, waiting for Soviet merchant ships to bring progress or dreaming of a different future in Miami. Today, it seems that Havana has no interests other than the waves breaking along the Malecón, its breathtaking beachfront. The Cuban capital is now effectively an "island" of two million inhabitants, the capital of an island that can only trust in its own capacities.

Anachronistic, beguiling and proud, Havana has managed to "absorb" its entire history, cloaking itself in a patina of decadence that merely enhances its charm. Its old buildings remains "conceptually" decadent even after restoration work, much of which funded by UNESCO, which added Habana Vieja to its World Heritage List in 1982. Plaza de Armas boasts enchanting views, like the Castillo de la Real Fuerza, the oldest fortress in the Americas, the Palacio del Segundo

299 center The Gran Teatro de la Habana is the official venue of the prestigious Ballet Nacional de Cuba. Sculptures by Giuseppe Moretti decorate the four domes of this Neo-Baroque masterpiece, which was built in 1914.

299 bottom The Capitolio Nacional is the stateliest building in Centro Habana. Designed by Otero and Bens, it was completed in 1929 and was the seat of Cuba's Congress until 1959; it now houses the Cuban Academy of Science and the National Library of Science and Technology.

300 top *An enormous white monument commemorates Maximo Gómez, the military leader of Cuba's revolutionary troops and one of the heroes of the struggle for independence from Spain between 1868 and 1898.*

Cabo and Palacio de los Capitanes Generales, both of which are masterpieces of the tropical Baroque style, and the Neo-Classical church commemorating the place where Havana's first Mass was celebrated. Beyond the square, Calle Obispo, Calle Mercadares and Calle Oficio boast elegant colonial residences dominated by the impressive 18th-century cathedral dedicated to San Cristóbal, the patron saint of the city.

Habana Vieja and the area known as Centro Habana are separated by the enormous tree-lined square of Parque Central, with sternly impressive buildings like the Tribunal Supremo Popular, as well as graceful examples of the colonial Art Nouveau style such as the Teatro García Lorca. The residential buildings behind them are more melancholy, despite their gaily-painted pastel façades. Set on a rise dominating the entire area is the Capitolio Nacional. Modeled after the Capitol Building in Washington, it was the seat of Cuba's Congress until 1959; it now houses the Cuban Academy of Science and the National Library of Science and Technology. Lastly, Plaza de la Revolución, in the Vedado area, is the capital's venue for mass events. The stage from which President Castro gives his speeches is in front of the Memorial José Martí, a monument that is 466 feet tall. Paradoxically, Vedado is also the location of the most evident architectural examples built by the "enemies" from the United States, like the skyscrapers of the Hotel Nacional and the Hotel Habana Riviera, and numerous American cars from the Fifties, with their chrome finishes that have miraculously survived time and the city's salt air, can be seen all over Havana.

Perhaps this is the same miracle that has allowed the people of Havana to do all they can – and with a smile – to survive the restrictions imposed by the government and make the many foreigners flocking to the city feel right at home. After all, Havana is a magnificent deception.

300 center top *The splendid Baroque building of the Catedral de San Cristóbal, originally consecrated to the Virgin Mary, was renamed to honor Christopher Columbus, whose remains were supposedly buried here from 1796 to 1898.*

300 center bottom *The work of Italian artist Giuseppe Gaggini, the Fountain of the Lions was built in Plaza de San Francisco in 1836. The church and convent of St. Francis of Assisi are located on the square.*

300 bottom Plaza Vieja is surrounded by the porticoed buildings of the wealthy 19th-century bourgeoisie.

300-301 Items from pre-revolutionary Cuba can often be found at the daily market held near Castillo de la Punta.

301 bottom left The Real Fabrica de Tabacos Partagas is a point of reference for cigar aficionados.

301 bottom right The 465-foot-tall monument to José Martí in Plaza de la Revolución is the tallest structure in Havana.

302-303 Installed in 1919, the cableway to Pão de Açúcar can transport 1360 people an hour to the top of the green hill (1293 feet) that marks the point where Guanabara Bay and the Atlantic Ocean meet. Its Portuguese name, which means Sugarloaf, is actually derived from the word pau-nh-acuqua, a Guarani term that means "tall hill." 302 bottom Nearly 100 feet tall and weighing 110 tons, the statue of Christ the Redeemer was supposed to be installed on Corcovado in 1922, but it was not completed until 1931.

303 top Largo do Boticário, on the slopes of Corcovado, was named after Joaquim Luiz da Silva Santo, the pharmacist of the royal family, who lived there in the mid-1800s. Dotted with picturesque colonial-style houses clad with azulejos, it is one of the city's most charming spots.

303 center The Maracaná, inaugurated in 1950, is the world's largest stadium (125,000 seats), but it is also a legend: this is where Pelé scored his 1000th goal in 1969.

303 bottom This tram – which the Cariocas call o bondinho – is always crowded. It leads to the picturesque barrio of Santa Teresa, following a route that goes through many of the city's historic districts.

304-305 This is one of the most famous views in the world: Christ the Redeemer and Sugarloaf Mountain overlooking Rio Harbor. Founded by the Portuguese in the mid-1500s, today Rio de Janeiro continues to evolve in many ways.

Rio de Janeiro

BRAZIL

In 1908, writer Colho Neto coined the name *Cidade Maravilhosa* for Rio de Janeiro. Fifty years later Vinicius de Moraes, Brazil's greatest poet, wrote a song that was destined to consecrate the legend of the marvelous city: *Garota de Ipanema*.

The girls of Rio dance to the sensual notes of the samba. They dance, and not only during the wildest Carnival celebration on the planet but also at Ipanema, Copacabana and Leblon, the city's most famous beaches – and, indeed, the most famous ones in the world.

They are dominated by the unmistakable profile of Sugarloaf Mountain and Mount Corcovado, from which the open-armed statue of Christ the Redeemer seems to bless all the beauty at his feet.

The panorama of Rio is simply stunning. Perhaps this explains the blunder of Portuguese captain Arturo Gonçalves when he arrived at Guanabara Bay on January 1, 1502. Thinking he had reached the mouth of a river, he named the place River of January: Rio de Janeiro. About sixty years later, the king of Portugal decided to found the city of São Sebastião do Rio de Janeiro there, and the Tamoio Indians who lived in the area named it Carioca, which means "white house."

Over the centuries, the Europeans mixed with the blacks brought in from Africa to work on the sugar and coffee plantations, and the Carioca lineage was established in Rio. Skin color aside (there are thousands of nuances), an ever-ready smile and a special talent for enjoying life are what best distinguish this group. Yet beyond its picture-postcard façade, Rio de Janeiro is a chaotic city of 6 million inhabitants, and 300 *favelas* have developed on its *morros*, or hills. Indubitably the *favelas* are not exclusive to Rio; nevertheless these precarious settlements rarely even have electricity or running water, and in many cases drug traffickers control their economy.

But one thing is undeniable. Even those who live in the "roughest" *favelas* smile, and that is because each of them can go and dance at the enormous entertainment arena known as the Sambodromo, built to host the Carnival parade, or they can go cheer their favorite team at the Maracanã. With a seating capacity of 125,000, Maracanã is the world's largest stadium, but it is also a legend, as this is where Pelé scored the 1000th goal of his career in 1969.

Because of its boundless vitality, Rio changes constantly, even in terms of city planning.

Rio de Janeiro

Only a few palaces and Baroque churches remain in the center of town, which until the 19th century was a colonial jewel and the seat of the court of Portugal's King John IV, who ruled his empire from here. Between 1900 and 1910 Francisco Pereira Passos, who was governor at the time, razed nearly everything to give Rio de Janeiro the monumentality of Paris under the Second Empire. More recent constructions include quarters like Cinelândia (1940-50), an extraordinary Brazilian "set" spawned by a passion for the Hollywood movie industry, and skyscrapers clad in mirror glass that have redesigned the cityscape. As Oscar Niemeyer complained, Rio has been overwhelmed by verticality. In 1937, the famous architect worked with Le Corbusier and Lucio Costa – thereby also sealing Niemeyer's alliance with

Costa, which would culminate with the Brasília project – to construct the Ministry of Education. For this building, he chose a "soft" approach in harmony with the surrounding landscape. However, the same thing cannot be said of the Catedral Metropolitana (1976), the pyramid-shaped work by Edgar de Fonseca that is 315 feet tall and can hold 10,000 people. Fortunately, across from this pachyderm are the 49 arches of the Lapa aqueduct, one of the few constructions in Rio that can boast 250 years of history. The tramway leading to the quarter of Santa Teresa moves up the aqueduct. Climbing aboard *o bondinho*, which is what the Cariocas affectionately call this tram, means feeling the magical beat of the city. Vinicius de Moraes was right when he said: "Rio is the drum of Brazil."

306 top As legend would have it, the beach of Copacabana was established in 1858 as a recreation spot. It is said that in August of that year, two whales were sighted and hundreds of people rushed from the city to see them. After the two whales left, the people stayed there for 3 days and 3 nights of festivities. In reality, the place that is now one of the most famous beaches in the world did not become a resort area until the early 20th century.

306 bottom A paradise for swimmers and surfers, the beach at Ipanema has also claimed it place in the history of swimsuits. The first thong bathing suit was supposed worn here at a beach party in 1972.

306-307 The beach at Ipanema — made famous by Vinicius de Moraes' lyrics, set to music by Antonio Carlos Jobim — extends for over 1 mile along the Rio shoreline. The Jardim de Alah canal divides Ipanema from Leblon.

307 bottom Nicknamed "Cidade Maravilhosa" because of its superb natural setting, Rio de Janeiro extends for approximately 12 miles along an alluvial plain, with the ocean on one side and mountains, covered with dense tropical vegetation, on the other. The Parque Nacional da Tijuca, covering an area of 46 square miles, extends from the city outskirts.

308 bottom right The city has
a population of over 10 million
(plus 8 million in the suburbs),
and as a result its residential
areas are also crowded with
skyscrapers.

309 top left Once the tallest
building in the city, the Altino
Arantes skyscraper is located at the
highest point in the center, and its
panoramic terrace is a tourist
attraction.

308-309 The sinuous structure in
the middle is Oscar Niemeyer's
Copán. Nicknamed o formigueiro,
it is listed in the Guinness Book of
World Records as the biggest
residential building on the planet.

308 bottom left The Pinheiros, in
the picture, runs through the
metropolitan area of São Paulo. The
Tamanduateí (the earliest settlement
was built on its banks in 1554) and
the Tietê also flow past the city.

309 top right *Little remains of the colonial city, and replicas have replaced many historic buildings. One example is the Catedral Metropolitana, inaugurated in 1956, which can hold 8000 people.*

São Paulo

BRAZIL

The 425-foot Prédio Martinelli, the city's oldest skyscraper, forms one of the tips of the Triângulo, the heart of São Paulo's financial district. The building was erected in 1929 and is a very faithful reproduction of New York's Empire State Building. Although history recounts that its first owner, the Italian magnate Giuseppe Martinelli, went bankrupt due to his extravagance in its construction, the skyscraper remains one of the imposing testimonials to the success of Italian immigrants in Brazil.

The Edifício Itália is situated in the same neighborhood, close to the Praça da República. This 500-foot triangular skyscraper with rounded corners was built in 1965 and has 4,000 windows. Several years ago it gained the honor of being added to the list of national monuments, as it is the highest expression of the "Verticalist" movement that produced the Palácio Zarzur Kogan, Altino Arantes and e-Tower, and consecrated São Paulo as Brazil's economic and financial capital, also from an architectural standpoint.

The population of approximately 16 million of the urban area of Greater São Paulo generates most of the country's wealth. Likewise, the city has sparked every major social and political renewal movement. It is no coincidence that the beloved and seasoned Lula da Silva, elected president in 2002, acquired experience here as an auto industry union movement leader. Whereas Rio is the city of play, São Paulo is the city of work. Since 1870, one million Portuguese, Galicians and Italians (who not only have "their" own skyscrapers, but also a large and very lively district, Bela Vista) have flocked here, in order to build themselves a future. Libertade, the quarter housing the largest Japanese community outside the homeland, has also arisen here since the Fifties. Traders of Syrian and Lebanese descent still prosper in the city, with stores in the Praça da Sé, but are now threatened by the industriousness of the latest and feistiest wave of immigrants, the Koreans.

São Paulo has been an enterprising city from the very beginning. Its first courageous inhabitants were the Jesuits, who founded a mission in the wild and inhospitable territory of the Guaraní Indians with the intention of converting them. They were followed by the cowboy-like *bandeirantes*, who explored the mineral resources of the territory and opened up a route between the Paraná Basin and the coast. The next to arrive were the farmers, attracted by the fertility of the *terra roxa* of the São Paulo countryside, where they planted coffee. During the second half of the 19th century, the vitality and industriousness of what was still a small town of 60,000 inhabitants witnessed the arrival of the British, who chose it as the linchpin for the construction of the Brazilian railway system.

Over the past fifty years this effervescence has been followed by massive industrialization. Needless to say, this process has spared little of the original city. Although its elaborate Baroque style can be misleading, the Pátio do Colégio, in Praça da Sé, is simply a 19th-century replica of the first Jesuit mission. Only the name of the *bandeirantes* survives, in the form of the new and very tall telecommunications tower, although the daring cast-iron Art Nouveau building of the Estação da Luz, the first railway station built by the British architect Charles Henry Drive, is original.

However, the city's most famous building is the Copán, an enormous structure with sinuous forms designed by the famous Oscar Niemeyer and listed in the *Guinness Book of Records* as the largest residential building on the planet. It houses 1,160 apartments and has so many residents that the city council has decided to give it its own ZIP code: a city within the metropolis. The locals call it *o formigueiro*, the anthill, but are truly proud of it, because it is one of the symbols of their greatness. As Marlene Dietrich once said, and with no offense to the Cariocans, "Rio is a beauty. But São Paulo – São Paulo is a city."

310 top The statue of Juan
Lavalle, the hero of Argentina's
struggle for independence and the
governor of the provinces of Río de
la Plata in 1828-29, dominates the
square named after him. The Teatro
Colón, known for its graceful Belle
Époque architecture, faces the
square.

Buenos Aires
ARGENTINA

From an etymological standpoint, porteños are "people of the port." From a poetical one, however, *porteños* are people who alternate melancholy with unbridled enthusiasm, and nostalgia for their origins with the wish to build something new. And though their sights are set on the horizon, they remain anchored to a land that still offers hope for the future. In short, *porteños* are the people of Buenos Aires. After all, Buenos Aires was a port long before it became a city and then the metropolis that is home to 40 percent of Argentina's 33 million inhabitants. Paradoxically, the first to reach it did not come by sea. In 1536 the Spaniard Pedro de Mendoza, heading an expedition of 1,600 men sent to

colonize strategic areas along the course of the Río de la Plata, pitched camp on a curve of the river and called the precarious settlement Espiritu Santu, and its port Nuestra Señora de Buen Ayre. Despite the name dedicated to the patron saint of sailors, the small colony was not successful: The scarcity of food and the unfriendly attentions of the fierce natives convinced the Spanish to abandon it after just a few months.

Forty years passed before another Spaniard, Juan de Garay, returned, this time more successfully. Nonetheless, it was not until the mid-18th century that the small river port of Santa María de Buenos Aires, as it had been renamed, grew into a town. It was governed by a series of viceroys appointed by the Spanish Crown, due to its growing importance as a port of call for trade between South America and Europe. Indeed, British troops tried to conquer it in 1806 and 1807.

During those years the Spanish Empire was in decline and engaged in conflicts with several other European powers. The citizens of Buenos Aires, the offspring of Iberian immigrants who by this time felt closer to their port than their distant homeland, rebelled in the May Revolution. The event took its name from the date of the viceroy's deposition – May 25, 1810 – and led to the independence of the Río de la Plata provinces four years later, a fundamental step toward creating the nation of Argentina. Seventy years later Buenos Aires was declared the country's capital. It had undergone great change in the meantime. Its architecture effectively makes it the "clone" of a European city, mixing the style of Paris with the austerity of London and the Mediterranean allure of Barcelona. This striking blend reflects the ethnic composition of its population, which came here from all parts of Europe. It has been calculated that at the end of the 19th century 72 percent of the city's inhabitants were foreigners. The earliest arrivals were the Basques, followed by the Italians, and subsequently Poles, Czechs, Croatians and Ukrainians, many of whom were Jewish. Finally, the 20th century witnessed the arrival of enormous numbers of Chinese and Middle-Eastern immigrants (Carlos Menem, Argentina's controversial recent president, is of Syrian origin). In the past one hundred years, Buenos Aires has been the theater of dramatic events alternating military dictatorships with the government of Juan Domingo Perón, elected as the country's leader three times since 1946. It was he who gave voice to the workers and inspired Peronism, the extraordinary movement whose icon was the president's legendary wife, Evita. Following

310 center and bottom The Casa Rosada (top) and the Cabildo are respectively the seat of Argentina's executive power and the old Spanish government building, constructed in (1765) and now the location of the city's historical museum.

311 An imposing allegorical monument commemorating the abolition of slavery in 1813 and the independence of the provinces of Río de la Plata in 1816 stands in front of Palacio del Congreso, which is a copy of the Capital Building in Washington.

a series of ups and downs, he was ousted in 1976 by the coup d'état of General Jorge Videla, who for six years paralyzed the country with the terror of his regime. Although the road to democracy was long and painful, today the end seems to have been reached. The same cannot be said for the economy, however, judging from the colossal crisis that hit Argentina in 2001 and whose serious consequences are still felt by its citizens. Buenos Aires bears clear signs of its anguished history, along with a never-placated penchant for grandeur. Although at night its streets revert to the hunting ground of the *cartoneros*, the new poor seeking refuse to recycle, the *porteños* do everything they can to make their capital worthy of the title of Latin America's most noble and European city. And they have good reason. Buenos Aires expresses elegance, energy and culture at every turn, with its 47 *barrios*, each of which has a distinctive personality, and its *Microcentro*, which actually covers a large area, despite its name.

The city's heart, and site of major political and social events, is the Plaza de Mayo. Flanking it are the Cathedral (1827), the Cabildo, the ancient seat of Spanish power that now houses the History Museum of the May Revolution, and the Casa Rosada. This 19th-century building is the country's center of power and owes its name to the color it was painted at the end of the 1800s. During his presidency, Domingo Faustino Sarmiento decided to combine the colors of the flags of the two opposing political parties, the Federalists (red) and the Unitarians (white). The result, of course, was pink. Avenida de Mayo links Plaza de Mayo with Congreso, which is home to the monumental Parliament Building. Midway between the two squares, the Avenida de Mayo intersects Avenida 9 de Julio: 460 feet wide, it is one of the most spacious streets in the world. It stretches for over a mile and a half, and is lined by superb Neo-Classical and *Belle Époque* buildings (such as the Teatro Colón). Further ahead is Manzana de las Luces, the quadrilateral where the Jesuits founded the university during the colonial period, and skyscrapers built during the 20th century, including the splendid Edificio Kavanagh. Although the monumental buildings of the institutional center are very interesting, it is in the *barrios* that Buenos Aires reveals its most attractive features. Several of these are noteworthy. San Telmo is the birthplace of tango, the poignant local music that has conquered the world. La Boca is the quintessential Italian *barrio*, whose brightly painted old *conventillos* (poor corrugated-iron houses built to accommodate immigrants) now house art galleries, restaurants and meeting places. Recoleta is the trendiest district of the capital and is famous for its cemetery, the burial place of Eva Perón and the king of tango Carlos Gardel, who are both the subject of popular devotion. Palermo is rich in romantic squares and

spacious parks, whereas Puerto Madero is the *barrio* on the river. Following a period of neglect that lasted several decades, an ambitious recovery program was commenced for this area of port warehouses, which was completed in 1998. Its streets were given musical women's names, and the slender and equally feminine Puente de la Mujer was built across the river to the designs of Santiago Calatrava. Despite the economic crisis, Puerto Madero immediately became the most glittering, expensive and fashionable entertainment area of Buenos Aires, exuding creativity and optimism. Perhaps this is because the *porteños*, who are first and foremost "people of the port," come here to breathe the *buena ayre* that gave their city its name.

---

312 *The 230-foot Obelisk that towers over the intersection of Avenida 9 de Julio and Avenida Corrientes was dedicated to commemorate the 400th anniversary of the founding of Buenos Aires.*

313 top *The Caminito is a picturesque pedestrian route in the barrio of La Boca. The houses are decorated with murals portraying tango scenes, and they are examples of a tradition started by painter Benito Martín.*

313 bottom *La Boca's hallmark is its festive atmosphere. Today, the conventillos – poor houses made of wood and corrugated metal that housed the first Italian immigrants – now hold shops, bars and art galleries.*

BIBLIOGRAPHY

Diamond Jared, *Armi, acciaio e malattie*, Turin, 1998.
State of World Population Report, United Nations Population Fund, 2004.
World Population Prospects: The 2004 Revision, United Nations Population Division, 2005.
Torres Marco, *Luoghi magnetici. Spazi pubblici nella città moderna e contemporanea*, Milan, 2005.
Vicari Haddock Serena, *La città contemporanea*, Bologna, 2004.
Rykwert Joseph, *La seduzione del luogo. Storia e futuro della città*, Turin, 2003.
Benevolo Leonardo, *La città nella storia d'Europa*, Rome-Bari, 2002.
Benevolo Leonardo, *Storia della città. Voll. 1-3*, Rome-Bari, 1993.
Calabi Donatella, *Storia della città. L'età moderna*, Padua, 2001.

Zevi Bruno, *Controstoria e storia dell'architettura. Vol. 1: Panoramica dell'Architettura mondiale. Paesaggi e città*, Rome, 1999.
Yatsko Pamela, *New Shanghai*, New York, 2001.
Dalrymple William, *City of Djinns*, London, 1993.
Dal Co Francesco, Forster Kurt W. and Soutter Arnold Hadley, *Frank O. Gehry, tutte le opere*, Milan, 1998.
Tzonis Alexander, *Santiago Calatrava*, Milan, 2005.
Buchanan Peter, *Renzo Piano Building Workshop. Voll. 1-4*, London, 2003.
Pawley Martin, *Norman Foster. Architettura globale*, Milan, 1999.
Lahuerta Juan J., *Antoni Gaudí (1852-1926). Architettura, ideologia e politica*, Milan, 2003.
Wiseman Carter, *I.M. Pei: A Profile in American Architecture*, New York, 2001.

INDEX

PHOTOGRAPHIC CREDITS

Franz Aberham/Anzenberger/Contrasto: page 259 center

Adenis/Gaff/Laif/Contrasto: pages 64 top right, 66 top left

Aisa: pages 35 top, 46-47, 47 bottom left, 62-63, 64 bottom, 74 bottom left and right, 80-81, 84 top, 166-167, 167 top, 172 top left, 192 center and bottom, 196-197, 200-201, 207 bottom right, 208 top left, 293 top center, 294 bottom, 295 top right, 295 bottom, 296 top, 297 bottom right, 312

Alamy Images: pages 11, 28 top left, 28 bottom, 31 left, 52-53, 52 bottom left, 54 center, 56 top left, right and bottom, 56-57, 57 bottom right, 59 top right, 60-61, 60 bottom, 61 center, 62 top left, right and center, 80 bottom right, 83 top, 83 bottom, 84-85, 116 bottom right, 117 top center, 117 bottom, 122 bottom, 173 bottom right, 184 bottom left, 191 top right, 195 bottom, 197 bottom, 198 top, 198 center, 214 center, 216 bottom, 217 bottom, 220 bottom, 224 top left, 234 bottom left, 236 center, 243 top left, 261 top right, 265 top left, 267 center, 273 top left, 280 top left, 282-283, 283 bottom right, 303 top right, 303 center, 304-305, 306 top and center, 307 bottom

Glen Allison/Agefotostock/Contrasto: pages 212-213, 216-217

Antonio Attini/Archivio White Star: pages 2-3, 12-13, 14-15, 18 left, 19 top center, 19 top right, 19 bottom, 20 right, 21 top left, 21 top right, 47 bottom right, 49 bottom right, 66 top right and center, 102-103, 102 bottom left, 103 center, 105 bottom, 106 center, 132 top center, 133 bottom left, 134 top, 134 center top, 134 bottom, 141 top right, 149 center, 151 bottom, 152 bottom left, 153 top, 174 top left and center, 174 center, 176-177, 176 bottom right, 177 top left and right, 178 bottom right, 179 top, 179 center and bottom, 203 top left, 218-219, 219 center, 220 top, 220 center top, 221 bottom left, 221 bottom right, 223 top left and right, 228 top left, 228-229, 229 bottom left and right, 232 top left, 232 center, 232 bottom, 232-233, 233 bottom left, 233 bottom right, 237 bottom left, 242 center, 243 bottom, 246 top right, 247 bottom right, 248-249, 248 bottom, 249 top left and right, 249 bottom, 250 top, 250 center, 251 top left and right, 254-255, 254, 255 top center and right, 255 center, 257, 260, 261 center left, 261 bottom, 262 top left and right, 262 bottom, 262-263, 263 bottom left, 272-273, 273 center right, 276 top left, 276 center, 277 top left and right, 278-279, 278 bottom, 279 top, center and bottom, 280 top right, 280 center and bottom, 280-281, 281 bottom left, 284 top left, 286 top and bottom, 287 bottom left, 288 top, 288-289, 289 bottom left and right, 290-291, 290 bottom, 291 top left, top right and center, 293 top right, 298-299, 298 bottom, 299 top center, 299 center, 299 bottom, 300 top, 300-301, 301 bottom right, 320

Anzerberger Toni/Contrasto: page 18 right

Atlantide/Agefotostock/Marka: page 267 bottom left

Atlantide Phototravel: page 188 center

Craig Aurness/Corbis/Contrasto: page 239 bottom left

Patrick Aventurier/Gamma/Contrasto: page 160 bottom left

Pallava Bagla/Corbis/Contrasto: page 155 center bottom

David Ball/Agefotostock/Marka: pages 198-199, 198 bottom

Dave Bartruff/Corbis/Contrasto: pages 70-71, 144 bottom left

Glenn Beanland/Lonely Planet Images: page 172 center

Neil Beer/Corbis/Contrasto: page 191 bottom

Marcello Bertinetti/Archivio White Star: pages 1 left and right, 17 center and right, 33 bottom, 36 center top, 36 bottom, 38-39, 39 center bottom, 48 center right, 51 top left and right, 54-55, 55 bottom left, 59 center, 64 top center, 65 bottom left and right, 75 top left, 77 top, 86-87, 96-97, 96 bottom left and right, 97 top left, 97 center and bottom, 98 top left and right, 99 bottom left and right, 100 top left and right, 100-101, 104 bottom, 104-105, 106-107, 108 bottom left and right, 109 top right, 109 bottom, 110 top right, 110-111, 111 bottom left and right, 112 top right, 112 center and bottom, 112-113, 115 top and center top, 115 bottom, 118 center, 119, 125 top center and right, 129 center top and center bottom, 130 bottom, 131 bottom, 132 top left, 132 center, 132-133, 133 bottom right, 134 center bottom, 134-135, 135 bottom, 148 bottom left and right, 149 bottom, 151 top right and left, 151 center, 152 bottom right, 160 bottom right, 161 top left and right, 176 bottom left, 178 bottom left, 235 center, 281 bottom right

Yann Arthus-Bertrand/Corbis/Contrasto: pages 32-33, 142 bottom, 144-145, 162-163, 268 bottom left, 293 top left, 309 top left

Walter Bibikov/Agefotostock/Contrasto: pages 269 top, 270-271, 272 bottom right

Alberto Biscaro/Sime/Sie: page 270 top right

Anders Blomqvist/Lonely Planet Images: pages 154, 155 top left, 156 bottom right

Tibor Bognar/Corbis/Contrasto: page 118 bottom

Massimo Borchi/Archivio White Star: pages 112 top left, 142 top center, 145 bottom, 146 center, 146 bottom, 156-157, 156 bottom left, 157 top, 157 center, 244 top left, 244 bottom, 245 bottom left and right, 246 top left, 246 center, 246-247, 247 bottom left, 272 bottom left, 273 top right and bottom right, 274-275, 275 top and center, 284 center and bottom, 284-285, 285 bottom, 286 center top and center bottom, 286-287, 287 bottom right

Livio Bourbon/Archivio White Star: pages 17 left, 32 right, 33 center, 34-35, 34 right, 35 bottom, 36 top right and top, 36-37, 37, 38, 39 top and center top, 39 bottom, 40 top left and top right, 42-43, 44 bottom, 45 bottom, 120 bottom, 121 bottom left and right, 158 top left, 158 center and bottom, 159 bottom, 162 bottom left and right, 163 top left and right, 163 center, 299 top left, 300 center top, center bottom and bottom, 301 bottom left

A. Bracchetti/P. Zigrossi/Musei Civici Vaticani: pages 114-115

Wojtek Buss/Agefotostock/Contrasto: page 181 bottom

Cameraphoto: pages 98 center, 98 bottom, 98-99, 100 center, 101 bottom

Angelo Cavalli/Agefotostock/Marka: pages 264 bottom left, 264 bottom right

Stephanie Colasanti/Corbis/Contrasto: page 206 top

Dutton Colin/Sime/Sie: page 50 bottom right

Anne Conway/Archivio White Star: page 86 top left

Alan Copson/Agefotostock/Contrasto: pages 168-169

Marco Cristofori/Corbis/Contrasto: pages 92-93, 93 bottom left, 125 top left

Richard Cummins: pages 44-45, 240 bottom, 241 top, 241 bottom, 243 top right, 243 center, 252 top and bottom, 252-253, 253 bottom, 271 bottom right

Richard Cummins/Corbis/Contrasto: pages 44 top, 226-227, 236-237, 258-259, 258 bottom, 259 bottom, 265 center, 289 center right

Richard Cummins/Lonely Planet Images: page 263 bottom right

Dennis Degnan/Corbis/Contrasto: pages 302 bottom, 306-307

Slone Douglas/Corbis/Contrasto: page 239 bottom right

Krzysztof Dydynski/Lonely Planet Images: pages 206 bottom, 206-207

John Elk III/ Lonely Planet Images: pages 219 top right, 234-235

Emmler/Laif/Contrasto: pages 138 top right, 208 bottom, 208-209, 213 top

Abbie Enock/Corbis/Contrasto: page 155 bottom

Enzo/Agefotostock/Marka: page 95 top

Estock/Sime/Sie: pages 6, 240-241

John Everingham/Art Asia Press: pages 160-161

Macduff Everton/Corbis/Contrasto: pages 164 top left, 295 center, 303 bottom

Michael AND. Feeney/Agefotostock/Contrasto: pages 48-49

Fabrizio Finetti: pages 22 top left, 22 bottom, 22-23, 23 left, 23 right, 24 bottom, 25 left, 25 right, 26-27, 26 right, 27 top, 27 center, 27 bottom

Nigel Francis/Corbis/Contrasto: page 29 left

Stuart Franklin/Magnum Photos/Contrasto: pages 9, 308-309, 308 bottom left

Franz-Marc Frei/Corbis/Contrasto: pages 30 bottom, 30-31

Rick Friedman/Corbis/Contrasto: page 274 bottom right

John Frumm/Hemispheres-Images: pages 67 right, 242-243

Jose Fuste Raga/Agefotostock/Marka: pages 83 center, 195 top left, 197 top right

Jose Fuste Raga/Agefotostock/Contrasto: pages 64-65, 82-83, 190-191

Jose Fuste Raga/Corbis/Contrasto: pages 18-19, 63 bottom, 137 top right, 139 bottom, 190 bottom right, 192-193

Jose Fuste Raga/Zefa/Sie: page 309 top center

Gaasterland/Laif/Contrasto: page 68 bottom

Bertrand Gardel/Hemispheres-Images: pages 141 top center, 180 bottom left, 182 center, 183 top, 238 top left

Ron Garnett: pages 224-225

Alfio Garozzo/Archivio White Star: pages 120 top left, 120 center, 120-121, 122-123, 122 top left and right, 123 bottom, 126, 127 bottom, 128, 129 top left, 129 bottom, 130 top left and right, 130 center, 130-131, 132 bottom, 310 top left, 310 center and bottom, 311, 313 center top and center bottom

Cesare Gerolimetto/Archivio White Star: pages 108-109, 109 center, 113 bottom right, 115 center bottom, 150 bottom, 234 bottom right, 235 top, 236 top, 236 bottom, 282 top, 282 center, 282 bottom

Gil Giuglio/Hemispheres-Images: page 256 top

Gollhardt &Wieland/Laif/Contrasto: page 218 bottom right

Grafenhain/Sime/Sie: pages 72-73

Sylvain Grandadam/Hoa-qui/Grazia Neri: page 180 bottom right

Kim Grant/Lonely Planet Images: page 237 bottom right

320 *Twin antennas mark the apex of the John Hancock Center in Chicago. The tapering high-rise building is 1131 feet tall. Sweeping urban development began in the "Windy City" with the advent of railroads in 1870. Above all, however, it was stimulated by a major catastrophe: the Great Fire of 1871, which made it necessary to redesign the urban layout. This laid the groundwork for the great modern city of Chicago, whose first skyscraper was built in 1885.*